EarthLight

Spiritual Wisdom
for an Ecological Age

Edited by Cindy Spring
and Anthony Manousos
with Eric Sabelman and Sandy Farley
Introduction by K. Lauren de Boer

Friends Bulletin is the official publication of Pacific, North Pacific and Intermountain Yearly Meetings, the three independent Yearly Meetings of the Religious Society of Friends.
Opinions expressed in this book are those of the authors,
not necessarily of the Yearly Meetings.

For more information, please contact
Friends Bulletin editor at friendsbulletin@aol.com
www.westernquaker.net
www.earthlight.org

Cover design by Anthony Manousos
Cover art © Jean Triol

ISBN-10: 0-9700410-2-0

ISBN-13: 978-0-9700410-2-9

First printing 2007 in the United States of America.
Printed on 100% recycled paper by Alonzo Printers, Oakland, CA.

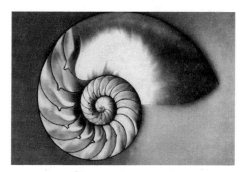

Contents

Earth Light Principles

Conscious Evolution

We actively explore how we as individuals and as a species can move toward a way of living that embodies mutually enhancing relations with all Earth's life-forms and natural systems. In so doing, we live in connection to and with reverence for all life.

Sacred Relationship

We acknowledge and honor the Spirit that brings us forth in interdependence. In so doing, we live in sacred relationship.

Collective Wisdom

We honor the essence of the world's wisdom traditions as important sources for learning values of compassion, reverence, and gratitude. In so doing, we awaken to a deeper, contemporary wisdom.

Mutual Learning

We engage in mutual learning experiences as we create an Earth community listening and speaking from the heart. In so doing, we are informed by one another's wisdom and compassion.

Conscious Choice

We recognize that our daily choices, even the small and habitual ones, have an impact on Earth's species in both beneficial and destructive ways. We seek to promote lifestyles that lead to social justice, sustainability, and ecological security for all life on Earth. In so doing, we live with conscious intent.

Inclusivity

We embrace the challenges and joys of truly diverse viewpoints and values in all areas of life in order to more fully accept and understand the depth of each other's experience. We value Earth's diversity of life and respect the rights of each species to flourish in its unique expression. In so doing, we foster and encourage the unique gifts in one another and in all life.

Celebration

We celebrate the human role as a positive, life-enhancing agent in Earth's unfolding story. In so doing, we live in the wonder and mystery of the living Universe.

Preface

I invite you to cross the threshold with me from the planet we're living on to an emerging planet—part dream, part reality. Are you searching for a world and a way of life that hold compassion and wisdom as core principles? So am I. This book contains guidance for the healing of our terribly fractured world. Its most basic teaching is to live in sacred relationship with all else. We've chosen some very fine thinkers, poets, artists and visionaries as guides.

If our species survives this century, I'm convinced that the era we are living in today will be considered one of those "dark ages." During the European dark ages of the 6th through 10th centuries, scribes were preserving the wisdom traditions of the past. During the dark times of the Middle Ages, scientific discoveries and revolutionary visions were squashed by authoritarian structures. But courageous thinkers were nurturing the seeds of a way of being that came to be called "The Enlightenment" in the 18th century. With that new dawn came the realization that an individual person had much more intelligence and potential than the institutions of the time allowed. So too, many of us are realizing that the Earth Community, as manifested through its ecosystems and myriad species, has much more intelligence and creativity than humans have appreciated. We sapiens are one species among many. What can we learn from each other's survival strategies as we co-evolve on this small planet?

The articles, poems and graphics in this anthology were chosen from 54 issues of *EarthLight* magazine plus many fine Quaker sources. We've done our best to sequence them within a matrix of seven principles drawn up by the EarthLight community in 2005. Letting each article or poem flow from one to the next, we've chosen to have you discover linkages between them, rather than provide written bridges.

Temenos is a Greek word that describes a sanctuary, a sacred place and time within which to connect to the Source of Life. Ordinary surroundings and routines fade into the background. May you find *temenos* as you settle into these pages. May you move more deeply into that core of collective consciousness, shared by all beings, that continues to survive, dream and carry on.

—*Cindy Spring, October 2006*

Introduction
Spiritual Ecology:
a Practice of the Heart

by K. Lauren de Boer

When I was asked to write an introduction to *EarthLight: Spiritual Wisdom for an Ecological Age,* I faced a challenge. What, from out of the rich experience of ten years as editor of *EarthLight*, might the focus of such an essay be? Where could I go for guidance? Eventually, it occurred to me to go to my original source of inspiration, the natural world.

So here I am, sitting along the shoreline of San Francisco Bay. As I pass the afternoon in contemplation, the mudflat before me slowly widens with the ebbing tide, drawing willets, stilts, curlews, and godwits in growing numbers. Brown pelicans and least terns cruise the shoreline, periodically free-falling into the water to feed on small fish. The air is alive with the smell of the sea and the sounds of gulls, and a fresh wind cools me. An occasional flock of sandpipers throws itself into the sky like a cast net, then circles, swooning back and forth over the silvery water of the channel several times before settling, each bird in perfect synchrony with the others, onto the shore again.

Watching this movement of birds gradually draws me into a state of reverie, and I remember one of my early inspirations. As an undergraduate at the University of Iowa, I had been fascinated by the relationship of landscape to the human imagination and was voraciously reading everything I could find written on the topic. One day, I attended a talk by writer Barry Lopez, just after he had completed his book *Arctic Dreams*. Drawing on a passage from the book, he spoke of being at Tule Lake in the Klamath Basin on the California-Oregon border. He spoke of the flight of flocks of snow geese numbering in the tens of thousands, and how the sweep of one flock across the sky would interlock with that of a second flock with perfect grace, not one

11

bird colliding with another.

My imagination soared with the simple elegance of this image. There was an intelligence there, and a spirit, I felt. I thought back to my own experience of countless hours in the fields and forests of my home bio-region in the Midwest. I especially recalled a bright October day on the banks of the Des Moines River when migrating birds passed all day overhead, moving in and out of my sight and hearing like thoughts and images in those fragile moments between sleep and waking. Their movement and presence changed me.

I left the talk that day with a sense that I had found my calling. As a writer, I couldn't imagine a more compelling work than that of attempting to communicate the sacred interplay of landscape and human imagination. That calling would eventually converge with the mission of *EarthLight*, a magazine of spirituality and ecology started by West Coast Friends (otherwise known as Quakers).

EarthLight was founded from a conviction within the Friends community that the environmental challenges facing the Earth community are spiritual at their root. It was felt that this reality needed to be explored, discussed and—more importantly— deeply felt, for lasting cultural transformation to take place. From that conviction, *EarthLight* grew to be a bridge-builder in many ways, with the practice of spiritual ecology as the common ground. I've come to know spiritual ecology as a practice that anyone, from any cultural background, religious tradition, or spiritual inclination can adopt. I also believe that it is a practice that can help us to face the tensions of our time in creative ways.

More than just a theory, spiritual ecology describes a way of being in the world. It is ancient in the sense that peoples have lived it in many times and places. It is contemporary in that it integrates the discoveries of science and a new sense of our evolutionary story. It draws both from knowledge of the ecology of the planet and from deeper sensitivities to the spiritual dimension of the Earth. As such, it forms the basis for an ethical code of conduct. It brings us out of the trance of our human-centered wonder-world, expanding our circle of concern to include other species. We begin to see a relationship between our spiritual condition and the planetary ecological crisis. And from this discernment, we seek to cultivate a conscious, sustainable lifestyle of simplicity and ecological integrity.

These are some of the basic ideas of spiritual ecology. However, it is its actual *practice* that makes a difference in people's lives. One can speak of the spiritual ecology, for instance, of growing food. The spiritual ecology of diet and the growing of food includes not only what nourishes us but also health of growers, workers, and the land, as well as the relationships of plants, pollinators, microorganisms, weather, sun, soil, water, and the energy flowing through the system It is both ecological and sacred work. One can also speak of the spiritual ecology of child-rearing, communication, lovemaking, and city design through which our spirituality becomes integrated into everyday life.

For many indigenous peoples whose cultures are relatively intact today, spiritual ecology is such a practice, although these cultures would not generally use the term to describe what for them is a way of life. While you can't really apply all practices equally to the cultures of all indigenous peoples, past and present, it is possible to distinguish a consistent orientation toward spiritual ecology as a way of life within these cultures worldwide. These include a sense of kinship that extends beyond the human; a systematic observation and knowledge of plants and animals passed from generation to generation through story and myth; the notion of a living planet and of Earth as Mother; sacredness of place; humans seen as just one part of a created order; and shamanic rites which draw on the primal powers of the natural world. These are present in all of us to some extent as indigenous mind.

While it is important not to idealize these cultures, we can recognize that their experience is an indispensable part of our human heritage and a wisdom source we need very much to draw on at this time in history. There is indigenous mind in all of us. We all come out of some lineage, some ancient culture that was, at one time, in alignment with the powers and graces of the natural world. We don't need to go back to hunting and gathering and living on the land to access that wisdom. Just spending a little time in the natural world can awaken us from our psychological, cognitive, and spiritual sleep, opening us to the sacred wisdom that surrounds us.

We need this wisdom source to help us face the tensions of our time creatively. One of the deepest tensions we live with today is the one that arises from simultaneous feelings of profound grief and joyful inspiration.

We all have a sense of the loss and destruction brought to the planet by human activity. E.O. Wilson and other scientists have estimated that we are losing 20,000 species a year to extinction. "Ecological overshoot" has now become a reality.[1] Humanity now consumes over 20 percent more resources than the Earth can produce, causing rapid declines in wild animal populations. Human activities threaten the Earth's ability to sustain future generations.[2] Sixty percent of the planet's ecosystem-support systems have been severely degraded. The wetlands, forests, savannas, estuaries, coastal fisheries, and other habitats that recycle air, water, and nutrients for all living creatures are being irretrievably damaged. Nutrient pollution from agricultural runoff has led to coastal dead zones measuring thousands of square miles. An estimated 12 percent of bird species, 25 percent of mammals and more than 30 percent of all amphibians are threatened with extinction within the next century. Humans now use between 40 and 50 percent of all available freshwater running off the land. Flow from rivers has been reduced dramatically. For parts of the year, the Yellow River in China, the Nile in Africa, and the Colorado in North America dry up before they reach the ocean. An estimated 90 percent of the total weight of the ocean's large predators—tuna, swordfish and sharks—has disappeared in recent years. Since 1980, 20 percent of the world's coral reefs have been destroyed and another 20 percent are badly degraded.

Our hearts are broken again and again when we hear these facts. "How shall the heart be reconciled to its feast of losses?" writes poet Stanley Kunitz. Spiritual ecology is a way of cultivating heart, of finding the courage (from the French *coeur*, or heart) to act. Instead of simply broken, we are broken open and become big-hearted and courageous, qualities needed to face loss creatively.

At the same time, there are sources of joyful inspiration that come from the growing community responding to the crisis and from having, for the first time, a common story of our origins. Scientifically based, this story tells us that the Universe isn't simply a place or a vast mechanism, but a sacred story, an event in which we play a meaningful part. It's a story that continues to unfold with greater beauty and complexity over time. Points of transformation in this story have brought about moments of grace in the face of crisis; we may be living in just such a moment. We are key characters in the narrative of the Universe, a purposeful event permeated with intelligence. Perhaps even more important, we have seen the planet as a whole. We've seen the NASA photos of Earth taken from space, and they have permanently shifted human consciousness.

We can also take heart in evidence of a kind of Earth *sangha* (to draw on a Buddhist term for spiritual community) that I saw mature over the ten years I was privileged to edit *EarthLight*. I've seen this sangha forming through the acts of hundreds of individuals. I've seen it in the emergence of initiatives like the International Forum on Globalization, an alliance of activists, economists, scientists, and writers from over 20 countries that formed to question the assumption that globalization is inevitable and to explore local, community-based economies as an alternative.

The Bioneers conference, organized by Kenny Ausubel and Nina Simons, is another such initiative that took root during this time. *EarthLight* was a partner with Bioneers from their early years and served to bring a spiritual influence to the conference's "visionary and practical solutions for restoring the Earth." The conference has grown to over 3,000 participants each year and now organizes satellite conferences in dozens of other locations simultaneously.

The *Forum on Religion and Ecology* grew out of a series of conferences organized by religious scholars (and *EarthLight* advisors) Mary Evelyn Tucker and John Grim. The conference series, focusing on eleven major world religion traditions, led to the publication of books on religion and ecology based on each tradition.

When I first began this work in 1995, there were only a handful of centers like Genesis Farm in New Jersey, founded by Dominican sister Miriam MacGillis, that integrated ecology and cosmology into a spiritual vision of the land. *EarthLight*, in its final four issues, published a directory of over 60 such centers. More have been identified since then.

These and other initiatives comprise the growing movement dedicated to cultivating "mutually-enhancing relations" with Earth's community of species, as envisioned by cultural historian Thomas Berry years ago. Like the elegant sweep of birds in the Klamath basin, we are all part of a larger body of unique voices and sensitivities dedicated to the well-being of the unborn. We are brought together in the communion of the whole through our shared love for the planet.

Ultimately, spiritual ecology comes down to what we each can do, moment to moment, to support this vision. Perhaps the most simple and yet most powerful act of spiritual ecology is the bow. The bow is an act of humility and reverence, and it can be carried out anywhere, at any time. It draws the recipient into our compass of gratitude and says: "I hold you, as part of the sacred community, in my widening circle of compassion and concern." For the significance of the bow, I return again to writer Barry Lopez: "The bow is a technique of awareness. We often address the physical dimensions of landscape, but they are inseparable from the spiritual dimensions. It is in dismissing the spiritual dimensions that we are able to behave like barbarians. If the land is incorporated into the same moral universe that you occupy, then your bow is an acknowledgment of your participation in that universe and a recognition that all you bow to is included in your moral universe. If you behave as though there were no spiritual dimension to the place, then you can treat the place like an object."[3]

I bow to the Earth and her family of species. I bow to all those who made sixteen years of *EarthLight* possible, to the Quaker community, the founders, the editors who served before me, and to all of the many volunteers and supporters whose advice and generosity inspired me and previous editors to a labor of love. I bow to all those who made this anthology possible, to the authors, the artists, the compilers, and to you—the reader—without whose sensitivities and discernment this labor would be lost.

Spiritual ecology is a creative response in a time of crisis and opportunity. I end with one of my poems about the source of that creativity, the wildness found in both our inner and outer landscapes.

The Good Story

The wild will come to you
Like a good story
Peopled with creatures
If you are still long enough

Like a gift of grace, a giving
That renews the marrow
And provides a home

For those occupied with alien stories
For those distracted by the search.

We have too long been occupied and distracted with the alienating story of greed and consumption. May we find the stillness that, through a practice of spiritual ecology, will allow a new story to live among us. The freshness, depth, clarity, and insight of the voices in this anthology are a bow in that direction.

Endnotes

[1] *The Living Planet Report,* issued by the World Wildlife Fund in September 2004 using scientific analysis from the Global Footprint Network.

[2] *The Millennium Ecosystem Assessment,* a report issued by the United Nations in May 2005, involving over 1,300 researchers from 95 nations. The report is the most comprehensive survey ever into the state of the planet.

[3] *Sierra Magazine,* Nov 1998, "On Sacred Ground: Writer Barry Lopez Respects Alaskan Environment," by Nicholas O'Connell.

The Genesis of EarthLight and of the Quaker Environmental Movement

by Anthony Manousos

with help from Eric Sabelman

Quakers (or Friends, as we prefer to be known) are usually fairly low-key when we gather for worship or business, but when a Colorado Friend named Marshall Massey spoke about the environment at Pacific Yearly Meeting's annual session in 1985, many Friends responded with uncharacteristic fervor. They were so moved by Massey's message that they unanimously decided to provide funds so he could write a book about environmentalism and Quakerism. This is something that Pacific Yearly Meeting had never done before, and it has never done since.

Many felt as if a prophet were in their midst. Robert Schutz, former editor of *Friends Bulletin*, the official publication of Western *unprogrammed** Friends, was especially taken by Massey's message:

> Have you ever been seized by an urgent enthusiasm? One that was triggered by a speech, no less? That's what happened to a whole lot of us at Pacific YM in 1985. And the speaker was a Prophet, who came to us under the broad-brimmed leather hat of Marshall Massey.

So compelling was Massey's message, and Western Friends' response to it, that he was asked to address the annual gathering

---

*Unprogrammed refers to Quaker meetings in which there is no set order of worship or paid minister; worshippers simply gather in silence and wait on the Spirit. *Programmed* Quaker meetings (which comprise the majority of Quakers in the USA) have pastors and worship services resembling those of typical Protestant churches.

of Friends General Conference in 1987. There his prophetic words energized the entire North American Quaker community, convincing many that environmental concerns should be taken as seriously as the abolition of slavery and nuclear weapons. Together Massey and Schutz helped to launch *EarthLight* magazine as well as a Quaker ecological movement called Friends in Unity with Nature Committee, later renamed Quaker EarthCare Witness.

Although rooted in Quakerism, *EarthLight* has always sought to embrace a wide variety of religious and spiritual perspectives. In that first issue of *EarthLight* (Spring 1990), Schutz wrote the following:

> What we mean by "Spirit and Ecology" is that we are pasting together—all of us who think hard about the meaning of words—a vision of the earth restored, the earth sustained, the earth as our mother, the earth as a fair and beautiful place to live in, not to perish in. Without our vision of the earth as it ought to and must be, we and it will perish. And we must not perish.

This vision evolved and expanded throughout *EarthLight's* fifteen years of publication. The first four issues were edited by Chris Laning, a Friend with a deep commitment to Quaker spirituality as well as to environmentalism. A botanist by training, she had just completed a certificate in graphic design at the UC Davis extension when she came to Pacific Yearly Meeting's annual session with a prototype for the magazine. Various titles for the publication were proposed—including "Noah," "Rootings," and "Webbings"—until finally Laning proposed "EarthLight," a title that resonated with Friends. As Laning explained:

> "EarthLight" seemed to have all the virtues: it's short, it's unusual enough to stand out, and it combines "Earth," our main concern, with "Light," which is a term often used by Friends for God or Spirit.

Laning saw the magazine as primarily Quakerly in its mission and focus. In her essay, "Back to the Garden" (Fall 1990), she observed that the founder of Quakerism, George Fox, felt a deep, almost mystical connection to God's creation. During his religious awakening, Fox said that he entered into "that state that Adam was in before he fell" and that "all the creation gave another smell unto me than before." Laning wrote: "All creation was 'opened' to him ... and he had regained ... a profound sense of *unity with nature.*"

During this period, *EarthLight* published many outstanding articles by Friends who were trying to understand environmentalism from a Quaker spiritual perspective.

EarthLight soon evolved into something more than simply a vehicle for exploring the ecological dimension of Quaker spirituality, however. It became truly interfaith in its outlook. Its next editor, Paul Burks, was a Methodist minister deeply influenced by the ecumenical movement and by process theology. During Burks' five-year tenure as editor (1991-1996), *EarthLight* published many timely articles dealing with the connection between environmentalism and religion. *EarthLight* helped to foster a new consciousness by bringing together "environmentalists, astronauts, astronomers, politicians, economists, Native Americans, and people on the cutting edge of religion."

In 1996 the editorship passed to K. Lauren de Boer, who broadened (and deepened) the spiritual perspective of *EarthLight* even more. A gifted essayist and poet, Lauren was a founding board member of the Epic of Evolution Society and director of the Center for Sacred Ecology in Oakland, California. He sits on the advisory board for the Center for Ecozoic Studies. Lauren's ecological perspective was shaped to a great extent by philosopher/paleontologist Teilhard de Chardin, cultural historian/"geologian" Thomas Berry and mathematical cosmologist/visionary Brian Swimme—the founders of the "Ecozoic movement." Their endeavor to see evolution and cosmology from a spiritual perspective (sometimes called "The Great Story") is evident in Lauren's description of *EarthLight's* purpose:

EarthLight magazine celebrates the living Earth and our thirteen billion year story of the universe. The magazine's mission and focus is to cultivate the awareness that Earth is a sacred community of life to be cherished, protected, and restored, not a commodity to be exploited. We seek to catalyze the personal and global consciousness required to ensure a healthy Earth for future generations of all species (#51, Autumn 2004).

EarthLight has published articles by many of the world's seminal figures in secular and religious thought about the place of humankind in Creation. By intention, most have been non-Quakers: Joanna Macy, Thomas Berry, Brian Swimme, John Cobb, Vic Yellowhawk White, and Connie Barlow—to name only a few who have served on *EarthLight*'s advisory board as well as written articles. Among the many notable Quaker environmentalists whose work appeared frequently on *EarthLight*'s pages were Keith Helmuth, Alain Strain, John Yungblut, Alex Wildwood, Rex Ambler, Francis Hole, Mary Coelho, Louis Cox, and Ruah Swennerfelt.

This book embodies what we feel is the best of *EarthLight* and of Quaker writings on spirituality and ecology during the past 20 years, a period that some see as the beginning of a new era in environmental consciousness, the "Great Turning" or the "Ecozoic Age."

No Quaker environmental writing during this period has had more influence than Marshall Massey's article, "The Defense of the Peaceable Kingdom." Originally published in *Friends Bulletin* in March 1984, it was republished as a pamphlet that circulated widely. Although some Friends do not find Massey's apocalyptic tone or prophetic style compelling, there is no doubt that Massey helped to launch the Quaker environmental movement. More than any other Quaker writer, Massey made it clear that environmentalism is, or should be, a deeply spiritual and religious concern.

The Defense of the Peaceable Kingdom

by Marshall Massey

There have been times in recent years when we Quakers have been wonderfully quick to spot ...new evils and to fashion a response. Such has been the case with our response to the draft in the Vietnam War, with our response to the needs of refugees from American wars, and with our efforts to challenge the "reasonableness" of our nation's possession of nuclear arms.

But these are the sorts of issues to which our traditions sensitize us: issues of war and peace, of cruelty and compassion toward our fellow human beings.

We are not so sensitized to environmental issues, and the result has been that we are now only slightly more awake to their significance than the average American is. We have certainly noticed that there are environmental problems; we have responded with Advices and Queries, and Guides to Practice; as individuals, many of us have become involved with environmental organizations, or have spoken out on special concerns within the environmental arena.

But we have failed to see the overall magnitude and urgency of the environmental crisis—a magnitude and urgency which are *at least* as great as that of the nuclear arms crisis, and possibly even greater. We have failed to see that the environmental crisis has a towering spiritual dimension, which *must* be addressed if the crisis is to be resolved; and we have failed to notice that there is not one spiritual movement anywhere in the world that has spoken adequately to that spiritual dimension.

In these respects, we have been every bit as deceived by that collective delusion against which John Woolman spoke as anyone else in our society.

The list of civilizations that have destroyed or severely diminished themselves by their unwise use of the environment is a long one: it includes, among others, the Sumerians and

Babylonians, the Mycenaean Greeks, the Romans in North Africa, the Mayans of Guatemala, the Easter Islanders, the medieval Chinese, the Hohokam of Arizona, the inhabitants of India, the inhabitants of the Sahel, and—not so long ago—the farmers of the American Dust Bowl. Not one of these societies foresaw its danger and avoided its end. The power of the collective dream claimed each and every one. The danger that confronts us is not new. Nothing is new but its scale and its extent.

But the scale and the extent are precisely where we Friends have been deceived.

The present environmental crisis is actually three crises, not one. The least of these crises—the *crisis of carrying capacity*—is the one that extinguished those civilizations of the past: it is capable this time of bringing down the curtain on all civilization throughout the globe, bringing on a Dark Age that can be expected to continue for millennia.

The middle crisis, which is the *crisis of extinctions and gene pool destruction*, promises to go a bit further, and to render the end of civilization almost totally irreversible.

The greatest crisis—the *threat to our planet's oxygen factories*—will, if not dealt with, literally sterilize the planet of all life except anaerobic bacteria.

Unlike the threat of nuclear war, the destruction wrought by these crises is not potential. It is happening right now. It does not hang upon a single bad decision that we may hope will never occur. It is the cumulative effect of a billion small decisions made by people who believe that their part in the destruction "doesn't count."

And unless the destruction is halted, it now appears that we will pass the point of no return, as regards each of these three crises, in somewhat under a hundred years. This fact is fairly well established by ecological studies.

On the other hand, like the nuclear arms crisis, these three environmental crises are totally unnecessary.

...Unlike nuclear war, unlike the host of lesser environmental issues, the three big crises are not discussed by candidates for public office or debated at any length in the media. No TV special such as *The Day After*, no movie such as *Testament*, has made them an object of concern to the general public. Indeed, prominent arms freeze activists have from time to time made speeches declaring that if World War III happens there will be no more environment (which is true), and that therefore nuclear war is the one real crisis we should all be working on (which is not true, since it ignores the urgency of the three great environmental crises, but which is widely accepted and believed even within the environmental movement).

The neglect of these three crises in political forums and the media is mirrored by a lack of public awareness. There is no question that environmental issues have become a major public concern in recent years; poll after poll taken in this country has found that substantial blocks of voters—in many cases, overwhelming majorities—want to see the environment properly protected regardless of cost,[1] and there are numerous indications that a similar shift of opinion is taking place all over the world.[2]

...Yet this new general environmental awareness does not extend to awareness of the crises. A typical demonstration of this came in a national survey of registered voters taken in early 1982 by the Democratic National Committee. The survey showed that 67% of registered voters want stronger environmental regulations. It revealed that environmentalism is the *only* issue on which voters think of themselves as being to the left of the Democratic Party. But, nevertheless, the voters surveyed generally agreed that environmental issues are not among the most important matters this country faces.[3] Other surveys have reported comparable findings....*

Why is there this selective blindness? Is it that the three crises are not real? Hardly. Jacques-Yves Cousteau, the founder of the Cousteau Society, has spoken out about the oxygen-factory

---

*Although poll results vary and are open to question and interpretation, it appears that American attitudes have grown more sympathetic to environmental concerns since the 1980s. According to recent Harris polls, in 1981, 45% of Americans strongly or somewhat agreed with the statement: "Protecting the environment is so important that requirements and standards cannot be too high, and continuing environmental improvements must be made regardless of cost." In 2005, 74% agreed with that statement.

crisis and also about the carrying-capacity crisis, and he is a conservative environmentalist who generally plays down his concerns in order to reach a broader audience. Both the carrying-capacity crisis and the extinctions crisis have been extensively explored in environmental literature and have become major continuing concerns of such organizations as the Sierra Club, Friends of the Earth, the Worldwatch Institute, and Environmental Action. No serious student of ecology would be likely to deny that all three crises are real and important, though plenty of uncertainty exists about the time frames involved.

So what remains? Only the power of the collective dream—which we already know is powerful enough to have convinced many early Friends that slavery is not really all that bad and to have convinced an enormous number of American voters that there is every reason to station Pershing and Cruise missiles as close to Moscow as possible.

I would suggest that there are values and convictions built into our society and culture and, as Woolman would put it, well suited to our natural inclinations, that make it very difficult for us to believe that we could be so extremely dependent on so many different parts of the global ecosystem, or that the parts we depend on could be so much at our mercy.

These values and convictions might, perhaps, include a conviction that nature is something to triumph over, and that indeed we have already triumphed and do not need to worry any more. They might also include a conviction that wilderness is unimportant, insignificant, and nature not worthy of a normal person's attention. They might include the idea that the world is too big for us to harm permanently. They might include the decision to grab what you can for yourself and let the next generation take care of itself....

To the extent that we think our present daily routines, our careers and recreations, are important, we may not believe we have "time" to worry about anything else. R. Duncan Fairn had a wonderful response to that, which he attributed to A. Neave Brayshaw and which is quoted in the London *Faith and Practice:* "We have as much time as there is, and when we say we haven't time we merely mean that we choose to do other things instead."[4]

But it takes a certain amount of maturing in giving things up to God to understand what this means; it is not a wisdom most adults seem anxious to acquire.

We are not well educated about nature in this society. Our education generally consists of a few lessons in elementary school, perhaps a course in high school biology, plus whatever we pick up from newspapers and television. Most of us live in suburbs, where grass, flowers, shrubs and trees, birds, squirrels, and bees are employed to give us the illusion of a lush, intact ecosystem without the fuss and bother of the reality. Most of the rest of us live in cities. Nearly all of us spend most of our time within four walls, with our attention directed either to artifacts or to ideas; even outdoors we have no urgent reason to understand the world in which we move.

This way of life perpetuates our ignorance and encourages us to underestimate the importance of the environmental crisis. Is it any wonder then, that while a 1982 poll of Americans found that the great majority want stronger environmental safeguards, the same poll found that 45 percent think pollution control measures are an unfair burden on industry?[5] Is it any surprise that our nation's most respected economists still believe, with few exceptions, that our environmental problems are irrelevant to predictions of what the economy will look like in ten years? As Paul Ehrlich has written, "the problem probably is that economists have stared too long at the ... standard economics texts ..." [6] We form our ideas of the importance of the environment, not from any actual experience, but from listening to one another—or from sheer imagination: as no less a personage than Ronald Reagan has said, "Trees cause pollution."

This, then, is the situation in which ecological and biological experts, with some part-time aid from a few concerned organizations, have been attempting to alert the world to the magnitude of the environmental crises. The emphasis in their efforts has been on presenting the facts. But the facts, the three crises, are only Cerberus' heads; it is his body, our collective dream, our collective refusal to see, that gives the three heads their existence. The experts and the organizations have failed to address the nature of the entire beast. And as a result, though they have added fuel to the general concern about pollution, they have failed to get their essential message across. The power of the dream has overwhelmed them.

To address the dream-body of Cerberus is a spiritual task, as Woolman and Burroughs and a host of other Friends understood very well. It is for this reason that the presence of Quakers *as a body*, a new and coherent Friends' testimony, is now so urgently required.

Endnotes

[1] In 1981, a *New York Times/CBS News* poll found that "more than two out of three people...[agree] that 'we need to maintain present environmental laws in order to preserve the environment for future generations'" (quoted in "Econotes," *Environmental Action*, Nov. 1981, p. 8). In 1982, a poll commissioned by the Continental Group showed that 60 percent of the general American public "favors continued environmental clean-up, even if companies have to charge more for their products" ("Econotes," *Environmental Action*, Feb. 1983, p. 5). In April 1983, a *New York Times/CBS News* poll found that 58% of Americans believe "protecting the environment is so important that requirements and standards cannot be too high and continuing environmental improvements must be made regardless of cost" (Deborah Baldwin, "Playing Politics with Pollution," *Common Cause*, May/June 1983, p. 15).

[2] The rise of the Green Parties of Australia and Europe is one sign. Another is the fact that, at international conferences such as the 1982 World Congress on National Parks, it has increasingly been the nations of the *third* world—not those of the first or second—that have taken the lead in the search for effective conservation strategies.

[3] "Econotes," *Environmental Action*, April 1982, p. 4.

[4] London Yearly Meeting of the Religious Society of Friends, *Christian faith and practice in the experience of the Society of Friends* (1960, 1966), p. 309.

[5] "Econotes," *Environmental Action*, Feb. 1983, p. 5.

[6] Paul R. Ehrlich, "An Ecologist Standing Up Among Seated Social Scientists," *CoEvolution Quarterly*, no. 31, fall 1981, p. 29.

New Quaker Environmental Awareness

Marshall Massey's prophetic witness caused many Quakers to revise their thainking and attitude towards the environment. Prior to the 1980s, Quaker books of disciplines, called Faith and Practice, *hardly mentioned the environment as a spiritual concern. But in the 1990s, new sections on the environment were added to most Quaker books of discipline. The following passage on "Harmony with Creation" from Pacific Yearly Meeting's* Faith and Practice *places environmentalism within a religious context and traces this concern back to early Quakers such as William Penn. Our book follows the Quaker practice of using quotations (advices) and questions (queries) as a way to stimulate reflection.*

Harmony with Creation

It would go a long way to caution and direct people in their use of the world, that they were better studied and knowing in the Creation of it. For how could [they] find the confidence to abuse it, while they should see the Great Creator stare them in the face, in all and every part thereof?
—William Penn, *Some Fruits of Solitude*, 1693

God is revealed in all Creation. We humans belong to the whole interdependent community of life on earth. Rejoice in the beauty, complexity, and mystery of creation, with gratitude to be part of its unfolding. Take time to learn how this community of life is organized and how it interacts. Live according to principles of right relationship and right action within this larger whole.

Be aware of the influence humans have on the health and viability of life on earth. Call attention to what fosters or harms earth's exquisite beauty, balances and interdependencies. Guided by Spirit, work to translate this understanding into ways of living that reflect our responsibility to one another, to the greater community of life, and to future generations.

In what ways do I express gratitude for the wondrous expressions of life on Earth?

Do I consider the damage I might do to the Earth's vulnerable systems in choices I make of what I do, what I buy, and how I spend my time?

In our witness for the global environment, are we careful to consider justice and the well-being of the world's poorest people?

Does our way of life threaten the viability of life on Earth?

Conscious Evolution

We actively explore how we as individuals and as a species can move toward a way of living that embodies mutually enhancing relations with all Earth's life-forms and natural systems.

In so doing, we live in connection to and with reverence for all life.

In what ways has my awareness of my relationship to the natural world evolved over time? Self consciousness — not self or no self

How has this changed consciousness affected my behavior and life choices? What is important

What does "reverence for life" mean to me, and how can this sense of reverence make a difference in the way I live my life?

What can we do as a human community to come into right relationship with other life forms on this planet? stop listen, learn.

"The forests are dying, the rivers are dying, and we are called to act. To return Earth to harmony is to restore the harmonious principles within ourselves and to act as responsible caretakers—to save the forests and the waters for future generations."
—*Dhyani Ywahoo*

"I am now setting out to uncover or rediscover a whole world that lies around me, and to discover it in such a way that the outer landscape might shape and mold the inner landscape. "
—*Esther de Wall*

"We abuse land because we regard it as a commodity belonging to us. When we see land as a community to which we belong, we may begin to use it with love and respect."
—*Aldo Leopold*

"We do not inherit the earth from our ancestors, we borrow it from our children."
—*Native American Proverb*

"I know of no restorative of heart, body, and soul more effective against hopelessness than the restoration of the Earth."
—*Barry Lopez,* Helping Nature Heal *(1990)*

"And Man created the plastic bag and the tin and aluminum can and the cellophane wrapper and the paper plate, and this was good because Man could then take his automobile and buy all his food in one place and He could save that which was good to eat in the refrigerator and throw away that which had no further use. And soon the earth was covered with plastic bags and aluminum cans and paper plates and disposable bottles and there was nowhere to sit down or walk, and Man shook his head and cried: "Look at this Godawful mess.'"
—*Art Buchwald, 1970*

The Great Turning

by Joanna Macy

I imagine that future generations will look back on the closing years of the twentieth century and call it the time of The Great Turning. It is the epochal shift from an industrial growth society, dependent on accelerating consumption of resources, to a sustainable or life-sustaining society. There is no guarantee that we will make it in time for civilization, or even complex life forms, to survive; but it is clear that there's no alternative, because now we are, in systems terms, "on runaway," consuming our own life support system. I consider it an enormous privilege to be alive now, in this Turning, when all the wisdom and courage we ever harvested can be put to use and matter supremely.

Lester Brown of the Worldwatch Institute says that, while the agricultural revolution took centuries and the industrial revolution took decades, this ecological revolution must happen within a few years. At the same time, it will be, of necessity, more thoroughgoing—involving not only our political economy, but the attitudes and habits that sustain it.

Scientists—at least those who are not in the pay of the corporations—see more quickly than the politicians that there is no technological fix. No magic bullet, not even the Internet, can save us from population explosion, deforestation, climate disruption, poison by pollution, and wholesale extinctions of plant and animal species. We are going to have to want different things, seek different pleasures, pursue different goals, than those that have been driving us and our global economy. New values must arise now, while we still have room to maneuver—and that is precisely what is happening. They are emerging at this very moment, like green shoots through the rubble. It's not in the headlines or the evening news, but if you open your eyes and fiddle a bit with the focal length, you can see it, like a faint green haze over things, intensifying here and there in pools and pockets of grass, cress, clover.

The Great Turning is occurring on three simultaneous levels or dimensions. Recognize how they are gaining momentum through your own life. On the most visible level are holding actions in defense of Earth, including all the political, legislative, and legal work required to slow down the destruction, as well as direct actions—blockades, boycotts, civil disobedience and other forms of refusal. Work of this kind buys time. It helps save biological and cultural systems, and the gene pool, for the sustainable society to come; but it is insufficient to bring that society about.

This first level is wearing. You can get stressed out of your mind, by both the urgency and increasing violence against activists. In point position, you take a lot of punishment; and when you step back to take a breather, you often feel as if you are abandoning ship. But to the extent you still care what's happening to the world, you're probably just slipping back to continue the work of the Great Turning in another form — the way the head goose, when she's tired, slips back and flies in the windstream of others, and another flyer takes her place.

The second or middle level of the Great Turning addresses structural causes of the global crisis, and creates sustainable alternatives. Only a couple of years ago, it was hard slogging to raise any opposition to, or even interest in GATT (the Global Agreement on Trade and Tariffs); people's eyes glazed over. But now they are rapidly becoming aware of the rape of the world, and the attack on democracy, built into corporate privilege. Novel types of teach-ins demystify economics, engage the practical imagination. At the same time new social and economic arrangements are mushrooming, from local currencies to local marketing and consumer cooperatives, from eco-villages to renewable, off-the-grid energy generation. They may look fringe, but they hold the seeds of the future.

These nascent institutions cannot take root and survive, however, without values to sustain them. They must mirror what we want, and think we are. That paradigmatic shift—at the third, most basic level of the Great Turning—is happening all around us. Some choose to see it as an influx of spirit from above, others as "hitting bottom" in our doomed and addictive society. Either way, we are opening our senses to the web of relationships, the deep ecology, in which we have our being. Like our primordial ancestors, we begin again to see the world as our body, and (whether we say the word or not) as sacred.

We hardly have words for the cognitive, spiritual, and perceptual revolution that is occurring now at a stunning rate of speed. These lines from the late California poet Robinson Jeffers catch some of its flavor:

> I entered the life of the brown forest,
> And the great life of the ancient peaks,
> the patience of stone,
> I felt the changes in the veins
> In the throat of the mountain,
> and, I was the streams
> Draining the mountain wood; and I the stag
> drinking:
> and I was the stars,
> Boiling with light, wandering alone,
> each one the lord of his own summit
> and I was the darkness
> Outside the stars, I included them.
> They were a part of me.
> how can I express the excellence
> I have found, that has no color but clearness;
> No honey but ecstacy...

We can't tell which will happen first, the final unraveling of life on Earth, or the moment when the elements of a sustainable world cohere and catch hold. But even if the Great Turning fails to carry this planetary experiment onward through linear time, it still is worth it. It is a homecoming to our true nature.

Just a thousand years ago a theologian wrote a poem. Amidst the apocalyptic fears and hopes of the first millennium, he experienced and expressed a new vision of the holy—not as a remote, justly angry judge, but as an immanent presence, creative and loving. Now at the end of the second millennium, we can receive his poem and let it speak to our own inklings of that which presses within us to be born. So attend now to Symeon the Theologian (949-1022 C.E.), knowing that where he said "Christ" and "God," I am substituting "Earth" and "planet":

> We awaken in Earth's body
> as Earth awakens our bodies.
> And my poor hand is Earth, she enters
> my foot, and is infinitely me.
> I move my hand, and wonderfully
> my hand becomes Earth, becomes all of her
> (for our planet is indivisibly
> whole, seamless in her planethood).
> I move my foot, and at once
> she appears like a flash of lightning.
> Do my words seem blasphemous?
> Then open your heart to her,
> and let yourself receive the one
> who is opening to you so deeply.
> For if we genuinely love her,
> we wake up inside Earth's body
> where all our body, all over,
> every most hidden part of it,
> is realized in joy as her,
> and she makes us utterly real,
> and everything that is hurt, everything
> that seemed to us dark, harsh, shameful,
> maimed, ugly, irreparably
> damaged, is in her transformed
> and recognized as whole, as lovely,
> and radiant in her light,
> we awaken as the Beloved
> in every last part of our body.

Odyssey of a Quaker Earthpeace Activist

by Louis Cox

In 1970 I had a "conversion experience" that altered the course of my life.

I was sitting in an adult forum after Meeting for Worship. The guest speaker, a chemistry professor from a local college, was one of the early voices crying in the wilderness, trying to convince Americans of the seriousness of the global ecological crisis. He faced a hard sell, however. The year before, US astronauts had landed on the moon. Our nation's faith in science and technology reigned supreme. People tended to be very optimistic about the future.

Like many others I was aware of and concerned about specific environmental problems—the smog that hung over the city, news of a river so polluted that it once caught fire. I had read about brown pelican and eagle populations that seemed to be headed toward extinction because a pesticide had invaded the food chain and was weakening their egg shells.

But up to that point I had viewed these problems as *local* issues, appropriately addressed by appropriate technology, education, and legislation. And I trusted that "they," our leaders, were doing what needed to be done to solve those problems.

There had been an element of denial in my outlook as well— the tendency that many people have to tune out "inconvenient truths" in order to maintain their psychological comfort zones. For example, as a young teenager, I persisted in swimming in a creek in my neighborhood after several warnings from my father that the water was polluted by effluent from nearby homes that lacked adequate septic systems. My mind at that time was incapable of fathoming the notion that anyone would dare to do something so awful to a resource that served everyone.

But our guest speaker that day showed very effectively how

the world scientific community was assessing the overall health of the planet. Because of the combined effects of all the local environmental problems, all of the earth's interconnected life support systems were now in serious decline. More startling was the speaker's explanation that the current economic system depended on depleting the earth, not on its continued good health. At the heart of this crisis was a mode of thinking that seemed to be out of touch with the natural processes of the planet.

It was devastating for me to realize that the earth, our mother, was dying, and that I was part of the cause. The future I had envisioned for myself suddenly vanished like a mirage. As I walked out of the Meeting House that day, I knew that I must begin changing my life *immediately*. I needed to stop doing those things that were robbing the future and to dedicate my life to restoring the earth's health.

My vulnerability to this message at that particular moment had a lot to do with the spiritual sensibilities that had led me to Quakerism and were being nourished there. All my life I had wanted to live with integrity, that is, to make my personal behavior a reflection of my professed values. But it did not occur to me to seek support for this newfound environmental concern within my Quaker Meeting. Some Friends in my Meeting were practicing a form of simple living, which they linked to the testimonies of Peace and Equality. But no one talked about the Quaker faith itself as a primary source of guidance and inspiration for living more lightly on the planet.

Acting as best I could on my own, I started reducing, reusing, and recycling. I drove less and bicycled more. I joined a local citizens group that lobbied legislators and handed out leaflets in front of stores. I attended many rallies and demonstrations. However, after a year or two of frantic activism, I began feeling burned out, overwhelmed by the apathy and inertia of US society. It all seemed so utterly hopeless.

I finally decided that the best way to lighten my impact on the earth was to leave the big city and join the "back to the land" movement. I spent the next 12 years developing an organic homestead in the rural Ozarks. Anticipating a worsening ecological situation, I worked to make my household more self-reliant in food production, heating fuel, water, etc. I studied the plants and animals on my land and picked up practical country living skills from old-timers of the area.

For cash income, I worked as staff writer for a local daily newspaper, which gave me an opportunity to publicize environmental issues. But I also observed that many natives of the region tended to view the new wave of homesteaders and their environmental concerns with distrust or disdain. I began to doubt that my isolated household would be very secure with the rest of the world going pieces and while I was surrounded by less-than-sympathetic neighbors, many of whom were heavily armed!

My doubts deepened during a Friends gathering in the Midwest that I attended in the late 1980s. Elise Boulding, the main speaker, shared an experience that had influenced her decision to become a lifelong peace activist: She and her family had emigrated from Norway when she was a young child, only a couple of years after the end of World War I. She remembered being horrified whenever she saw photographs of the destruction and suffering caused by the Great War. Her anxiety grew when, as a teenager in the late 1930s, another major war in Europe seemed likely. But she took comfort in the thought that she could always go back to Norway, where, she assumed, it would be safe.

The Nazi invasion and occupation of Norway at the outset of World War II therefore left her deeply shaken. She suddenly realized that there was no longer any place in the world where a peace-loving person could simply hide from trouble. The only way to be safe, she concluded, is to work for peace and justice for all, to eliminate the root causes of violent conflict. Out of this realization, her life's calling as a peace activist emerged. Significantly, she found the support and guidance she needed in the traditions and practice of the Quaker faith.

I saw a parallel between Elise's story and my own role as a "conscientious objector" to modern industrial society's "war against nature." I saw the truth that the world had become too small for individual withdrawal to be a viable option. I felt a leading to take what I had learned as a homesteader and journalist and to engage the powers as an "Earthpeace" activist.

Fortunately, it was about this time that I learned of a group of Quakers who had started a North American environmental organization called Friends Committee on Unity with Nature (FCUN, later renamed Quaker Earthcare Witness). To quote Quaker founder George Fox, "my heart did leap for joy" at the prospect of finding both a spiritual home and supportive community for my environmental concerns, and I began subscribing to their newsletter. When I visited their Unity with Nature Center at the FGC Gathering in 1990, I had the same feeling that many people report after attending a Friends Meeting for worship for the first time—that I had "come home." I reveled in finding committed Friends who were talking about Earthcare as a Quaker testimony. This is what had been missing in my earlier frantic environmental activism—an understanding of the spiritual transformation that is essential to curbing our ecologically disruptive behavior. I started doing volunteer publications work for FCUN and eventually became a part-time staff member. This was the answer to my earlier problem of activist burnout—faithful response to a leading without having to feel like all the world's problems are on my shoulders.

Over the years, FCUN/QEW has done a respectable job, through its publications and programs, of articulating the connection between ecology and spirituality and highlighting ways that Quaker values and practices enable us to witness effectively for an earth restored. We have also provided the impetus for and support for many local Earthcare groups across North America.

But what about our ultimate goal of stopping humankind's reckless endangerment of God's creation? Environmental consciousness has grown in the last four decades, but the forces of destruction seem to have been growing even faster. Most of us encounter numerous obstacles to leading an ecologically correct lifestyle—jobs, family situations, economic constraints, etc.—that we see as keeping us stuck in a system that exploits both the earth and other people. We may not have all the answers, but we can try to understand and support one another as we struggle with individual choices and systemic issues.

Several years ago I was given an opportunity to get a little less stuck and to move a little closer toward earth-friendly living. I was invited to live in an off-grid solar-powered home in a beautiful rural area of Vermont, with Ruah Swennerfelt, a life partner who shares my deep concern for the Earth as well as many other values. We now live in a loose-knit community, where neighbors support one another. For me this new direction is not only a personal joy, but also an opportunity for a new kind of witness: a ministry of showing others what an alternative way of living on the earth might look like.

At the same time my life is an example some of the frustrations we all face because we live in an imperfect world. Because of the lack of adequate public transportation in my county, I have to rely a lot on a private automobile. Many of my purchases still exact a toll on the Earth because I am still linked to a larger world that hasn't yet learned to care. But at the heart of my new spiritual journey is finding joy in what is positive rather than focusing just on difficulties or making excuses. That's the Quaker Earthpeace activist's answer to burnout.

In my current part-time job as publications coordinator for Quaker Earthcare Witness, I experience the satisfaction of having paid work that is contributing to a better world. When I think back to that day in 1970 when I walked out of the meeting house praying for guidance to live with greater ecological integrity, I know that my prayers have been answered.

The Great Work – Thomas Berry in His Own Words

Selections from Thomas Berry's writings

Many readers of EarthLight *felt our prayers had been answered for a clear direction in spiritual ecology when we began reading the insights of "geologian" and cultural historian, Thomas Berry. Here are quotations from several of his books.*

The Great Work of our time is to reinvent the human...

Humans, more than any other living form, invent themselves. Other species receive their basic life instructions at the time of their birth... Some species, especially mammalian, do need some teaching from an older generation. Yet this is quite minimum if compared to the extent of teaching and action humans need to arrive at maturity. That is the purpose of the long childhood had by humans.

at the species level...

The issues that we are concerned with seem to be beyond the competence of our present cultural traditions, either individually or collectively. What is needed is something beyond existing traditions to bring us back to the most fundamental aspect of the human: giving shape to ourselves. The human is at a cultural impasse...Radical new cultural forms are needed. These new cultural forms would place the human within the dynamics of the planet rather than place the planet within the dynamics of the human...We must find our primary source of guidance just now in the inherent tendencies derived from our genetic coding. These tendencies are derived from the larger community of the Earth and eventually from the Universe itself.

with critical reflection...

This reinventing of the human needs to be done with critical competence. Originally there was a certain instinctive, spontaneous process whereby the early cultural formations were established. Now we need all our scientific insight and technological skills. We must, however, see that our sciences and technologies are coherent with the technologies of the natural world...

We insist on the need for critical understanding as we enter the Ecological Age in order to avoid a romantic attraction to the natural world that would not meet the urgencies of what we are about. The natural world is violent and dangerous as well as serene and benign. Our intimacies with the natural world must not conceal the fact that we are engaged in a constant struggle with natural forces. Life has a bitter and burdensome aspect at all levels. Yet its total effect is to strengthen the inner substance of the living world and to provide the never ending excitement of a grand adventure.

within the community of life systems...

This is the primary condition for reinventing the human. Because the Earth is not adequately understood either by our spiritual or by our scientific traditions, the human has become an addendum or an intrusion. We have found this situation to our liking since it enables us to avoid the problem of integral presence to the Earth. This attitude prevents us from considering the Earth as a single community with ethical relations determined primarily by the well-being of the total Earth community...

There are great difficulties in identifying just how to establish a viable context for a flourishing and sustainable mode of being.

Of one thing we can be sure, however. Our own future is inseparable from the future of the larger life community which brought us into being and sustains us in our aesthetic and emotional sensitivities, our intellectual perceptions, our sense of the divine, as well as in our physical nourishment and our bodily healing.

in a time-developmental context...

The universe is revealed to us as an irreversible emergent process. We no longer live simply in a spatial mode of consciousness where time is experienced as a seasonal renewing sequence of realities that keep their basic identity in accord with the Platonic archetypal world. We live not so much in a cosmos as in a cosmogenesis; that is, a Universe which is an irreversible sequence of transformations moving in general from a lesser to a greater order of complexity and from a lesser to greater consciousness. Our sense of who we are and what our role is must begin where the Universe begins. Not only do our physical shaping and our spiritual perception begin with the origin of the Universe, so too, the formation of every being.

by means of story...

The story of the Universe...is our most valuable resource in establishing a viable mode of being for the human species as well as for all those stupendous life systems whereby the Earth achieves its grandeur, fertility, and capacity for self-renewal...This story, as told in its galactic expansion, its Earth formation, its life emergence, and its self-reflexive consciousness manifested in the human, fulfills in our times the role of the mythic accounts of the Universe that existed in earlier times when human awareness was dominated by a spatial mode of consciousness.

and shared dream experience...

The creative process, whether in the human or the cosmological order, is too mysterious for easy explanation. Yet we all have experience of creative activity... out of the formless condition a formed reality appears. This process can be described in many ways, but the most appropriate way seems to be that of dream realization. The Universe seems to be the fulfillment of

43

something so highly imaginative and overwhelming that it must have been dreamed into existence.

But if the dream is creative we must also recognize that few things are so destructive as a dream or entrancement that has lost the integrity of its meaning and entered into exaggerated and destructive manifestation. There is no dream or entrancement in the history of the Earth that has wrought the destruction that is taking place in the entrancement with industrial civilization. Such entrancement must be considered as a profound cultural disorientation. It can only be dealt with by a corresponding deep cultural therapy.

—from "Reinventing the Human at the Species Level" and "The Earth Story," *The Great Work*

We need to understand that we ourselves activate one of the deepest dimensions of the Universe. We can recognize in ourselves our spiritual capacities for understanding. That these capacities exist from the beginning of the Universe is clear since the Universe is ever integral with itself in all its manifestations throughout its vast extension in space and the full sequence of its transformations in time. The human is neither an addendum nor an intrusion into the Universe. We are quintessentially integral with the Universe. In our selves the Universe is revealed to itself as we are revealed in the Universe.

—from "The Earth Story"

...the real issue before us is no longer finding its expression in terms of liberal and conservative but in terms of the ecologist or environmentalist on the one hand and the commercial-industrial establishment on the other. A new alignment of forces is taking place throughout every institution and every profession in our society.

What I am concerned with—and this is at the center of the Great Work as I envisage it—is that the human and the Earth form a single community of life. I am concerned that we recognize that the planet and all its modes of being have their rights independent of the human. The intimacy of humans with the various other components of the planet is the fulfillment of each in the other and both within the single Earth community. It is a mystical fulfillment, as well as a working arrangement. It is a commitment, not simply a way of survival. Anything less, to my mind, will not work...If we communicate to the next generations anything less than a truly inspiring vision of the wonder and grandeur of life, with all the natural phenomena that surround us, then we will be failing in our responsibility.

—from "The New Political Alignment," *The Great Work*

There is much to be done before this last decade of the twentieth century fulfills its designation as a Moment of Grace in the actualities of the Earth story. What can be said is that the foundations have been established in almost every realm of human affairs. Finally the mythic vision has been set into place. The distorted dream of an industrial technological paradise is being replaced by the more viable dream of a mutually-enhancing human presence within an integral ever-renewing organic-based Earth community. The dream drives the action.

—from "Moments of Grace," *The Great Work*

Our Children, Their Future

by Thomas Berry

Our children will live not in our world, but in their world, a future world that is rapidly taking on its distinctive contours. Our exploitative industrial world, despite all our scientific discoveries, is in a state of decline. The long-term survival of our children will depend on a new relationship between the human and the natural worlds. A change is taking place from exploitative relationships to one of mutual enhancement between the natural and human worlds. The type of prosperity known in the better moments of the 20th century will never again be available.

A new prosperity, however, will be available. Our children must activate this prosperity in the great variety of human activities. Indeed we have begun this process. Already we are aware of the following needs of our children.

Our children need a healthy Earth on which to live. A sickened planet is not conducive to healthy children physically, or to emotional or psychic security. They need pure air and water, sunlight, fruitful soil and all those living forms that provide the context in which human existence can be properly nurtured. Only if we provide this context will we fulfill our obligations to our children.

Our children need to become members not only of a local or even of the human community, they need to become conscious members of that wonderful society of all the living and nonliving beings of the natural world about them.

The refusal of human beings to become intimate members of the community of the Earth is leading to destruction of the entire planet. The next generation can survive only as functional members of this larger community. Our children are instinctively aware of this. We need only foster this awareness.

Our children need to learn not only how to read books composed by human genius, but also how to read the Great Book of the World. Again, reading this Great Book is natural to children. Alienation from this primary educational experience has been, in our generation, the source of unmeasured disaster to every aspect of human existence. The New Prosperity requires a new language, a language of nature that presently begins to be understood by those involved in solar energy, by the new architects, the new educators and the environmentalists. This new language is primarily the language of the Earth, a language of living relationships that extend throughout the universe.

We have here on the North American continent a superb natural setting in which our children can become literate, capable of understanding what their world is telling them. Above all, this natural world is telling them about a new prosperity, a new richness of life, new energies that are available and new perspectives to enjoy.

In a special manner our children need to observe and esteem the spontaneities of nature in our own bio-regions of North America, spontaneities that give expression to genetic diversity, the most precious endowment of the living world. Without the marvelous variety of living forms that swim in the seas and live and move upon the Earth and fly through the air, our own human understanding, our emotional life, our imaginative powers, our sense of the divine, our capacity for verbal expression: these would all be terribly diminished. If we lived on the moon our sense of the divine would reflect the lunar landscape; our emotions, sensitivities and imagination would all in a similar manner be limited to a lunar mode of expression.

Our children need to learn gardening. The reasons for this reach deep into their mental and emotional as well as their physical survival. Gardening is an active participating in the deepest mysteries of the universe. By gardening our children learn that they constitute with all growing things a single community of life. They learn to nurture and be nurtured in a universe that is always precarious, but ultimately benign. They learn profound reasons for the seasonal rituals of the great religious traditions.

Elementary education might very well begin and be developed in a gardening context. How much the children could learn! A language related to life! Emotional responses to blossoming and fruitful plants, social cooperation and death as a source of life. They could learn geology, biology, and astronomy. They could learn the sources of poetry and literature and the arts. They might even be saved from the sterile, ephemeral world of electronic games.

Our children need to understand the meaning, grandeur and sacredness of the Earth as revelatory of the deep mysteries and meaning of the world. Rather than teaching them to disdain the natural world as unworthy of their concern, it would be most helpful if our religious traditions would move toward a stronger emphasis on the glorious phenomena of the universe about us as modes of divine communication.

Our children need a sense of their unique historical role in creating a new ecological age. This future world is something that has never existed before. We are involved in an irreversible sequence of planetary developments. For the first time an integral form of the planet Earth with all its geological contours, its living forms and its human presence has become possible as a vital, functioning reality expressing itself in its unborn sequence of splendors in movement and song and an infinite variety of color in the sky, in the sea, and throughout the five continents.

There is a certain truth in the expression: "The dream drives the action." The greatest contribution we can make to our children is to assist them in their dreams of the world of pure air and water and sunlight and soil, where the company of living beings would flourish.

Science as Wisdom: A Way Forward

Interview with Scientist Brian Swimme

by K. Lauren de Boer

My first encounter with Brian Swimme came at a time when I was on an active search. As a graduate student in the late 1980s, I was interested in the human-earth relationship, wanting to explore how landscape affects the human imagination. If I had any sense of the sacred, it was unconscious. Then I ended up studying at the Institute in Culture and Creation Spirituality in Oakland where I took Brian's class "Cosmos as Primary Revelation." Here was a scientist talking about the great mysteries of the Universe in the most passionate way I could imagine! By the time I left the program, I had come to understand that the human imagination was not something

"out there," separate from some great matrix called the Universe. It is a deeply embedded expression of a great unfolding of creativity—the epic of evolution. And I, as a human being, had an astounding role to play as the way in which the Universe reflects on and takes joy in its existence. It helped heal what for me had been a significant missing piece of my upbringing as a Christian Reformed minister's son: the sacredness of the human-earth relationship. The ICCS program in general gave me hope that the Christian tradition contained seeds of earth renewal for those willing to search them out. I hope the following interview imparts something of the gift of someone who I feel is one of the great teachers of our time.

K Lauren de Boer: You began your teaching career at the University of Puget Sound in Tacoma after you got your PhD in gravitational dynamics, mathematical cosmology and singularity from the University of Oregon. What happened there? What subsequently brought you to want to tell the story of the Epic of Evolution through what you've called the "poetry of science?""

Brian Swimme: I didn't understand at the time but I could never really feel at home in the classroom of the university. I look back now and I can tell you what it was. But at the time I said something's odd, something's strange, not right. I realize that I really wanted to teach the mysteries of the Universe. The whole idea of teaching the mysteries of the Universe in the university meant that I ran into one difficulty after another because the focus there is a curriculum that will lead to employment. There are two things that you have to give a university student: employment, or entrance into another educational program where they will get employment. I thought, there's something wrong with that. I hated the thought of taking all the knowledge of the universe and using it to get a job. I wasn't against people working, but it was amazing how much is bothered me. It just felt sacrilegious. So that alone I would say is what ruined me as a regular university scientist.

If you grow up in America or Japan or France—any of the modern countries—you have been given the most advanced training in a very particular form of consciousness. We read about these Tibetan Llamas. At two years old they start to train them and by the time they're in their 30s, they've really gone somewhere in this particular form of consciousness. We do the same thing. And our form of consciousness is materialism, or consumerism. Our whole society gives a really advanced training in it. That's what I've come to understand. What is necessary, I think, is to have a process that goes deeper than that, and it has to liberate a human from the hold which is very deep in the soul—the hold of the modern materialistic, capitalistic, consumerist worldview. For myself, part of what I'm doing in education is working with the roots of consciousness, attempting to liberate the confinement, and ease humans into the magnificence of the universe. The very fact that the human—especially Americans— cannot easily slide into ecstasy, that fact alone is a symptom of the diseased consciousness of consumerism. I'm attempting to provide an antidote and an introduction to this more fulfilling and ecstatic mode of consciousness.

K. Lauren de Boer: When did you first have a sense that the Epic of Evolution, the Universe Story might be an antidote?

Brian Swimme: My sense of the power of the Epic, but even more, my sense of the ecstatic side of life and the infinity of the mysteries—that you can go directly into an infinite, bottomless intimacy in the universe—that's something that goes back all the way to childhood. The idea of science as a way of moving us into an intimate understanding, as an antidote or a way forward, that wasn't until I talked to Thomas Berry who really named it and said the story of science is the way into the future. What I was doing was sort of unconscious and intuitive. I had no real understanding of it in a cultural framework. Thomas (Berry) understood it completely, explicitly. Working with him enabled me to deepen this understanding of the cultural significance of the new story of science.

K. Lauren de Boer: The notion of science moving into a new phase, that it no longer has to be the handmaiden to technology, no longer a mere process of collecting data and facts—what would that mean for a culture which is so oriented toward buying things, so oriented toward a world that's always "getting better," at least in material sense?

Brian Swimme: I think for scientists and for other people it's a question of "is the universe valuable? Is it sacred? Is it holy? Or is the human agenda all that matters?" I just don't think we're that stupid to continue in a way that continues to destroy. I'm hopeful that the Epic of Evolution will be yet another strategy in our culture that will lead our consciousness out of a very tight, human-centered materialism and that we'll just sort of ease into seeing the magnificence of the whole.

Of course there are indigenous cultures all over the planet that don't need scientists to tell them that the universe is holy. Some indigenous people are working with both the most advanced concepts in their indigenous culture and the most advanced ideas in science. One of the reasons we don't recognize indigenous science as science, is because we don't recognize natural history as science! This to me is part of the lopsided orientation of the modern mathematical scientist. I'm one of them—I know. It's a great honoring and valuing of mathematics and a denigration of the specific. We're so impressed with our human minds for coming up with mathematics and so unimpressed by the marvels of a fern or an ant. Again, we don't recognize that as being of supreme significance. Or holy. As we can once again recognize the power of the naturalist tradition, we'll see that inside that tradition itself is indigenous knowledge. Indigenous people who are working with the Epic of Evolution tell me this: that the young people on the reservation don't listen to them when they're telling them traditional stories. Until they put it in the context of the new science. Then suddenly they're interested. They don't want to be behind the times or out of it. They want to be hip and with it, with the modern culture. Then they find out that the cutting edge of modern culture is a profound recognition of the truth of their tradition. And suddenly, it comes together for them. Finally they can see the depths of their own tradition! Indigenous science is in a leadership position within this particular natural history tradition.

K. Lauren de Boer: They're in a leadership position because of centuries and centuries of building that body of knowledge from direct observation...

Brian Swimme: Direct observation. And cherishing that local knowledge. And passing it on. And teaching the form of consciousness that can see it.

K. Lauren de Boer: E.O Wilson states that he wrote his book *The Diversity of Life* in epic form because he believes that it is absolutely essential to strike "the inner mystic chord of emotion" when telling the story of the epic, not to just present the story in a book of facts. What do you think he's getting at here?

Brian Swimme: That's such a deep question. My whole life is devoted to that question. How do you break through a form of consciousness that doesn't see that we are destroying everything? Joanna Macy is convinced that because we refuse to grieve, we remain in denial. I think that's an important insight into the collective psyche. We refuse to grieve. And we're afraid that if we begin to grieve, we will become so overwhelmed, we'll become catatonic and useless.

K. Lauren de Boer: When in reality, there's a kind of empowerment that happens when one moves into grieving.

Brian Swimme: Exactly. So I think there's something important about that, it's through our woundedness that we really see it. By taking into consideration where the suffering is greatest. You could begin anywhere. It depends on where your heart lives. For me, it's the all, the unborn. I'm somehow terrified by what they are going to see, when they emerge, when their moment comes, say in a thousand years or so. And it just seems so horrendous that we would act in a way that would ruin their chances of living. Thomas Berry sees a lot of the destruction as an attempt to put together human life without a cosmic, vast story. So he thinks our way forward, then, is to begin to see our lives, in all the details, as part of a vast story.

53

K. Lauren de Boer: Part of the narrative for me that's most exciting is the notion that we as a species are the Earth actually reflecting on her own stunning beauty. Somehow through that crucible of the evolutionary story, the universe came to "taste itself," I think is how you've phrased it. It's a part of the story that really grabs me on a deep level.

Brian Swimme: Me too. This goes back to your first question—why was I just not happy teaching in a regular university? What I can say now is, I am just so profoundly happy serving out the role of the human as the realm in which the universe and the earth reflects upon and tastes its beauty. It's just so satisfying. We've been given this great gift and we're not quite capable of believing that this really is what we're to do. We're ready to bask in beauty. When I talk about just basking in beauty, it's not to suggest that it's dissociated from hard work. There are all kinds of hard work involved here, but if a person is working with food and agriculture, say permaculture, and the primary motive is to produce the food, then there's something missing. The primary motive has to include this opportunity of being stunned by the amazing reality in which we're dealing. For me, it's becoming a parent. I never stop being amazed at participating in giving birth to a human. It's just unbelievable that we would be given that kind of power. And we're not just given the power, we're also given the power to become aware that we have that power.

We've only recently developed this power of conscious self-awareness. So there is a challenge to maintain it. What happens is that we tend to collapse into older strategies, evolutionary strategies and we drop away from conscious self-awareness, become more reptilian or, even machine-like. But if the conscious self-awareness can be maintained, there is just this deep sense of satisfaction and joy that is the natural birthright. If we find ways to ease out of compulsion, then we have all of this energy for creating a life that's simple, that's compassionate, that's ...

K.Lauren de Boer: ...profoundly spiritual...

Brian Swimme: Profoundly spiritual. Moment by moment. And

then instead of all of that energy being trained on destruction, it would all be drawn back into the true work of the human—which is to be where beauty is deeply felt.

K. Lauren de Boer: Creativity is at the core of what you do and seems a process so essential to the story. Is creativity a link between the larger cosmic process and our personal lives?

Brian Swimme: It's really interesting—the word "creativity" wasn't even used before the 20th century. As a concept, it's new, even though we're kind of immersed in it. True creativity is breath. It's each moment. Because each moment really arises new, we're participating again in creating the ultimate reality. It's not a question of "Gee, can I be creative?" Everyone's creative. Constantly. Every second.

Creativity has to do with breath, and walking, conversation and lovemaking, and childrearing. And for humans to enter into creativity fully means to also enter into an awareness of its awesome power! The only way you can do that is by reflecting upon what creativity has accomplished in 15 billion years. It's the same creativity that gave birth to the stars, the galaxies, the angiosperms. If you really get into that and then you begin to see the whole thing as a flame, you just feel it as this ongoing fire. And here we are in the middle of it! It's just like being part of a whirlwind and it's only a choice of how you want to creatively participate.

You can enter into it in the ecstatic sense, the sense that, "Wow! I am that power!" The universe is permeated with self-organizing dynamics at a variety of levels at work—elementary particles, stars, galaxies, consciousness. We live within that realm. I think the self-organizing dynamics of the universe have us. We don't have them. Within the evolutionary point of view, you realize, holy toledo, the mind itself is just an expression of the powers of the universe!

Scientists find universe awash in tiny diamonds

by Pat Mayne Ellis

But haven't we always known?
The shimmer of trees, the shaking of flames
every cloud lined with something
clean water sings right to the belly
scouring us with its purity
it too is awash with diamonds

"so small that trillions could rest
on the head of a pin"

It is not unwise then to say
that the air is hung close with diamonds
that we breathe diamonds
our lungs hoarding, exchanging
our blood sowing them rich and thick
along every course it takes
Does this explain
why some of us are so hard
why some of us shine
why we are all precious

that we are awash in creation
spumed with diamonds
shot through with beauty
that survived the deaths of stars

*The title is based on a quotation found in a newspaper clipping
on the subject.*

Declaring the Holy

An Interview with Poet Pattiann Rogers

by Maryanne Hannan

I had never heard of Pattiann Rogers when I attended her poetry reading at Sienna College in upstate New York in 1998. I went with friends, and our minds were not on poetry, but on all the things we would talk about afterwards. By the end of the reading, we were all fans.

If I had to say what I most admire about her work, I would say it is unfailingly interesting. Whenever I begin a Pattiann Rogers poem, I know I am going on an intellectual adventure. It will not dissolve into treacly emotion or ineffable ponderings. I am always curious what she will do in the poem, where she will bring me, what intellectual surprises await me.

In the tradition of great philosopher poets, Pattiann Rogers writes her own contemporary de rerum natura ["on the nature of things"]. In language matching the fecundity of the world she describes, she shows the power of imagination to deepen thought. Images from her poems have stayed with me, becoming the thoughts themselves.

Maryanne Hannan: Much of your poetry takes as its starting point the raw physicality of life. How did you come to this reverence for and attention to the physical world?

Pattiann Rogers: I'm not certain what you mean by raw physicality. We are physical creatures immersed in a physical world, a world we come to know through our bodies, through our senses. We were born from the Earth and have inherent connections with it—strong pre-verbal connections that we feel and are affected by everyday. We are surrounded by and within the physical world, sunlight and shadows, wind or the still lack of it, the motion of clouds in the sky, the fragrance of rain, the silence of snow, the sound of a river, a bird calling in the background, grasses covered in frost, grasses in the wind, a fly at the window, a flowery weed by the roadside, the outline of a familiar tree at dusk, the sound of a door slamming, a dog barking in the distance, frogs or crickets or locusts beginning their calls as night comes on. Those living in cities are no less involved in the physical world. The city is full of life of all kinds and the energy of life. Food is obviously physical. Taking nourishment is something humans have in common with all life forms. I believe we come to know ourselves better the more we are aware of all the facets of the Earth, its life and its processes, and all the elements of the Universe that encompass us.

Maryanne Hannan: You have written that "the world provides every physical image and sensation we will ever need in order to experience the sacred, to declare the holy, if we could only learn to recognize it."

Pattiann Rogers: The more we observe, the more alert we are to the details of the physical world around us, the more we come to value and revere it. I'm curious about the history of the Earth, the origin of life on Earth, and the ways those many lives maintain themselves. I'm extremely grateful for those among us who carefully study the Earth in all of its manifestations and those who study the heavens and its elements. Many who do this work describe their discoveries as religious experiences. I remember reading a quote from an astronomer viewing the first images coming from the Hubble Space Telescope. He said, "It was like seeing the face of God." We are spiritual creatures too. We delight, we grieve, we extol, we worship, we love. We hold to justice, honesty, compassion, grace. These are not abstractions. They are actions, states that are felt in our bodies. They are present in our blood, our pulse, our bones, our cells, our breath. We sometimes speak of them as if they had no connection with our bodies. I believe this is a mistake. The spiritual and physical are one.

Maryanne Hannan: I love your poem "The Immortal Soul," which concludes "the soul then believes/ with all of its body in its own immortality." But it always begins with the body, does it not?

Pattiann Rogers: Often an uplifting experience occurs for me when I'm least expecting it. I wrote of this in an essay, "Surprised by the Sacred." Sometimes a fleeting experience lasting only moments can stun the heart, and I sense something very important has been encountered. But exactly what? And exactly why am I moved? It may be as simple as watching the way a bird veers by overhead against an evening sky or being shocked at finding a toad in the toe of a boot or noticing the sudden fragrance of wet field grasses or seeing the morning shadows of a tree on the curtains. It happened once for me when I heard roofers working on the roof next door begin to sing together in the hot summer sun.

Many of my poems begin with my investigating such an experience. "Why was I moved by what happened in what might have seemed something ordinary? What was my body reacting to?" I ask. Almost always, it's the reaction of my body that comes first and then the verbal acknowledgment of the incident. My poems don't attempt simply to describe the incident but to probe more deeply to try to discover what it was about the incident that so completely captured my soul. Poetry is the tool I use in this investigation.

Maryanne Hannan: Many of your poems use the vocabulary of science. What does science have to offer poetry?

Pattiann Rogers: It's finally become apparent to me that science is not quite the right word to be using in regard to my poetry. A better word, and one I'm trying to use more often, is cosmology. It's cosmology that's at the heart of my poetry, a vision of who and where we are and reflections on what it means to be human. All cultures have possessed a cosmology, beliefs about the Universe and the physical world, its origins, processes, and its future. Often in the past, the cosmology of a culture was synonymous with its religious beliefs, one and the same, or at least the two worked closely together. Today the story of the physical Universe, our contemporary cosmology, comes from science. Our cosmology is a story, an amazing story that is still in the process of being told, a story that modifies itself and scrutinizes itself. It's a vision, and we are included in the vision.

Maryanne Hannan: Not many poets write as you do about our contemporary cosmology.

Pattiann Rogers: We and our culture have assimilated this story. It is part of our being, whether we've acknowledged that or not. I know that's true because we make decisions and we act everyday in accord with our cosmological story. For instance, we believe our body is made from the dust of old stars and that it is composed of tiny living cells, and we know something about how those cells function. We have seen images of blood coursing through veins, living sperm swimming toward an ovum, one reaching its goal. We've seen the bones of our own bodies in x-rays and MRI's. We've seen ultrasound images of living fetuses in the womb. These are images of our physical bodies not seen by other generations. We believe every living creature possesses a genetic code and that we are related to all the life forms on Earth. We believe we live on a turning globe called the Earth and that our Earth revolves around our star, the Sun, along with the other planets in our solar system. We believe day and night are the results of our Earth turning on its axis. We believe the landmasses of the continents float on tectonic plates and move very slowly, sometimes encountering each other, causing mountains to rise and earthquakes to occur. We believe that the Universe contains billions of galaxies, which in turn contain billions of stars. We know we are extremely small in relation to the size of the Universe and that our sun is a very ordinary star. These are just a few of the details of our cosmological story that almost all of us accept.

This story of the physical world, as much as we know of it, is stunning, and glorious. I find it beautiful and frightening, full of wonder and mystery. I've tried to explore in poetry what the vision of our contemporary cosmology means to beauty, to the human spirit, to our spiritual needs. It seems crucial to me that this be done, not just by me but by all of us.

Maryanne Hannan: Does poetry have anything to offer this cosmology?

Pattiann Rogers: Poetry is the only medium in which the language and the music of words is flexible enough to allow experimentation and hypotheses about these issues which are so important to how we define ourselves as human beings, how we imagine who we are, and therefore what we value and how we act.

I've made guesses in my poetry about the nature of divinity within our cosmological story, and about the nature of beauty and love, about our obligations as conscious creatures in the Universe. I don't give answers. I try to ask the right questions or to provide an evocative experience of the physical world in order to perceive it anew. Who are we in this Universe as we have come to envision and understand it? What is the creative power? What is divinity?

Maryanne Hannan: Your poem "The Possible Suffering of a God During Creation" toys with the idea of a god who is not omnipotent. Is this something you believe?

Pattiann Rogers: What satisfies me now is to imagine a divine power that is involved in every aspect of the Universe, interwoven and in union with it, not separate. We know the Universe is in constant change and flux, it is in motion, not static, it is in a process of evolution. It seems to follow then that this also must be the state of the power within it. That's crudely said, and it's simply a guess. It's a guess that pleases me because it appears to meld with our contemporary cosmology and because it eliminates the paradoxes that arise when we posit an all-knowing, all-powerful, loving, perfect God who controls everything like a master puppeteer. If this latter is our definition of God, then we must account somehow for the sufferings and deaths of infants, children, and the innocent from diseases, droughts and floods, violent weather, earthquakes and other "natural" phenomena. The efforts to explain this paradox seem contorted and contrived to me and not satisfying.

The idea of a divine power who needs us as the Universe needs us to reflect upon it, to praise it, to invest it with meaning and, by our actions, to create compassion and justice, honor and love, is satisfying and sustaining to me. It is liberty not to obey because we are commanded to obey but to try to live a constructive and righteous life in order to aid in fulfilling the promise of the Universe and bringing divinity into its full realization.

It seems important to me to remember that I can be both believer and seeker. I can believe and yet continue to question and search at the same time. I can believe and still be willing to modify or refine or enhance my beliefs in order to strengthen them, or more exactly conform them to the truth of my experiences in the contemporary world. Belief to me does not mean rigidity, inflexibility, being static and unchanging. The Earth, the Universe, the physical world we live in is none of these things. Why should spirituality be so? If spirituality is alive and vital, then it, too ,will evolve if we allow it, always with care and circumspection.

Maryanne Hannan: Do you have any particular spiritual practice underlying your work and sustaining you in the process?

Pattiann Rogers: When I'm able, I go to those places that have given me spiritual renewal in the past, places that have offered me reaffirmation of my own integrity and belief again in the basic goodness of humankind and the possibility of a high purpose to our existence. Music, especially classical music, is almost always such a source for me, also, the perspective the vast physical world provides—ocean, mountains, the intense activity in the multiplicity of life forms. Van Gogh, in a letter to his brother Vincent, wrote: "I have a terrible need—dare I say the word?— of religion. Then I go out at night and paint the stars." I, too, find the starry night sky a source of awe and inspiration, a release from boundaries.

Not all people find spiritual renewal in the same places or in the same ways. Sometimes I'm uplifted and renewed by watching the joy people take in their creativity—whether it's flying kites or sailing or roller-blading or making ice sculptures or collecting the largest ball of string in the world or rock climbing or embroidering or molding pottery or building a chair.

We get up out of bed every morning, almost every one of us, knowing we are going to die, and yet we get up and try to fulfill our obligations and do what we believe is right and important, and we try to do this without harming others, and we try to do this knowing that we have been born in ignorance and we will die in ignorance, knowing we will never solve the great mystery of life or understand the horrible majesty of the Universe. We create, we play and rejoice, we praise. There is nobility in this, the highest nobility.

The Possible Suffering of a God During Creation

by Pattiann Rogers

It might be continuous—the despair he experiences
Over the imperfection of the unfinished, the weaving
Body of the imprisoned moonfish, for instance,
Whose visible arms in the mid-waters of the deep sea
Are not yet free, or the velvet-blue vervain
Whose grainy tongue will not move to speak, or the ear
Of the spitting spider still oblivious to sound.

It might be pervasive—the anguish he feels
Over the falling away of everything that the duration
Of the creation must, of necessity, demand, maybe feeling
The break of each and every russet-headed grass
Collapsing under winter ice or feeling the split
Of each dried and brittle wing of the sycamore
As it falls from the branch. Maybe he winces
At each particle-by-particle disintegration of the limestone
Ledge into the crevasse and the resulting compulsion
Of the crevasse to the grain by grain, obliterating self.

And maybe he suffers from the suffering
Inherent to the transitory, feeling grief himself
For the grief of shattered beaches, disembodied bones
And claws, twisted squid, piles of ripped and tangled
Uprooted turtles and rock crabs and Jonah crabs,
Sand bugs, seaweed and kelp.

How can he stand to comprehend the hard, pitiful
Unrelenting cycles of coitus, ovipositors, sperm and zygotes,
The repeated unions and dissolutions over and over,
The constant tenacious burying and covering and hiding
And nesting, the furious nurturing of eggs, the bright

Breaking forth and the inevitable cold-blowing-away?

Think of the million million dried stems of decaying
Dragonflies, the thousand thousand leathery cavities
Of old toads, the mounds of cows' teeth, the tufts
Of torn fur, the contorted eyes, the broken feet, the rank
Bloated odors, the fecund brown-haired mildews
That are the residue of his process. How can he tolerate
knowing
There is nothing else here on earth as bright and salty
As blood spills in the open?

Maybe he wakes periodically at night
Wiping away the tears he doesn't know
He has cried in his sleep, not having had time yet to tell
Himself precisely how it is he must mourn, not having had
time yet
To elicit from his creation its invention
Of his own solace.

The Motherhouse of Reinvention

by Sharon Abercrombie

An old adage says that "necessity is the mother of invention." The necessity of our time, the Immaculate Heart of Mary Sisters of Monroe, Michigan, "the Blue Nuns," are finding, is the health and sustainability of planet Earth and future generations. Thus, invention based on a vision of sustainability is at the heart of the renovation of their Motherhouse. But even beyond that, sustainability is becoming the over-arching concept for their community's charism in the 21st century.

When EarthLight's *assistant editor, Sharon Abercrombie wrote this story a few years ago, the "green Motherhouse" was under construction. The project is up and running. In the words of a recent* Toledo Blade *reporter, the sisters are "in the green." They've cut utility bills by $187,000 a year through a one-half reduction in their use of water and of natural gas. "Sustainability pays. And not just earthly dividends," notes Martha Weise, campus administrator for the order. Gas usages is down by 54 percent; water usages by 50 percent.*

Savings go beyond reduced utility bills. The nuns have netted $2,000 by using recycled paper and other recycled office supplies; $2,200 by selling empty inkjet cartridges to a recycler; and $4,100 by cutting the number of dumpsters used and increasing paper and household recycling.

A "greening committee" oversees the activity. It has initiated other measures, such as fueling vehicles after 6 PM. To pay for the project, the committee is selling T-shirts made with recycled materials.

The sisters' activities have not gone unnoticed. Last October, the Sisters won a 2005 Design Honor Award from Faith and Form *magazine and the Interfaith Forum on Religion, Art and Architecture. It was their sixth award. The renovation has also won the Clean Air Excellence Award from the US Environmental protection Agency; the Build Michigan Award; a Building Award*

*from the Michigan Historic Preservation Network, and the 2004
Pyramid Award for Best Project Team.*

During the Great Depression of the 1930s, the poorest of
the poor in Monroe, Michigan didn't have to worry about their
children going to bed hungry every night. The kind sisters across
town dropped by each week with vegetables, fruit, and meat—
the generous bounty from their own motherhouse farm. The
sisters were truly living out the Christian Gospel mandate to
feed the hungry.

These same women were a familiar sight downtown as well.
Each day, a couple of the sisters would drop by the local bank to
make fifty-cent deposits to their community's savings account.

It was a deliberate gesture, an example-setting move to
encourage townsfolk to support their US banking system—
despite people's understandable feelings of mistrust, cynicism,
and betrayal which had erupted following the stock market crash
of 1929.

Seventy years later, the Sister Servants of the Immaculate
Heart of Mary continue to live out their role as vibrant, visible
pacesetters. This time around, they have opened the doors of
their religious outreach to Earth Herself.

The 650-member religious order has embarked upon the
largest environmental sustainability building project in the
United States. Costing "lots of millions of dollars," in the words
of Sister Paula Cathcart, its initiator and a member of the
Leadership Team, the project entails a wholesale renovation of
the community's retirement center for 250 senior sisters in
residence, using cutting-edge ecological design features.

The community envisions turning the project into a real
ecological laboratory experience as well as an educational site,
said Sister Janet Ryan, also a member of the Leadership Council.

Expected to be completed in 2003, the first phase of the
project is bringing in the most energy-efficient resources around
lighting and water use reduction, including a 240-well
geothermal heating and cooling system.

That's just the beginning. The sisters also plan to restore
native plants to the property. According to Danielle Conroyd,

project director, the Monroe bioregion was a deciduous swamp in its natural state. No wonder the nice, green, well-manicured lawns so beloved in the Midwest and South never worked well. Taking this into account, five acres now managed as mowed lawn in front of the Motherhouse will be diversified and restored as meadow savanna, planted with seasonal grasses, wildflowers, and a bordered lawn. Meadows will also buffer existing woodlands.

The community has already begun implementing some of those outdoor dreams. This past summer they turned several acres of their land into an organic community garden—a Community Supported Agricultural (CSA) endeavor.

It was staffed, in part, by retirees in wheelchairs, who volunteered to shuck beans during the bountiful harvest season, and by residents of Freedom House, an interdenominational charity that provides food, clothing, shelter, and social and legal services to refugees.

How best to describe the IHM sustainability project? Several terms come to mind: "leaving no footprints upon the Earth" is one. "Reinventing the human," in the words of venerable geologian Father Thomas Berry, is another. Each explains what the sisters are about. However, one does not learn to walk lightly and reinvent oneself overnight. The project traces its inception back several years ago when the community realized that its old motherhouse building, constructed during the early 1930s, needed extensive renovations.

When architects and engineers told them the structure had 18-inch concrete and brick walls and would likely be standing into the 23rd century, the sisters concluded that it would be better to work with what they had rather than build a new, more costly, lower-quality structure.

Here, in fact, was an opportunity to expand their mission of social justice to include the ecological perspective, so "that the quality of life would be guaranteed for future generations," Sister Janet explains. But to reach out to the seventh generation, as envisioned by native people of this continent, one must live in harmony with Earth.

The Sisters invited Father Al Fritsch, a sustainability expert from Appalachia, to do a series of land audits, to explore the possibilities for their building and property. Next, they started a series of theological discerning sessions for their sisters to help in the decision-making. "Spirituality is at the core of who we are," notes Sr. Paula, "and we needed to understand the project in the light of that call."

It became a five and a half year study. The sisters brought in ecological designers of the caliber of architect William McDonough. McDonough is a pioneer in the international sustainability movement in the area of ecological design. They studied the works of Thomas Berry, Teilhard de Chardin, and Brian Swimme, and consulted the writings of contemporary ecofeminists. They pored over religious texts of all the world spiritualities, to see what they had to say about the place of Earth in their respective cosmologies.

And they combined Scripture reading with Dr. Suess. At one point, as a community, the sisters read *The Lorax*, the tale of a greedy businessman who chops down all the trees in his bioregion, sending all the animals and birds into exile—and finally the people as well. As an old man, he finds himself totally alone. He realizes his terrible mistake. When a visitor stops by, the old man sends him out to find some seedlings to begin replanting the devastated area.

The Sisters' discernment process took a hard look at the effects of environmental racism upon the poor. They traced the progress of contemporary theology, noting that the language used to describe the central mystery of Christianity moved from "salvation" to "liberation" of the individual soul to the salvation/liberation of human history. And they prayed every step of the way. "God, source of energy, meet us in our deepest hearts."

Many of the sisters grieved, as the beloved motherhouse they'd lived with all their lives was to be no more. And they kept praying. "God source of all energy, show us the next steps…energize us anew."

Community newsletters chronicled each step of the journey. "Now we are at a new point," Sister Mary Ann Hinsdale wrote in one of the publications. "We are realizing that transformation in Christ extends to the whole universe." Another Sister reflected that "our very beings are knit to the crucified and risen Christ as he returns to God the creation that groans to be set free." It was becoming clearer and clearer that environmental degradation was the overarching moral issue of the 21st century, notes Sister Janet.

During the process, the sisters brought together 130 of their members who had volunteered to become a part of the discernment. Two years ago, ninety-two percent of them voted "yes" to sustainability as their new community charism for the 21st century. This over-arching concept of sustainability, after all, was not inconsistent with their heritage; in fact, "it was to be found in the liberating and transforming mission of Jesus," notes Sister Paula.

They voted "yes," even though they would be taking a major financial risk, putting their limited resources on the line. "But if you don't put your money where your mouth is, how can you truly model ecological sustainability?" observed Sister Janet Ryan.

The final upshot of this discernment process: "The entire campus would be a Center for transformation of consciousness demonstrating that we are all One, and that who we are [as individuals] makes a difference," states Sister Paula.

The Practice of the Presence of the Wild

by David Oates

The first time I attended a Quaker meeting there was something strangely familiar about it. It took me a long time to discover what it was.

The first meeting was in 1980. About that time I had also been taking hikes by myself in the Sierra Nevada mountains. They varied from a few days to a few weeks in duration, and from easy strolls to arduous explorations up high, beyond trails and signposts.

Eventually I began to understand that the two experiences, seemingly so unlike, shared something essential. It was wildness: the uncontrolled and uncontrollable.

Alone on a mountainside it is an obvious meditation to recognize how big the world is, and how much bigger the cosmos beyond it, and beyond that how encompassingly small the little life is that holds the beholding mind. Small and easily damaged.

In a silent meeting there sometimes comes a similar recognition. Out of the dark into which the mind descends, a becoming humility settles over one. There is much in that dark silence, much that is not understood or understandable. Some of it emerges during a well-gathered meeting, either to stir the individual with unexpected intuitions or to impel someone to stand and speak words that are just a little truer than his ordinary talk.

The silence is wild. No one controls it or measures it. Without this silence, Quaker meetings would be shallow talk-societies. In the silence is the depth and the profundity. In it one encounters the truth: a person is a small bit of intellectualizing jetsam afloat on a mighty and incomprehensible stream.

This is distressing news to the Faust in us. Which is precisely why it is such important news.

Typical city-folk today apparently believe that if anything goes wrong, it must be someone's fault. They suppose that we humans control all: if someone is hurt, some official must have screwed up. It can never just be the fact that humans are mortal, and life is dangerous. Skiers who run into trees blame resort operators rather than the laws of physics. Earthquakes are followed by lawsuits.

Civilized life fosters this delusion. City lights blot out the starry sky, that insult to mortal pride. Day and night can be ignored. Weather is minimized. Edges are rounded. Health care is good enough, with a little luck, for one to go for months and years without an obviously unsolvable problem.

What losses these comforts are! What a revelation simple hunger can be—how sharpening to the senses, how bracing to the mind. What sleepy, deluded, dull people we turn into under such a regimen of toasty quilts and surfeit. What a silly theory it is to think that all hazards are, or ought to be, marked with red triangles and registered with the appropriate authorities. How badly we need a sharp pinch now and then to bring back to us the reality: though we try to provide for our needs, life is nevertheless both uncertain and painful. Best not to forget it.

The common thread in all these urban delusions is denial of

nature as an independent and superior reality. Our handling of wilderness is symptomatic of this denial: we label it "natural resource" and chop it up for raw materials. Where human desire is the measure of all things, all the world is a consumable commodity, a playpen for the infantile appetite.

But nature is present all the while. It is undeterred by our silly denial. Sickness, accident, old age, and death remind us, eventually, if nothing else does.

But the systematic loss of awareness of this reality leaves us unable to comprehend. We think there must be some mistake.

It is the urban/civilized lie that humans can control all, much, or even an important part of life. Most of what counts is far beyond our reach. By limiting our focus to a few trivial elements which we can manipulate, we shrink our lives to pitiable smallness. And all the rest of the cosmos goes unnoticed.

It is a high price to pay for the illusion of safety.

If the reality of nature is as present as all that, then we do not have far to look for deliverance. Which is not to say there is no need for plain old outdoor trees-and-mountains wilderness. Contact with the *real* wilderness of uncivilized nature is an unmatched vehicle for awakening and deepening the mind. In many non-Western cultures one leaves the village to encounter the natural world alone and in its full reality—and to gain the depth and serenity which that encounter brings. The modern world needs places for this reason, along with all the other good other reasons.

But even right now, in the dregs of the Dark Ages of twentieth century, in the middle of the city, opportunities for encounter surround us. The wild is everywhere, despite the city-lie. Wildness is the medium in which we swim, as near as the night sky, a brush with death on the freeway, a dream. By learning to welcome the unplannable, uncontrollable, and the incomprehensible as nature itself, we can refresh and renew ourselves daily. Thoreau knew what he was saying—that in *wild-ness* (not wilderness) is the preservation of the world.

Tracts of unexplored land are wonderful: but the wild is within us, as well.

A few places to look:

Silence

Thoreau again, from his journal for 1841:

"I have been breaking silence these twenty-three years and have hardly made a rent in it. Silence has no end: speech is but the beginning of it. My friend thinks I *keep* silence, who am only choked with letting it out so fast. Does he forget that new mines of secrecy are constantly opening within me?"

The Body

Almost everything about it defies will and intention. Health and ill-health, equally, are mysteries. I get spooked when I so much as lay abed for a day with a cold; it makes me think of dying, and of the frailty of my daily happiness. These are good thoughts.

A little exercise feels as good as a walk in the woods. It keeps me in my body, this amazing, difficult, recalcitrant, biological marvel. Myself my own zoo.

And sex, too. What a rollercoaster it is, and how far from rational control! It seems a perfect wilderness to me, a place where one goes along for the ride and is grateful for it.

The Mind

Our cultural theory, derived from Descartes, holds that the mind alone is free and apart from nature. This is baloney: the mind itself ranges far beyond our civilized control. It is a wild place, as every night's dreams prove. Even what we call "reason" is hidden from us. Try to trace how a conclusion arises! A sensible owner of a mind would welcome the whole thing, reason and unreason, waking and dreaming, bound and loose, known and mysterious. To explore it is, I think, to go on a vision quest.

Language

How could this most human of artifices also be wild? Because it is an organic process that operates by its own logic. Because it uses us as much as the other way around—because our thought and our sense of reality are built as much out of language as out of our own perceptions. And because it comes to us unbidden and uncontrolled. "Language is simply alive, like an organism," suggests Lewis Thomas, a student of both biology and language.

Poetry

And all the other arts, no doubt. The reason they refresh us is precisely that they go beyond the merely measured and calculated response. To dive into a poem is to go places you cannot predict or control. That is what makes it a poem. Its resonances are wacky, like those in a cavern. It talks back to you from the strangest angles.

No matter how reasoned and clipped and formalized their above-ground manifestations, mind and language possess a deep taproot of wildness. The poet who wishes to explore there must perform an act of awful courage: he must abandon the control our waking lives are based on. She must loosen the strings that tie together the personality and make the world safe and comprehensible. He must allow the carefully-made whole to fragment. No one who has even fleetingly experienced the vortex of the unreasoning mind will underestimate the attempt.

The creative journey is perilous because it encounters the unknown and uncontrolled forces of nature residing deep within us. It is for this very reason that the creations of art, literature, and music are renewing and redemptive.

Failure

By my accounting, the little death. The ego comes crashing down. Plans fall apart. Goals recede, unreached and perhaps forever unreachable. Shame and embarrassment crowd out the mellow feeling of social worth and acceptance. Bereft of the social clothing, one is reduced to the basics—a poor, naked, forked animal. A beast that eats, sleeps, and thinks beneath the sun and the seasons. No longer a Controller of Destiny; now just an inhabitant, wandering among the marvels and dangers. It's an experience we all need, periodically, lest we forget.

There are, no doubt, many more of these potential encounters, many ways to catch sight of the wild. They are the antidote to the accelerating madness of our war-making, wall-building, money-hoarding culture. What craziness is produced by unacknowledged fear; by the mad attempt to control all, whether in the group mind of civilization or the private mind of individuals. What bliss when the doors are opened, the sweet fresh air blows through, and all that energy of denial is released for peaceful, productive, and happy pursuits.

The human spirit is refreshed as it looks straight into the realities. In the presence of nature itself the fantasy of control and the neurosis of denial fall away. The open palm replaces the clenched fist. A sojourn in the wilderness is the primal way to learn this lesson (and to learn it again and again, as we must). But in between trips to the high country, the open sea, the desert, one can daily restore the vital balance of action and acceptance, planning and improvisation. One can always take a moment for the practice of the presence of the wild.

Camas Lilies

by Lynn Ungar

Consider the lilies of the field,
the blue banks of camas
opening into acres of sky along the road.
Would the longing to lie down
and be washed by that beauty
abate if you knew their usefulness,
how the natives ground their bulbs
for flour, how the settlers' hogs
uprooted them, grunting in gleeful
oblivion as the flowers fell?

And you—what of your rushed and
useful life? Imagine setting it all down—
papers, plans, appointments, everything—
leaving only a note: "Gone to the fields
to be lovely. Be back when I'm through
with blooming."

Even now, unneeded and uneaten, the
camas lilies gaze out above the grass
from their tender blue eyes.
Even in sleep your life will shine.
Make no mistake.   .
Of course
your work will always matter.
Yet Solomon in all his glory was not arrayed like one of these.

Sacred Relationship

LONE WOLF
CIRCLES

We acknowledge and honor the Spirit
that brings us forth in interdependence.

In so doing, we live in sacred relationship.

Have I experienced the pull of the Spirit to interaction with creation?

Where is my place in the world?

How do I perceive the Divine?

"As we lie in bed each morning, we wake to the fire that created all the stars. Our principal moral act is to cherish this fire, the source of our transformation, ourselves, our society, our species, and our planet."
—*Brian Swimme*, The Universe is a Green Dragon, *Santa Fe, New Mexico: Bear and Co, 1985.*

"Throughout history, it has been philosophers, religious leaders, and revolutionaries who have asked us to reexamine our relationships, our purposes, and the way we live. Now we are being asked by the ocean."
—*Ross Gelbspan, quoted in* EarthLight *45, p. 5.*

"What is it that has forced the deep contours of human consciousness? Surely it is our primal experience of Earth and all its particular forms and processes: the sheltering forests and the wide open plains, the deep valleys and the high mountains, the flow of rivers and the beauty of lakes, the bounty of plants, and the intelligence of animals."
—*Keith Helmuth*

"But ask the animals, and they will teach you, or the birds of the air, and they will tell you; or speak to the earth, and it will teach you, or let the fish of the sea inform you. Which of all these does not know that the hand of the Lord has done this? In his hand is the life of every creature and the breath of all humanity."
— Job 12:7-10

"Asking: 'Who owns the land?' would be like asking two fleas, 'Who owns the dog?'"
—*Anonymous*

"If we surrendered
To earth's intelligence
We could rise up rooted, like trees."
—*Rainer Maria Rilke*

Invocation

by John Seed

We ask for the presence of the Light, and pray that the breath of life continues to caress this planet home.

May we grow in true understanding—a deep understanding that inspires us to protect the trees on which we bloom, and the water, soil, and atmosphere, without which we have no existence.

May we turn inwards and stumble upon our true roots in the intertwining biology of this exquisite planet. May nourishment and power pulse through these roots, and fierce determination to continue the billion-year dance.

May love well up and burst forth from our hearts.

May there be a new dispensation of pure and powerful consciousness and the charter to witness and facilitate the healing of the tattered biosphere.

We ask for the presence of the Light to be with us here: to reveal to us all that we need to see, for our own highest good and the highest good of all.

We call upon the spirit of evolution, the miraculous force that inspires rocks and dust to weave themselves into biology. You have stood by us for millions and billions of years; do not forsake us now. Empower us and awaken in us pure and dazzling creativity. You who can turn scales into feathers, seawater to blood, caterpillars to butterflies: metamorphose our species

Awaken in us the powers that we need to survive the present crisis and evolve into more aeons of our solar journey.

Awaken in us a sense of who we truly are: tiny ephemeral

blossoms on the Tree of Life. Make the purposes and the destiny of the Tree our own purpose and destiny.

Fill each one of us with love for our true Self, which includes all the creatures and plants and landscapes of the world. Fill us with a powerful urge for the well-being and continual unfolding of this Self.

May we speak in all human councils on behalf of the animals and plants and landscapes of the Earth.

May we shine with an inner light that will spread rapidly through these dark times.

May we all awaken to our true and only nature—none other than the Nature of the planet Earth.

We call upon the power that sustains the planets in their orbits, that wheels our Milky Way in its 200 million year spiral.

Imbue our personalities and our relationships with harmony, endurance and joy.

And fill us with a sense of immense time, so that our brief flickering lives may truly reflect the work of vast ages past, and the millions of years of evolution whose potential lies in our trembling hands.

O Stars, lend us your burning passion.

O silence, give weight to our voice.

We ask for the presence of the Light.

Rainforest and Psyche

by John Seed

In the fourth World Rainforest Report, Queensland zoologist Peter Dwyer notes that the New Guinea highlanders find the rainforest wildlife not only good to eat, but also "good to think."

He goes on to say, "Whilst we don't eat our rainforests, we do become enmeshed in our perceptions and thinking about them, until they suddenly and vividly possess for us values that we can only identify as symbolic, intrinsic, and—with some desperation—as spiritual.

"The tropical rainforests are primitive and ancient ecological systems, whose origins stretch backwards through the emergence of the flowering plants in Jurassic times over 135 million years ago, to the plants preserved in the coal measures [*i.e. coal-bearing strata*] of the Carboniferous millions of years before that and which appear to us today in the form of plastics.

"Such is bio-geo-chemical continuity."

Dwyer's ability to see rainforests of hundreds of millions of years ago embedded in the plastics of the present age is a good example of the psychological effects of rainforests upon people who spend their time in them. Psycho-bio-geo-chemical continuity.

Why is this so? Why do we who spend our time in rainforests "become enmeshed in our perceptions and thinking about them?" I believe that contact with rainforests energizes, enlivens a realization of our actual, our biological self. They awaken in us the realization that it was "I" that came to life when a bolt of lightning fertilized the chemical soup of 4.5 billion years ago; that "I" crawled out of Devonian seas and colonized the land; that, more recently, "I" advanced and retreated before four ages of ice.

We are composed of the ashes of ancient stars weaving themselves into ever more brilliant complexity, weaving themselves into rainforests, weaving themselves into us.

I am that!

Yes, our psyche is itself a product of rainforests. We evolved for hundreds of millions of years within this moist green womb before emerging a scant five million years ago, blinking, into the light. When we enter the rainforest we become acutely and personally aware of the exquisite intelligence of Nature, holding millions of species in dynamic, evolving equilibrium.

In the light of these forests our puny human intelligence becomes aware of itself as a mere fragment of this vast compassionate web. Our tiny, momentary life finds a true frame of reference, against which our humanity can see itself. We realize the matrix within which (regardless of any arrogant fantasies we may have to the contrary) we are inextricably embedded. The intelligence of the rainforest which gave rise to human beings (as well as to other myriad creatures) remains accessible to humans who choose to surrender to it. Unfortunately, the thick insulation of social fictions that we call our "selves" may prevent us from recognizing that we are just one leaf on the tree of life, just one strand in the vast biological fabric, incapable of independent existence.

We may then labor under various delusions: the universe revolves around the Earth, the world was created for our benefit, or our relationship with the myriad creatures is to "subdue and dominate" them.

Thinking like a rainforest!

If we enter a rainforest and allow our energies to merge with the energies that we find there, then the rainforest may be a place where our roots are able to penetrate through the soft soil, reaching beyond the sad 16,000 year history and into the reality of our billions-of-years-of-carbon journey through the universe. Various truths which had been heretofore merely "scientific" become authentic, personal and, yes, spiritual. We may now penetrate to a truly deep ecology.

A few years ago I read a paper by Arne Naess called "Self-

Realization: An Ecological Approach to Being in the World."
Arne Naess is the person who coined the phrase "deep ecology."
For many years he was a Professor of Philosophy at Oslo
University and a radical environmental activist. In this paper he
pointed out the shortcomings of altruism or moral duty as the
correct motivation for the kind of work that we are doing to
protect the environment.

"Altruism," he says, "implies that ego sacrifices its interests
in favor of the other, the *alter*. The motivation is primarily that
of duty. It is said that we *ought* to love others as strongly as we
love ourselves.

"It is unfortunately very limited what people are capable of
loving from mere duty....Unhappily, the extensive moralizing
from environmentalists has given the public the false impression
that we primarily are asking them to sacrifice, to show more
responsibility, more concern, better morals.

"As I see it, we need the immeasurable variety of sources of
joy opened through increased sensitivity towards the richness
and diversity of life. Part of the joy stems from the consciousness
of our intimate relation to something bigger than our ego,
something which has endured for millions of years.

"The requisite care flows naturally if the self is widened and
deepened so that protection of nature is felt and perceived as
protection of ourselves.

"How is this to be brought about? The question needs to be
treated in another lecture. It is a question of community therapy.
Healing our relations to the widest community: the community
of all living beings."

What Naess is saying is that if we want to find the right
perspective to effectively protect nature, then we have to feel
that nature to be part of ourselves. We need an *ecological self.* It is
not enough just to have ideas about these things. What he is
talking about is who we feel and perceive ourselves to be. In
order to establish an ecological identity, we first need to
understand intellectually that we are a part of nature, that we
have no independent existence, that we are part of all of the
cycles of nature, and that by disrupting and polluting these cycles,
we are destroying ourselves. But knowing this is not enough—

we have to widen and deepen ourselves so that we deeply recognize our interconnectedness with all of life. Then care for nature flows naturally because it is now a matter of self-defense or self-protection.

For the last several years in New South Wales, we have been getting together for three or four days on Solstices and Equinoxes and designing processes and rituals which I think fit very well into this category of community therapy towards an ecological self. We get together around these turning points in the year in the bush, either up in the mountains or else down on the coast along a river. We set up camp and after introductions we break into affinity groups—earth, air, fire and water. As well as taking care of the housekeeping, these groups will present a dance or theater representing their element to the others. In this way we start to identify with the cycles of which we are composed and start to extend beyond our exclusively human identification.

We then go on a vision quest alone in the bush with the objective of finding a plant or an animal or a feature of the landscape which will be our ally during the remainder of the Council of All Beings. This may be something that we actually see in our walking through the landscape or it may be something that comes to us in a vision or a memory. When we return to the camp we construct a mask or other representation of our ally. Through this ally, we will represent all of the myriad species of plants and animals and all of the landscapes and bioregions of the Earth in the Council of All Beings.

One of the roots of the Council of All Beings is deep ecology. The other influence that gave rise to the Council was Dr. Joanna Macy's Despair and Empowerment workshops.

Dr. Macy points out that society discourages us from truly experiencing, let alone expressing, the kind of anguish, sorrow and despair that naturally arise in sensitive people when they find out the kind of things that are happening to our world. As well as such social inhibitions, many people fear that if they were to fully open themselves to these feelings, it would crush them— we fear that we would not be able to handle the strength of the feelings, and so we push them away.

What Joanna has found is that by releasing and giving

expression to such feelings in a safe and supportive environment (such as the Despair and Empowerment workshops), far from being crushed, or made numb or apathetic, we become empowered. To the extent that we allow ourselves to experience the pain that we feel for the planet, commitment, creativity and joy are increased. Often after Despair and Empowerment workshops, groups of people spontaneously come together and start to act for the planet.

In a despair ritual, we may put on our masks and walk to a ceremonial place which we've earlier consecrated. There, representing the myriad species, we stand in a circle and start to call out what we see happening to the nonhuman world. The dolphins call out what is happening to the sea, and the mountain gorillas tell us of the depletion of their rainforest home. As strong feelings arise, we may move to the center of the circle to weep and howl, expressing our sorrow, grief, despair and rage. As the feelings subside, we move back and hold the energy for the others.

An important element of the Council of All Beings involves work with processes to activate the older parts of our brain—our mammalian and reptilian brains. We recapitulate the evolutionary journey. For example, one of the sites where we gather for the Council of All Beings is by a river which has soft deep mud banks, and when we explore our reptilian ancestry, we slither around in this mud. The cumulative effect of such exercises is profound and enables us to progressively escape from identifying exclusively with the human part of our being and our frontal lobes.

We also use guided meditations such as the "Gaia Meditation" I wrote with Joanna Macy, which appears in *Thinking Like a Mountain.* As well as such meditations, people share songs, poems and other offerings to create an atmosphere where we can experience ourselves in a wider and deeper sense. To move towards feeling ourselves as we really are—leaves on the tree of life, part of the ecology of this planet.

Throughout the four days we work on different processes to extend our sense of self, to enable us to get in touch with the fact that the human part of our being is only the most recent addition, and that each of us is much, much older than our humanness.

Our breasts identify us as mammals and our navel as placental mammals. By looking at our bodies, by seeing the clues in our bodies, we can start to feel our way into the fact that we have truly traversed this path, that we actually are the products of millions and billions of years of evolution, and that we *can* start to experience ourselves in that way.

Each Council of All Beings is different because there are different people involved and we redesign them every time based on the feedback of those present. They always finish with empowerment games similar to those described by Joanna Macy in her "Despair and Empowerment in the Nuclear Age." We may call for a brainstorm by the assembled beings. We ask ourselves this question: "If it should turn out that there are any humans on this planet who *truly* wish to represent the interests of all of life, rather than some narrow sectional interest such as their own species, is there anything that such humans can do?"

Typically, lots of ideas pour out from the assembled beings of the kinds of things that they would like to see humans doing. The next day, after we "de-role," we examine the notes from this brainstorm. People then find themselves taking up ideas generated by the Council of All Beings and agreeing to carry out the tasks that the Council has set.

There are many ways each of us can experience our ecological self. I feel that the highest form of community therapy is for people to actually put their lives where their mouths are. This was how the awakening of ecological self took place for me at Terania Creek. Rapid change of consciousness took place as a result of participating in direct action and putting my own body between the machine and the wilderness. The Council of All Beings is based to some extent on the realization that direct actions and blockades in defense of nature don't attract everyone, and also that such events are not available all the time.

There is nothing esoteric about the Council of All Beings. It is a natural and easy way to help people expand and express their awareness of the ecological trouble we are in and to deepen their motivation to act. We do not need to be ecological experts ....The essential is already present in our desire that life go on.

Animal Allies:
Nature and Other Mothers

by Brenda Peterson

"My imaginary friend really lived once," the teenage girl began, head bent, her fingers twisting her long red hair. She stood in the circle of other adolescents gathered in my Seattle Arts and Lecture storytelling class at the summer Seattle Academy.

Here were kids from all over the city—every color and class, all strangers to one another. Over the next two weeks we would become a fierce tribe, telling our own and our tribe's story.

Our first assignment was to introduce our imaginary friends from childhood. This shy fourteen-year-old girl, Sarah, had struck me on the first day because she always sat next to me, as if under my wing, and though her freckles and stylish clothes suggested she was a popular girl, her demeanor showed the detachment of someone deeply preoccupied. She never met my eye, nor did she join in the first few days of storytelling when the ten boys and four girls were regaling one another with futuristic characters called Shiva and Darshon, Masters of the Universe.

So far the story lines we'd imagined were more Pac-Man

than drama. After the first two days I counted a legion of characters killed off in an intergalactic battle. The settings for all these stories portrayed the earth as an environmental wasteland, a ruined shell, hardly shelter to anything animal or human. One of the girls called herself Nero the White Wolf and wandered the blackened tundra howling her powerful despair; another girl was a unicorn whose horn always told the truth. All the stories were full of plagues and nuclear wars— even though this is the generation that has witnessed the fall of the Berlin Wall, the end of the Cold War. Their imaginations have been shaped by a childhood story line that anticipates the end of this world.

After three days of stories set on an earth besieged by disease and barren of nature, I made a rule: no more characters or animals could die this first week. I asked if someone might imagine a living world, one that survives even our species.

It was on this third day of group storytelling that Sarah jumped into the circle and told her story: "My imaginary friend is called Angel now because she's in heaven, but her real name was Katie," Sarah began. "She was my best friend from fourth to tenth grade. She had freckles like me and brown hair and more boyfriends—sometimes five at a time—because Katie said, 'I *like* to be confused!' She was a real sister, too, and we used to say we'd be friends for life."

Sarah stopped, gave me a furtive glance, and then gulped in a great breath of air like someone drowning, about to go down. Her eyes fixed inward, her voice dropped to a monotone.

"Then one day last year, Katie and I were walking home from school and a red sports car came up behind us. Someone yelled, 'Hey, Katie!' She turned ... and he blew her head off. A bullet grazed my skull, too, and I blacked out. When I woke up, Katie was gone, dead forever." Sarah stopped, stared down at her feet and murmured in that same terrible monotone, "Cops never found her murderer. Case is closed."

All the kids shifted and took a deep breath, although Sarah herself was barely breathing at all.

"Let's take some time to write," I told the kids and put on a cello concerto for them to listen to while they wrote. As they did their assignment, the kids glanced over surreptitiously at Sarah, who sat staring at her hands in her lap.

I did not know what to do with her story; she had offered it to a group of kids she had known but three days. It explained her self-imposed exile during lunch hours and while waiting for the bus. All I knew was that she'd brought this most important story of her life into the circle of storytellers, and it could not be ignored as if she were a case to be closed. This story lived in her, would define and shape her young life. Because she had given it to us, we needed to witness and receive—and perhaps tell it back to her in the ancient tradition of tribal call and response.

"Listen," I told the group as the cello faded and they looked up from their work. "We're going to talk story the way they used to long ago when people sat around at night in circles just like this one. That was a time when we still listened to animals and trees and didn't think ourselves so alone in this world. Now we're going to carry out jungle justice and find Katie's killer. We'll call him before our tribe. All right? Who wants to begin the story?"

All the Shivas and Darshons and Masters of the Universe volunteered to be heroes on this quest. Nero the White Wolf asked to be a scout. Unicorn, with her truth-saying horn, was declared judge. Another character joined the hunt: Fish, whose translucent belly was a shining "soul mirror" that could reveal one's true nature to anyone who looked into it.

A fierce commander of this hunt was Rat, whose army of computerized comrades could read brain waves and call down lightning lasers as weapons. Rat began the questioning and performed the early detective work. Katie, speaking from beyond the earth, as Sarah put it, gave us other facts. We learned that two weeks before Katie's murder, one of her boyfriends was shot outside a restaurant by a man in the same red car—another drive-by death. So Sarah had not only seen her best friend killed at her side, but she had also walked out into a parking lot to find Katie leaning over her boyfriend's body. For Sarah, it had been two murders by age thirteen.

With the help of our myriad computer-character legions, we determined that the murderer was a man named Carlos, a drug lord who used local gangs to deal cocaine. At a party Carlos had misinterpreted Katie's videotaping her friends dancing as witnessing a big drug deal. For that, Rat said, "This dude decides Katie's got to go down. So yo, man, he offs her without a second thought."

Bad dude, indeed, this Carlos. And who was going to play Carlos now that all the tribe knew his crime? I took on the role, and as I told my story I felt my face hardening into a contempt that carried me far away from these young pursuers, deep into the Amazon jungle where Rat and his computer armies couldn't follow, where all their space-age equipment had to be shed until there was only hand-to-hand simple fate.

In the Amazon, the kids changed without effort, in an easy shape-shifting to their animal selves. Suddenly there were no more Masters of the Universe with intergalactic weapons—there was instead Jaguar and Snake, Fish and Pink Dolphin. There was powerful claw and all-knowing serpent, there was Fish who could grow big and small, and a dolphin whose sonar saw past the skin. We were now a tribe of animals, pawing, running, invisible in our jungle, eyes shining in the night, seeing Carlos as he canoed the mighty river, laughing because he did not know he had animals tracking him.

All through the story, I'd kept my eye on Sarah who played the role of her dead friend. The detachment I'd first seen in her was in fact the deadness Sarah carried, the violence that had hollowed her out inside, the friend who haunted her imagination. But now her face was alive, responding to each animal's report of tracking Carlos. She hung on the words, looking suddenly very young, like a small girl eagerly awaiting her turn to enter the circling jump rope. "I'm getting away from you," I said, snarling as I'd imagined Carlos would. I paddled my canoe and gave a harsh laugh. "I'll escape, easy!"

"No!" Sarah shouted. "Let me tell it!"

"Tell it!" her tribe shouted.

"Well, Carlos only thinks he's escaping," Sarah smiled, waving her hands. "He's escaped from so many he's harmed before. But I call out 'FISH!' And Fish comes. He swims alongside the canoe and grows bigger, bigger until at last Carlos turns and sees this HUGE river monster swimming right alongside him and that man is afraid because suddenly Fish turns his belly up to Carlos's face. Fish forces him to look into that soul mirror. Carlos sees everyone he's ever killed and all the people who loved them and got left behind. And Carlos sees Katie and me and what he's done to us. He sees everything and he knows his soul is black. And he really doesn't want to die now because he knows then he'll stare into his soul mirror forever. But Fish makes him keep looking until Carlos starts screaming he's sorry, he's so sorry. Then...Fish eats him!"

The animals roared and cawed and congratulated Sarah for calling Fish to mirror a murderer's soul before taking jungle justice. Class had ended, but no one wanted to leave. We wanted to stay in our jungle, stay within our animals—and so we did. I asked them to close their eyes and call their animals to accompany them home. I told them that some South American tribes believe that when you are born, an animal is born with you. This animal protects and lives alongside you even if it's far away in an Amazon jungle. Because it came into the world the same time you did, it also dies with you to guide you back into the spirit world.

The kids decided to go home and make animal masks, returning the next day wearing the faces of their chosen animal. When they came into class the next day, it was as if we never left the Amazon. Someone dimmed the lights; there were drawings everywhere of jaguars and chimps and snakes. Elaborate masks had replaced the Masters of the Universe who began this tribal journey. We sat behind our masks in a circle with the lights low and there was an acute, alert energy running between us, as eyes met behind animal faces.

I realized that I, who grew up wild in the forest, who first memorized the earth with my hands, have every reason to feel this familiar animal resonance. But many of these teenagers have barely been in the woods; in fact, many inner-city kids are afraid of nature. They would not willingly sign up for an Outward Bound program or backpacking trek; they don't think about recycling in a world they believe already ruined and in their imaginations abandoned for intergalactic nomad futures. These kids are not environmentalists who worry about saving nature. And yet, when imagining an Amazon forest too thick for weapons to penetrate, too primitive for their futuristic Pac-Man battles, they return instinctively to their animal selves. These are animals they have only seen in zoos or on television, yet there is a profound identification, an ease of inhabiting another species that portends great hope for our own species' survival. Not because nature is "out there" to be saved or sanctioned, but because nature is in them. The ancient, green world has never left us though we have long ago left the forest.

What happens when we call upon our inner landscape to connect with the living rainforests still left in the natural world? I believe our imagination can be as mutually nurturing as an umbilical cord between our bodies and the planet. As we told our Amazon stories over the next week of class, gathered in a circle of animal masks, we could feel the rainforest growing in that sterile classroom. Lights low, surrounded by serpents, the Jaguar clan, the elephants, I'd as often hear growls, hisses, and howls as words. Between this little classroom and the vast Amazon rainforest stretched a fine thread of story that grew thicker each day, capable of carrying our jungle meditations.

When Elephant stood in the circle and said simply, "My kind are dying out," there was outrage from the other animals.

"We'll stop those poachers!" cried Rat and Chimp. "We'll call Jaguar clan to protect you." And they did.

This protection is of a kind that reaches the other side of the world. Children's imagination is a primal force, just as strong as lobbying efforts and boycotts and endangered species acts. When children claim another species as not only their imaginary friend, but also as the animal within them—their ally—doesn't that change the outer world?

This class believes it to be so. They may be young, but their memories and alliances with the animals are very old. By telling their own animal stories they are practicing ecology at its most profound and healing level. Story as ecology—it's so simple, something we've forgotten. In our environmental wars the emphasis has been on saving species, not becoming them. We've fallen into an environmental fundamentalism that calls down hellfire and brimstone on the evil polluters and self-righteously struts about protecting other species as if we are gods who can save their souls.

But the animals' souls are not in our hands. Only our own souls are within our ken. It is our spiritual relationship to animals that must evolve. Any change begins with imagining ourselves in a new way. And who has preserved their imaginations as a natural resource most deeply? Not adults, who so often have stripmined their dreams and imagination for material dross. Those who sit behind the wheel of a Jaguar have probably forgotten the wild, black cat that first ran with them as children. Imagination is relegated to nighttime dreams, which are then dismissed in favor of "the real world." But children, like some adults, know that the real world stretches farther than what we can see—that's why they shift easily between visions of our tribal past and our future worlds. The limits of the adult world are there for these teenagers, but they still have a foot in the vast inner magic of childhood. It is this magical connection I called upon when I asked the kids to do the Dance of the Animals.

The day of the big dance I awoke with a sharp pain at my right eye. Seems my Siamese cat Ivan, who has always slept draped around my head, had stretched and his claw caught the corner of my eye. In the mirror I saw a two-inch scratch streaking from my eye like jungle make-up or a primitive face-painting. "The mark of the wildcat," the kids pronounced it when I walked into the dimly lit room to be met by a circle of familiar creatures. Never in ten years had my Siamese scratched my face. I took it as a sign that the dance began in his animal dream.

I put on my cobra mask and hissed a greeting to Chimp, Rat, Jaguar, and Unicorn. Keen eyes tracked me from behind colorful masks. I held up my rain stick which was also our talking stick and called the creatures one by one into the circle. "Sister Snake!" I called. "Begin the dance!"

Slowly, in rhythm to the deep, bell-like beat of my Northwest Native drum, each animal entered the circle and soon the dance sounded like this: Boom, step, twirl, and slither and stalk and snarl and chirp and caw, caw. Glide, glow, growl, and whistle and howl and shriek and trill and hiss, hiss. Each dance was distinct—from the undulating serpent on his belly, to the dainty high-hoofing of Unicorn, from the syncopated stomps of Chimp on all fours to Rat's covert jitterbug behind the stalking half-dark Jaguar. We danced, and the humid, lush jungle filled this room.

In that story line stretching between us and the Amazon, we connected with those animals and their spirits. And in return, we were complete—with animals as soul mirrors. We remembered who we were, by allowing the animals inside us to survive.

The Dance is not over as long as we have our animal partners. When the kids left our last class, they still wore their masks fiercely. I was told that even on the bus they stayed deep in their animal character. I like to imagine those strong, young animals out there now in this wider jungle. I believe that Rat will survive the inner-city gangs; that Chimp will find his characteristic comedy even as his parents deal with divorce; I hope that Unicorn will always remember her mystical, truth-telling horn. And as for Sarah who joined the Jaguar clan, elected as the first girl-leader over much mutinous boy-growling, Sarah knows the darkness she stalks and the nightmares that stalk her. She has animal eyes to see, to find even a murderer. Taking her catlike, graceful leave, she handed me a poem she'd written, "Now I can see in the dark," she wrote, and she signed herself, "Jaguar—future poet."

Picking Up Roadkill

by Susan Tweit

Down the highway the other day, my husband and I spotted the humped form of a dead animal straddling the double yellow line. "Do you want me to stop?" he asked.

"Yes," I said, "please." He turned the truck around and parked on the shoulder. I hopped out, waited for a break in the traffic, then ran into the road.

"It's a porcupine," I said, returning and yanking open the rear door to dig for the folding shovel, "the biggest one I've ever seen."

It took both of us, one pulling, one pushing, to scoot that porcupine off the road. As we laid it in the grass on the verge, I admired its massive size—it must have weighed 40 pounds—and its profusion of golden quills. Then we hopped back into the truck and headed on our way.

I've been picking up roadkill for almost two decades now, since a wildlife biologist I used to work with started me on the habit. "If you move them off the road," he told me after picking up and carrying off a fresh jackrabbit carcass, "they don't go to waste, and it keeps the scavengers that feed on them from getting hit." It made sense, so I started picking up roadkill too.

Over the years, I've hauled an assortment of dead animals off the road: mostly jackrabbits, pocket gophers, and coyotes, but others too, including a cow elk that I could barely budge and a still-warm curve-billed thrasher, dead only minutes.

At first, I picked up roadkill simply for the reason my biologist friend gave. But the act has gradually come to have a deeper meaning: I see it as a ritual of connection and completion. Stopping to move the bodies of my wild neighbors out of harm's way says that I respect and value their lives, no matter how different from my own. By pulling them off the pavement, I can mitigate in a small way their horrific death by vehicular homicide and allow them the dignity of decomposition, of rejoining the cycle of life as their flesh nurtures other lives.

For several years, I quit picking up roadkill. My excuse was that I was too busy, in too much of a hurry. In truth, I'd been feeling too low to face death over and over again.

Last year, however, I resolved to resume the act, in response to two deaths: that of James Byrd, Jr., the black man who was dragged to death behind a pickup truck in east Texas by white supremacists, and that of Matthew Shepard, the University of Wyoming student who was brutally beaten and left to die on a fence outside Laramie simply because he was gay.

I don't mean to belittle or trivialize either Byrd or Shepard's deaths—or that of any other victims of violent hate crimes—by comparing them to the death of a creature hit on the highway. But to me, how we treat other animals says a lot about how we treat our fellow humans. Psychology research bears this out: people who commit violent crimes, it seems, are likely to have grown up abusing animals. Studies show that a high percentage of violent criminals got their childhood kicks from setting cats afire, beating dogs to death, or swerving to hit rabbits on the road.

We Quakers live by the belief that there is that of God (or whatever name you prefer to give that spiritual power) in each and every one of us, and thus we are all due respect and compassion. In my mind, "that of God" equals the sacred spark that animates all lives—whether other animals or people so different that we struggle to accept them as kin.

It may seem like a stretch to go from the brutal killings of James Byrd and Matthew Shepard to removing dead animals from the highway, but I believe that a civilized society is created as much by our private, everyday acts as it is by the laws we pass or the contracts we sign. It is our personal behavior that sets the model for what we expect of others. We get back what we give.

To me, picking up roadkill is an act of respect, a way to atone for the times when I fail to be the kind and compassionate human being I can be. Stopping to pick up animals hit on the highway is simply an extension of the philosophy of doing unto others— even those whose lives are very different from my own—as I would have them do unto me: caring for them. Caring sometimes involves dealing with blood and guts before breakfast or facing ridicule for standing up for what you believe.

I don't kid myself that the act of picking up roadkill will prevent thoughtless cruelty or erase hatred, but it's my witness for a more humane world.

Turning the Compost

by Barbara Meyn

It's all there—the tough ends of the broccoli,
cores and cobs of cabbages and corn
shared now with birds and slugs and worms.
A bright red millipede writhes away.
The resident scorpion, compost-hued,
digs himself deeper into the pile.
Millions of yet smaller beings live
in the dark, citrus-scented mold.
It sparkles with their presence.

What feeds on our winter leavings will enrich
the lettuces and leavings even now in the garden.
Sometimes I think there is no death, only change,
only our lives' tough ends becoming something new.

The Voice of the Turtle

by Linda Souma Seebeth

For, lo, the winter is past, the rain is over and gone; the flowers appear on the earth; the time of the singing of birds is come, and the voice of the turtle is heard in our land.
—Song of Solomon *2:11*

It is obvious that I love turtles. From the concrete sculpture sitting in my garden to the crystal carving upon my altar, turtles can be found almost everywhere in my home. Turtles made of clay, metal and pipestone. Turtles made of cloth, glass and wood. Plus, I am usually wearing turtle jewelry which, like most of my turtles, were gifts from friends and family. "Why did you pick turtle as your totem animal?" I am often asked. The truth is, I did not choose turtle. Turtle chose me.

Fourteen years ago, while courting, my husband often steered his motorcycle to a quiet dead end street beside a small, twelve-acre glacial kettle known as Stricker's Pond. One edge of the road met the banks of the water, a designated nature conservancy, while modest twenty-five-year-old homes overlooked it from a slope on the other side. "I love this street," Al would say as we admired the peaceful view of bufflehead ducks gliding in the sunstreaked water. Little did we know then, but a few years later we would be living in one of those houses, motorcycle traded for wedding rings.

Shortly after moving into our home, Al paused from the task of unpacking boxes to gaze out the large picture window at a muskrat swimming in and out of its mound of sticks. "You know, it's really a shame this street is going to become a busy road," he lamented. We had been told when we bought the house of plans to connect this quiet street to a future development. When Al learned the proposal had not yet received final approval, he decided to attend the city council meeting to voice his objections and concerns. David was about to meet Goliath. That naïve act of faith, Al's determination to participate in the democratic process, led us into a political battle that would last over four years.

The city of Middleton faced the same expansion problems as many other cities across the country. Located adjacent to Madison, the capital of Wisconsin, the larger city's rapid growth encroached upon its surrounding neighbors. And like anywhere, land near both the city and wildlife—land still bearing the presence of nature—was highly desirable. Although Stricker's Pond was in Middleton, the city of Madison bordered it directly to the south. Our street ran along the eastern shore and came to a dead end at the boundary between the two cities. The pending development would bulldoze through the pond street and increase traffic from less than a hundred cars a day to over several thousand.

"You don't have a snowball's chance in hell of stopping that road from coming through," a councilman said to Al at the meeting where plans for the development were easily approved. However, Madison had neglected to corroborate their plans with Middleton. They also neglected to realize the power of one motivated man.

Being the new kid on the block did not prevent Al from introducing himself to every household on our street. Our home soon became the location for organizational meetings where willing neighbors divided responsibilities. Convincing the city of Middleton to resist being swallowed by the neighboring big fish was the first order of business. Tension already existed between the two cities over other development issues, so Middleton had to carefully choose which fish it wanted to fry.

The alderman of our district supported our position and drafted a proposal to cul-de-sac our street, which would prevent it from being linked to the main artery.

Stricker's Pond is a 9,000-year-old wetland reserve and former home to the Woodland Indians. It is said the famed Sauk warrior, Black Hawk, camped along its banks while being pursued by the US government. When large new homes had been built along the Middleton shores, children collected shoe boxes full of arrowheads and Indian artifacts unearthed by the excavation. Knowing of the pond's historical significance made our determination to preserve it even stronger.

I felt a responsibility to speak for the plant and animal life that could not speak for itself. My presentation to the city council would address the ecological consequences of increased pollution. After numerous phone calls to the Department of Natural Resources, the Army Corps of Engineers, environmental lawyers, the Public Interveners Office and the Audubon Society (sometimes it felt like I spent the entire day on the phone), I was led to Dr. James Zimmerman, a great naturalist, who taught classes on wetlands ecology and environmental impact analysis at the University of Wisconsin. Jim, I discovered, often brought his students to Stricker's Pond because it was a rare and valuable resource, rich in a wide variety of plant and animal life. He informed me of the crucial role wetlands play in our watershed. Functioning like giant sieves, they filter the rainwater before it travels to underground water supplies and larger lakes. Fortunately, Stricker's Pond had survived the fate of other wetlands already filled-in and built upon before their significance was understood. But could it survive heavy metal contamination from car exhaust, along with increased runoff from driveways, roads, rooftops and chemical lawn treatments? The effect of this non-point pollution on a wetland is devastating but not easy to quantify because it does not take place all at once. Repercussions are subtle—a gradual disappearance of species over ten or fifteen years.

The city of Middleton was reluctant to go to battle over the pond. The engineers were concerned about traffic flow, the mayor about good relations. Our alderman informed us that after informally polling his fellow representatives, only two out of six were willing to vote for his proposal. And one of the votes was his.

At times, after months of discussion and hours on the phone, it seemed like it would just be easier to let the road go through so we could get on with our lives. For weeks before the final vote, I could hear the bulldozers beyond the end of our road where Madison had already begun the development, and I would be filled with agitation, thinking we could never beat city hall. When the neighbors and I became discouraged, my husband rallied our spirits. Throughout that time, Al set a constant example of the importance of putting beliefs into action.

I realized I had to develop an inner calm and be willing to accept whatever the outcome. After all, how could I be sure that in the greater scheme of things it wouldn't be more beneficial to have the road go through? Perhaps people traveling on the road would be moved by the beauty of the pond and be inspired to care about the Earth. It was difficult to let go of my personal desires, especially since they seemed so right! Jim Zimmerman's research convinced me that our ideas were best for the pond. Nonetheless, I had to trust that a greater life force knew what was best for all, and I must release my energies to that intelligence.

I spent many hours walking beside the pond, marveling at the sunsets while sitting near a hundred-year-old oak tree. Not a day passed without Al and I expressing thankfulness and joy for our glorious home. I developed the habit of sitting in my living room and "tuning in" to the pond. It was a form of meditation. Whatever I could do for the pond, I would do. My eight-year-old daughter came into the living room one day while the baby was napping and found me sitting quietly.

"What are you doing, Mom?" she inquired.

I tried to explain in child's terms about releasing my will and being open to whatever I could and should do.

"You mean you're listening to the pond to find out what to do?"

"Yes! I'm listening to the pond."

On the day the Middleton city council would be voting on whether or not to cul-de-sac our street, a friend stopped by with her children. As we were talking, I drifted over to the window and saw a movement in the grass. At first I thought it was a leaf. Then I asked, "Is that a turtle?" My friend said it was—a turtle in the front yard—and wouldn't the children like to see that?

We took the children out to the lawn and there it was, a painted turtle, digging through the grass with her hind feet. Specks of orange on the edges of her brown shell shimmered with each movement. What was she doing? Was she going to lay eggs? At that moment another friend drove up with two of her children and joined the captivated group. She said, "Where's your video camera? You should be taping this." So we filmed the turtle. We three women stood in a protective circle around her, like midwives, making sure she wasn't disturbed. We connected with that turtle and the common energies of birthing. Later, Jim Zimmerman would tell us that it is most unusual for a turtle to lay her eggs in front of humans. The whole process took about an hour from the moment she began digging until she finished covering the hole and walked back across the road to the pond.

When Al came home from work, I excitedly reported that the pond had spoken to me. With only three hours before the meeting, we edited the tape down to ninety seconds and added some of Paul Winter's "Sunsinger" to the background. That evening our neighborhood showed up in full force at the meeting. When it was time for me to present the environmental component, I showed the video. The music, the movie and the story created an unexpected hush in the room. I narrated only slightly, feeling tears welling up as I spoke. When I resumed my seat, I was uplifted when neighbor after neighbor stood and spoke against the road—neighbors who had never spoken at past meetings.

The council voted 6-1 in our favor. It was an unexpected victory. Al overheard a disgruntled Madison representative comment as he exited the meeting, "It was the damn turtle." Many people agreed. The turtle had changed their minds.

What other animal would be more befitting to demonstrate the destruction the increased traffic would bring to the pond? Watching the turtle slowly plod back to her pond home was far more meaningful than seeing a pheasant or rabbit dart across the road. And why did the turtle select our yard and not a more secluded spot in the vacant lot next door?

As the turtle story spread, I became the recipient of a beautiful assortment of turtle icons. The ordeal did not end there, however. The city of Madison sued the city of Middleton for preventing the connection of the two streets. Turtle has long been associated with the qualities of determination and steadfastness, which were exactly what we needed to plow through the following years of legal disputes. On the day the judgment (in our favor) was made in the circuit court, the turtle eggs hatched. Madison then appealed the decision and won in the appellate court. Finally, the case was tried in the state supreme court. After years of legal entanglement, during which time the houses had been built in Madison and those new neighbors joined in our effort to protect the pond, the courts made a final decision in favor of Middleton. The road would NEVER become a through street.

Looking back on this process, I learned many things. I have a renewed faith in the power of the individual. We each can truly make a difference. Also, everyone has a role to play. Al's outer organizational skills and practical tasks complemented my inner attunements. One would not have been as effective without the other. The turtle experience renewed a wondrous sense of awe about our connection with all life. That connection is available to each of us at every moment.

There are turtles on every continent of the world. Jim Zimmerman told us that turtles are an indicator species. A healthy turtle population means a healthy body of water. North American Indian stories state that the Earth rests on the back of Turtle, keeping the Earth stable. Gandhi may have learned nonviolence from the turtle because rather than engage in fighting, it retreats in its shell. Angeles Arrien stated, "In many ways, the Turtle may be the creature we can most learn from as we face change and transition in our lives. Perhaps like the Turtle, we are being asked to *walk the mystical path with practical feet*—to make time for going within and to bring out into the world, in practical ways, the richness of what is found inside."

As years passed I have heard many stories that increase my

respect for the essence of Turtle. One Ojibway creation tale explains the role that it played in our street's story. The Ojibway tribe (Chippewa) are native to the Great Lakes region, including Wisconsin. "…For this service to mankind and the spirit woman, the turtle became the messenger of thought and feeling that flows and flashes between beings of different natures and orders. He became a symbol of thought given and received. The turtle, slowest of all creatures, represented celerity and communication between beings."

Turtle and I are both incarnations of the Sacred. In that way, we stand on equal ground. Deep within, we share the same creative presence and are moved by the same life force. Turtle and I have met. Both of our lives have been altered. I am thankful that I listened to the pond and heard the voice of the turtle.

Garden of Eden on Your Dinner Plate?

by Connie Barlow

Those of us who nurture an evolutionary spirituality delight in knowing that all creatures are kin and that our ancestry reaches far into the heavens—that previous generations of stars forged the very atoms of carbon and calcium, of phosphorus and nitrogen, that have become us. We have given up a literal translation of the Genesis Story, yes?

Actually, no. Our relationship to food is, in many ways, still caught in the old mythology. We maintain a Garden of Eden view of the plant realm, and this can be unhealthy. How so?

Fundamentally, we assume that plants are, in a sense, here for us—that plants are here to be eaten and, preferably, in the raw. So deep is this assumption that we are not even aware of it. Evolutionary science, in contrast, informs us that plants are here for themselves; as with all forms of life, they have intrinsic value. The myriad species of plants each evolved and persisted by co-evolving with many other forms of life, including our primate ancestors.

Co-evolution moves in two distinct directions: to repel or to entice. Leaves, stems, and seeds of plants tended to co-evolve repellent relationships with our kind, but fruits co-evolved attraction.

Out of the Garden

First, how do plants repel would-be consumers? With the exception of the grasses (for whom grazing is helpful in eliminating shade-producing competitors and whose small seeds tend to pass unharmed through the intestines of a cow or horse), plants are not idly waiting to become somebody's snack or salad—be it a vertebrate or an insect. Many plant leaves are armed with toxins: oxalates (in spinach) that deprive animals of calcium, tannins (in tea leaves) that "tan" and thus destroy the proteins lining our intestines. And many seeds are packed with even stronger poisons, to protect their rich concentrations of proteins and fats from hungry animals.

Fortunately, our forebears evolved large and sophisticated livers to render many of these toxins harmless. They also evolved habits of eating that avoided over-consumption of any single toxin—including ingestion of toxins in small doses as medicinals. They mixed and matched foods, too, with one plant toxin sometimes counteracting another. And they regularly consumed clay (especially when pregnant), which renders many toxins harmless.

When hominids domesticated fire and began cooking foods, dry heat or wet heat sufficed to denature some of these toxins. And when we learned to add salt to water, or to manufacture pressure cookers, the boiling point was raised to levels that could denature even more toxins.

Making Peace with Legumes and Other Poisonous Plants

Every culture that has made the seeds of a legume (bean family) an important part of their diet has developed elaborate methods for maximizing nutrition and minimizing the toxins inherent in this protein-rich food. Because legumes uniquely are able to "fix" nitrogen, they can efficiently produce nitrogen-rich chemicals that are especially noxious. Traditional cuisines for preparing the vast diversity of legumes—as in soaking and changing the water, boiling with salt, sprouting, or fermenting—are thus not merely for taste.

For example, high and extended doses of many kinds of improperly processed legumes strip the body of essential B vitamins. This is why soybeans traditionally are cooked at very high temperatures or fermented. And this is why the German people suffered malnutrition following World War II, despite the bushels of soybeans provided by the US government. Those people received the beans but not adequate instruction in how to cook them.

Ditto for the Middle Eastern staple of lentils. Dahl is a cooked form of lentil in which the floating seed coats, the most poisonous part of the legume seed, have been skimmed away.

Meanwhile, East Asian cultures became masters at sprouting beans to the point that the embryo in each seed fully consumed the toxins and reformed these into benign plant tissues.

In South America, the indigenous peoples learned to roast the highly toxic seed of cashews and of chocolate in order to drive away the most terrible poisons, rendering these foods not only fit to eat, but fit for the gods to eat—in moderation.

And, of course, there is breeding. Common breeds of potatoes have only a fifth of the glycoalkaloids that were present in native Peruvian stock, which the peoples of the mountains used primarily as a famine food: de-skinned, boiled, and always dipped in clay. But a fifth of a toxin load is still to be reckoned with.

With the exception of the grasses (rice, wheat, oats, corn) and seeds that are aiming to be planted by squirrels (walnuts, acorns, chestnuts), virtually every other kind of seed has to find a way to deter potential consumers. If you have whole avocados in your kitchen, know that you have enough strychnine (in the seed) to kill a colony of rats. If you have a bag of whole apricots on the shelf, know that you possess enough cyanogens (if the seeds are crushed and swallowed) to cause yourself serious or lethal damage. But then, evolution has trained our senses to crave the pulp and to reject the bitter or pungent seed. We are pulp thieves extraordinaire of avocado and apricot, but for raspberry, strawberry, blueberry, perhaps grape: ah! we are evolutionarily wedded partners.

Back to the Garden—With a Fruit in Hand

When our hominid ancestors came down out of the trees and began walking the African savanna, we became God's gift to many species of plants. For now we could carry seeds in our intestines far away from forested groves, deposit them in fertile mounds, and thus give new forests an opportunity to grow well beyond the confines of primate-friendly canopy.

We thus became highly desirable harvesters of fruit. The plants were happy to feed us sweet and nutritious pulp in exchange for our ambulatory services. Of course, many birds and mammals had been fulfilling this function long before we became distance carriers of seeds. But now we eagerly joined this ecological guild.

But the seeds had to be small. Persimmon seeds encased in slippery orange flesh are swallowed and passed by bears, not us. Mango seeds that cling so tenaciously to their delectable packaging are looking for nothing less than a rhino or elephant. The avocado seed, native to South America, co-evolved with toxodons, giant ground sloths, and other giant creatures now extinct. As horticulturists with a taste for green flesh, we humans have simply (and crucially) taken their place.

Toward an Evolutionary Spirituality

Once we get over the initial shock of learning that plants are not here for us, but with us, we can open to the prospect of cultivating a truly evolutionary spirituality.

We can remember with gratitude our primate ancestors whose marvelous livers we inherited.

We can remember with gratitude our hominid ancestors who tamed fire.

We can remember with gratitude the ingenuity of our ethnic ancestors who invented pottery (independently in many parts of the world), and who generation by generation honed experience and experimentation in all the world's bioregions to forge prosperous new relationships with sometimes reluctant plants.

We can pay renewed attention to world cuisine, and resume preparing plants with the attention to proper processing that we and they deserve.

We can teach our young to look at a mango and appreciate the Asian elephant, and to dip into a bowl of guacamole and conjure up the image of a giant ground sloth.

And we can feel gratitude for the worldwide collaboration of botanists, anthropologists, and other scientists who have not only taught us new stories but shown us how important it is to value the wisdom of the old.

Grace at the Table

by Molly D. Anderson

Our tendency to think of food only as a commodity within a global economic system may be blinding us to effective approaches to hunger and malnourishment. Restoring the food system will involve restoring it, in large part, to the gift economy.

Food is essential to life. But do food production and exchange deserve special treatment or protection of some kind, different from the way we treat other things we buy and sell?

This question is part of a heated international debate over subsidies that support domestic agriculture in the United States, the European Union, and Japan. But more importantly, it is a vital question for the survival of our species, because food production and distribution are among the most powerful ways that humans affect the health of this planet.

To date, most of our impacts have been harmful. The modern food system takes a devastating toll on ecosystem services as well as human societies. We have disrupted the global nitrogen cycle, poisoned fish hatcheries, stripped away fertile topsoil, overgrazed pasture, dumped toxic chemicals into the water supply, and exterminated countless other species. If acknowledged at all, these costs are written off as unavoidable side-effects of feeding the world.

The rules of the global economic system dictate that food should be produced wherever it can be grown and processed most cheaply, then shipped around the world to wherever consumers are willing to pay the highest price. Although this system supposedly promotes greater wellbeing for all, it actually creates scarcity through the perverse logic that only people with money to buy food can have it.

While the world produces more than enough food and obesity rates are soaring, the numbers of people who are starving or malnourished have increased in recent years. Food aid, in the form of dumping surplus from overproducing countries on poor countries and thus undermining local markets, is not a real gift but a devil's bargain that weakens those who accept it.

Is there any alternative? Is the global market, its worst abuses patched with free food for starving people, the only place to look for answers to hunger? I believe that we have other options, but we must look outside the market economy to find our way. With grace, we can find a path out of this morass. We can bring grace to the table by acknowledging the holiness of food and Earth itself.

Food and Sacrament

Food is intimately connected with sacraments and religious observations in all faiths. In addition to the Lord's Supper, almost all holy days/holidays are celebrated or commemorated with fasts, feasts, and special foods such as lamb, wassail, matzoh, and horseradish. The homely ritual of "saying grace" reminds us of the holiness of every meal. But why does food have this special connection with sacraments?

Augustine defined sacraments long ago as a "visible form of invisible grace." They connect us with the mysteries of life, love, struggle, forgiveness, and death—a world that is bigger than we perceive with the senses and encompass with abstract thought.

They imbue our individual lives with meaning by reminding us that a Spirit greater than our small and insignificant efforts works through us. Sacraments mark our proper place in time and space, and our proper relationship with other people and the earth. Anthropologists have depicted the sacraments of primitive societies as rituals that serve to maintain the ecological health of a community's land and water. The celebration of sacraments in contemporary society functions in a similar way to maintain the ecological health of a community of faith.

Food has resonance with all of these attributes of sacrament. Harvest and slaughter, cooking and consumption frequently are social occasions that connect us with others through shared labor. Food links us with the cycle of seasons from planting to harvest, and reminds us of our relationship with the natural world.

It connects us literally with specific places. The molecules we consume—nitrogen fixed by a pea plant in a particular field, sugars produced as the sun ripens a pear in a particular orchard—become part of our bodies. Eating, drinking, and breathing are the most intimate connections we have with the world around us. They are the acts by which the world is made flesh.

The quality of being "set apart" distinguishes the realm of the sacred. What is sacred is set apart from either the secular or the profane. While "secular" seems relatively innocuous in its current use, "profane" is more jarring. But the roots of "profane" translate simply into "before the temple" and, therefore, not sacred. This distinction goes beyond the mere recognition that different things and activities have different rightful spheres.

As a verb, "to profane" means to misuse or abuse what ought to be held in reverence and respect, to violate, to defile, or to pollute. That is, profanity involves grave harm that ensues when a thing or behavior is out of the place or time where it rightfully belongs. This displacement is at the core of the ecological meltdown in our food system.

Our society regards food, by and large, as having nothing to do with the sacred. In almost all aspects of the global economy, food is merely a commodity or thing to be bought and sold. Its production, preparation, and consumption are mechanical processes we try to make as efficient as possible through research, technology, and government policies. "Efficiency" means producing the same or more food more cheaply—which usually means with less human labor. The logical outcome of this way of thinking about food is rural ghost towns and industrialized agriculture, replete with factory farms and processors, where acres of land and water are converted into calories and protein. Waste products from the factory pollute the surroundings and spread downstream. Rural people become "waste products" that flood the cities or flee to other countries where they hope to find work. Modern food comes out of the pipeline fast, cheap, convenient, and often laced with contaminants ranging from rodent hair to salmonella. Frequently it is consumed alone, while commuting to a job, at the desk, or in a tiny bubble of solitude in a crowded eatery.

Thinking of food as a commodity to be bought and sold is so common that many of us have trouble imagining any other mental framework. However, food belongs more naturally in a different economy altogether. Rather than a market transaction, eating is an ecological transaction. Like most biological processes, food production is complex and depends on myriad delicate interactions among living organisms. Modern economic efficiency is a paltry imitation of ecological efficiency, whereby the infinite diversity and glory of life are created and perpetuated from nothing more than water, sunlight, and a few chemicals.

Although fertilizing crops with sewage sludge containing heavy metals and other toxins is economically efficient, it is ecologically disastrous because those substances have moved into places where they do not belong. Animals eating the sludge-fed crops are poisoned, and the toxins become concentrated in their bodies, to the detriment of whatever eats them. Coal-fired power plants are economically efficient ways to make electricity; but the mercury they emit is taken up by ocean fish which, when consumed by pregnant women, cause developmental and learning problems in their children. Feeding cows waste products such as chicken litter, feces, and even the ground-up carcasses of other cows seemed to be a miracle of economic cleverness—until mad-cow disease entered the food chain in this way.

Food and the Gift Economy

The special qualities of food place it within the gift economy, a parallel economic universe alongside the world of buying, selling, and capitalist accumulation. The gift economy provides meaning—not just utility—to the exchange of goods.

Anthropologists and scholars of culture, most notably Lewis Hyde, have explored how the gift economy operates and defined its unique rules for the benefit of people who mostly see the world through market economy spectacles.

The most fundamental rule of the gift economy is that the gift must be passed along, from one person to another. Wealth is equivalent to the ability to give much, and a wealthy person who hoards for himself or his own family is considered rude or pathological.

If gifts are allowed to go out of circulation because someone tries to accumulate them, they lose value and the person responsible for this social breach loses status. A person who gives to another does not necessarily receive something in return from the recipient. But the wider community provides, in the long run, because gifts—like grace—tend to flow to empty places. A curious distinction between the gift and market economies is that the former creates abundance, as goods are constantly shared and redistributed, while the latter creates scarcity, as goods pile up for some people and diminish for most others. The story of the loaves and fishes is a story of the gift economy at work. God's grace, as the supreme gift of unmerited forgiveness and redemption, clearly lies in the gift economy.

Things that belong in the gift economy share certain characteristics. First, they tend to be priceless, in that their value cannot be captured in monetary terms alone. A frozen dinner from the grocery-store cooler never tastes as good as a homemade meal prepared with love. Second, things in the gift economy acquire value in the act of being given. A cup of tea and muffin in the home of a friend who listens to your story mean far more than a soda and bag of chips from the convenience store. Third, things in the gift economy increase in value as they are used again and again, and decrease in value as they are hoarded. Food rots when it is stored away for years.

Friendship deepens as it is expressed over and over in different ways, through shared meals as well as other gifts of love. When something belongs in the gift economy yet is treated as a commodity, a sense of wrongness or incongruity results. For example, hospitality may be proffered and accepted with pleasure, but the host is likely to be insulted by a guest who offers to pay for the favor. If a friend invites you to her house for a meal and you leave a tip on the table, she will think you are joking (if she is not offended). Putting a price on kindness or generosity coarsens and diminishes it. Sometimes the person who misinterprets a gift just seems clueless, but sometimes the mistake creates a deep rift in the social fabric.

By treating food as nothing but a commodity, we violate its inherent nature, thereby violating our own nature and the earth itself. The damage to the earth is perhaps most immediately apparent: polluted water and soil, mass species extinction, global warming. These phenomena destroy the very source of life on which we all depend. They rob the next generation of the wherewithal to survive.

But treating food as merely a commodity also damages the public good, our own spiritual health, and prospects for peace because it exacerbates the huge weight of inequity in the world. Should people continue to go hungry in countries that produce more than enough food?

Should food go only to people who can buy it? "It is God's gift that all should eat and drink and take pleasure in all their toil" (Ecclesiastes 3:13). The Protestant Reformation was triggered by outrage at profits made from the sale of grace, in the form of indulgences. Now we have giant supermarket chains and agribusinesses raking in enormous profits from the sale of food.

Four members of the family that inherited the profits of WalMart—now the largest food retailer in the world—rank in the world's top ten wealthiest people. Ultimately, the profanity of treating food only as a commodity and source of profit, and not as a gift to be shared freely with whomever is hungry, coarsens our own souls and diminishes our humanity. Can we possibly invoke a Reformation of the global food system before its grotesque inequities spark mass riots and war?

Reforming the food system will involve restoring it, in large part, to the gift economy. Food must become holy again, a gift of grace. The tenacious link of food, holiness, and gift is rooted in the reality of food. This link is a signpost that points the way into the gift economy. It shows us that the gift economy of food does not have to be built from scratch, just reinforced where it already exists.

We strengthen the gift economy with any action that strengthens communal bonds and the bond between humans and the natural world.

So grow your own food. Observe garden plants closely until you understand what they need and how they are adapted to their place. Prepare meals yourself, or with friends. Invent new menus and recipes. Teach children how to garden. Support local farmers who give priceless treasures to your community—open space, clean air, beauty, watershed protection—by using environmentally sound practices. Buy from them directly in farmers' markets and seek out locally grown food in your grocery.

Buy organic food from your own region. Arrange to trade your time for a bag of vegetables at a food co-op or farm. Eat more food when it is in season in your region, less food that is shipped from far away. Give food away to people who need it, as long as you don't diminish them and their ability to provide for themselves by doing so. Share food with friends. Say grace. Act to ensure that all people in your town can enjoy their right to food. Act to ensure that children worldwide have enough to eat.

The logic of the market economy will tell you that these actions are foolish and that others will take advantage of you if you give food away or sell it too cheaply.

But perhaps this is a risk worth taking. Ralph Waldo Emerson urged, "be a gift and a benediction." Giving of yourself and the things you possess, after all, is the most consistent and time-honored way to find real satisfaction and joy.

My Religion Is Rain

by Cindy Spring

My religion is Rain.
My religion is rain, wind, sun, earth.
Bind me to the numinous, to the Divine, to the Source of Life.
Make me whole, One with All Else.
Give me strength to carry on.

Rain...
gentle mist that moistens each leaf,
torrent of hail that flattens vegetables

Falling
falling
in gratitude to the cycles of ocean, clouds, rivers, creeks flowing
back to ocean.

Falling
falling
in praise of the Ark of Earth, sailing dark space,
on a co-evolutionary mission
between Venus and Mars.

Falling
falling
in service to the seeds, the bees, the totem redwoods, the humans,
and most of all,
the tiny fish that feed the whales.

My religion is Rain.

The title is taken from a line in a poem by Drew Dellinger, "Hymn to the Sacred Body of The Universe"

Collective Wisdom

We honor the essence of the world's wisdom traditions as important sources for learning values of compassion, reverence, and gratitude.

In so doing, we awaken to a deeper, contemporary wisdom.

By what truths am I living my life?
From what sources have I drawn my moral code?
Do I acknowledge the t/Truth, no matter where it is found?

"We should understand well that all things are the work of the Great Spirit. We should know the Great Spirit is within all things: the trees, the grasses, the rivers, the mountains, and the four-legged and winged peoples; and even more important, we should understand that the Great Spirit is also above all these things and peoples. When we do understand all this deeply in our hearts, then we will fear, and love, and know the Great Spirit, and then we will be and act and live as the Spirit intends."
—*Black Elk, a.k.a. Ekhaka Sapa (1863-1950)*

"The Torah is called the Tree of Life. Rooted in wisdom, it grows through understanding, and its branches spread out far and wide to produce leaves for shade, flowers for beauty, and seed-bearing fruit to replenish the world."
—*from the* Zohar

"Traditionally, when people wanted answers to life's ultimate questions—Where are we? Why are we here? What does it all mean? What, if anything, are we supposed to do?—they looked to their revealed texts, or to their ancestral myths if they were oral peoples."
—*Huston Smith*

"In each of us lives a way of knowing that far exceeds mental constructs alone. And in each group or society, there is a way of knowing that exceeds the knowledge of any one person or any one group. It is our shared work, therefore, to perceive the existence of, and to develop our inherent aptitude for, collective wisdom."
—*From* A Call to Collective Wisdom *published by the Fetzer Institute*

Confessions from the Buddhist Frontier: Theology & the Wild

by Kurt Hoelting

We are several days into our kayak journey now, and the pace is slowing. We are finally getting here. As agreed, we have been paddling for an hour in silence, threading the island tapestry toward a seemingly impenetrable wall of ancient forest that looms ahead. Our group of 12 travelers, coming from all corners of the continent, have settled into a remarkably cohesive community in the few days we have been together. Now, as we round a bend into the estuary, almost miraculously, a gateway appears in the forest, and even the sweep and cadence of our paddles are laid to rest.

Only now does the full force of the silence truly descend on us. It is a potent presence, pouring into our senses as palpably as the tidal current that carries us into the gate of the forest. Early in the trip the silence had felt strange, a little disorienting. But as our days unfold, we are falling under its spell.

There is a deep sense now of being held, both by the silence and by the flowing water, which grows even more luminous as our kayaks settle to the pace of the tide. Our gaze is drawn downward, beneath the surface, where schools of pink and chum salmon circle and scatter below our kayaks. The splash of leaping salmon echoes in the silence every few seconds. Each splash seems to linger in the air, almost as if a bell has been struck.

I smile to myself, thoughts circling and scattering like the salmon beneath me. It feels so right to be here, leading this trip, here in this coastal wilderness of Southeast Alaska. For years I have fished these waters commercially for salmon and halibut. Now I am seeking to be here in a new way, a way that accords more closely to my Zen practice. I now invite people to this pristine wilderness to explore meditation, in a setting that adds a new dimension to the Buddhist notion of "Original Nature."

In unexpected ways, my life has come full circle. My thoughts drift back in time to the early 1970s, when as a young theology student at Harvard Divinity School, I wrote a thesis paper entitled "Wilderness as an Ethical and Spiritual Imperative." In it, I suggested that the ecological crisis is at root a spiritual crisis, and that our reigning belief systems are dangerously out of step with the way ecosystems actually work. It was a perspective conspicuously absent from theological education at the time, one which seems only now to be finding a voice in our established religious institutions. These days I have plenty of company in this conviction. Still, I wonder to myself where I would have gone with that thesis if I had known more about Buddhism then.

In retrospect, my ordination as a Protestant clergyman, and my brief career as a university chaplain, were an awkward and unsettled time for me. I was sincere enough in my aspiration to the ministry. I was definitely responding to a call. But I know now that the call was toward a different path. I was swimming against my own inner current, frustrated in my yearning for an Earth-honoring spiritual tradition.

New commotion on the stream bank calls me back. Up ahead, where the estuary narrows, and the spawning salmon are concentrated in a large pool, a black bear has emerged from the forest. Oblivious to our presence in the silence, she plunges into the stream and quickly retreats with a ten pound chum salmon struggling in her jaw. Finding what she wants so easily, she withdraws back into the safety of the forest, carrying her lunch with her. She never saw us, or heard our astonished gasps. Soon we pass the spot where the bear snatched her meal. The surface of the pool is still roiling with hundreds of agitated salmon. I have seen this spectacle before, but rarely at such close range. I am wide awake now. This is closer than I like to come to a fellow predator who is clearly the one in charge here. I think of Daniel Goleman's observation that, through most of our evolution as a species, the big theological question has always been, "Do I eat it, or does it eat me?" At the moment the question feels uncomfortably relevant. Edging the group to the opposite side of the stream, I comment that, until the very recent past, this kind of wild encounter was a normal part of the experience of every human being, everywhere.

Further upstream the estuary widens again, and we breathe a bit easier. Ancient moss-draped Sitka Spruce and hemlock trees give mute testimony to centuries of standing watch over this place. A pair of bald eagles, a family of mergansers and a flock of Canada geese all retreat deeper into the watershed as we approach. Where the geese had been, a dusting of goose down feathers floats lightly on the water.

What we are seeing here is rapidly becoming, in Christina Desser's words, an "extinct experience." By driving this kind of wild nature to the far margins of our world, we have placed our own psychic lives on the endangered experience list. My evolution toward Buddhism has turned continually on this awareness. The tradition of my youth has offered scant protest or leadership as we consume and discard the biological bedrock of our own souls.

As a college student, working summers on a salmon seiner in Southeast Alaska, I stumbled on the writings of Gary Snyder and Thomas Merton, and my Christocentric thinking took a hard turn toward the East. From Snyder, a poet and ecologist, I found the bridge between human nature and wild nature. From Merton, a Trappist monk, I caught the scent of something essential in the life of disciplined solitude. Both drew heavily upon Zen Buddhist thought and practice. Both recognized an ecological spirit at the heart of Buddhism.

To a degree that is unique, I believe, among world religions, Buddhism has from its inception incorporated a kind of Deep Ecological view of the nature of Self. The thirteenth century Zen Master Dogen, in his *Mountains & Rivers Sutra,* declared:

> It is not only that there is water in the world, but there is world in water. It is not just in water. There is a world of sentient beings in clouds. There is a world of sentient beings in the air. There is a world of sentient beings in fire. . . there is a world of sentient beings in a blade of grass (Gary Snyder, *The Practice of the Wild*).

Buddhism has long understood what we are only now

learning in the West—that the self includes the entire material universe. The notion of a separate self is pure fiction, an invention of the human ego. As the Buddhist thinker Joanna Macy wrote in an essay, "The Greening of the Self":

> The conventional notion of the self with which we have been raised and to which we have been conditioned by mainstream culture is being undermined. What Alan Watts called "the skin-encapsulated ego" and Gregory Bateson referred to as "the epistemological error of Occidental civilization" is being unhinged, peeled off. It is being replaced by wider constructs of identity and self-interest, by what you might call the ecological self or the eco-self, co-extensive with other beings and the life of our planet. It is what I will call "the greening of the self" (*Dharma Gaia*, Parallax Press).

This "ecological self" fits seamlessly with what Buddhism has been teaching for 2,500 years. *Paticca-samuppada* (dependent co-arising), together with *anicca* (impermanence, ceaseless change), both core concepts in Buddhism, provide a perfect spiritual counterpart to the view of the universe now emerging from the ecological sciences. Albert Einstein declared: "If there is any religion that would cope with modern scientific needs, it would be Buddhism." It is a view, in Allan Hunt Badiner's words, in which the world is seen as "a massive interdependent, self-causing dynamic energy-event against a backdrop of ceaseless change."

In such a universe, how can we be "separate?" Where does "nature" leave off, and "I" begin? Wu Wei Wu put it bluntly when he asked, "Why are you unhappy? Because 99.9 percent of what you think, and everything you do, is for yourself. And there isn't one."

Western religious traditions are certainly not indifferent to this problem. In many ways they seek to mitigate our excessive preoccupation with the ego-based self. But in my view, they do not dig deeply enough to the core of the self and its delusions.

The Judeo-Christian streams, for all their inherent beauty and depth, essentially leave intact a concept of the self as separate, an entity that stands apart from and above nature, that can somehow be "saved" or "lost" independent of its fellow creatures, independent of its total environment. They also substantially fail to disentangle themselves from the legacy of anthropocentrism, from a moral universe that Theodore Roszak has said "stops at the city limits." Many individual Christians and Jews care passionately for the Earth. However, because of this fidelity to a human-centered world, leadership in confronting the full implications of the environmental crisis has been slow to emerge from our traditional religious institutions.

Buddhism, on the other hand, recognizes these errors up front as core delusions of the human mind. It intuitively grasps the tenacity with which the human ego seeks to advance its own flawed agenda, and offers practical, no nonsense tools with which to confront and transform the delusions of the mind. These tools form what is commonly called "practice." They are experientially based in meditative discipline, in the cultivation of intimate, non-judging engagement with the present moment.

Pascal has said that "All of man's difficulties are caused by his inability to sit alone in a room by himself." Our fear of being alone, of ceasing activity and opening to the voice of silence, is fundamentally a fear of intimate contact with the real, ever-flowing and transient world. In fact, a word that is sometimes used interchangeably with "enlightenment" in Zen is "intimacy."

Buddhism recognizes that intimacy is a prerequisite to love, that we cannot truly love that with which we are not intimate. And real intimacy can only be achieved by a kind of deep listening that stills and transcends mechanisms of our ego-based mind. The despoliation of the natural environment that we have loosed on the world in our time is thus no accident, in the Buddhist view, but an extension of our limited view of self. It is an inevitable result of our failure to identify deeply enough with the world's interbeing, to watch and listen in this fundamental way. As we wake up in the West to the magnitude of the environmental crisis, and recognize in it a challenge that supersedes all merely human crises, Buddhism steps forward with important missing tools and perspectives for the task at hand. Though I am far from this level of knowing myself, I feel the spaciousness of my mind opening bit by bit as I learn to just sit and listen to my world, as I gradually wean myself from the "inner newsreel" of my own mind.

Even these thoughts are a digression from the essential moment at hand, which calls me back now in the guise of a loon's lilting voice. I look around again at this place that feels ancient and new at the same time. I gently stroke my paddle to bring the kayak back into alignment with the current, then sink back into a place of deep stillness.

Over and over I wake up thus, or try to, anyway. There is no end to it, no real "enlightenment," no point at which the ego's hold on my mind is finally overcome. I don't know why, but I know it's so. Somewhere in me the conviction grows that my desire to "heal the Earth" is no other than my desire to be present to myself, to be truly alive in this precious moment. It is one and the same work.

Buddhism has been a great help to me in claiming this deep intention. In spite of every digression, every setback, every unthinking act or unkind word, it always comes back to this. Where am I now? What is needed now? What is to be done?

How to Regain Your Soul

by William Stafford

Come down Canyon Creek on a summer afternoon
that one place where the valley floor opens out
You will see
the white butterflies. Because of the shadows
come off those vertical rocks in the west, there are
shafts of sunlight hitting the river and a deep
long purple gorge straight ahead. Put down your pack.

Above, air signs the pines. It was this way
when Rome was clanging, when Troy was being built,
when campfires lighted caves. The white butterflies dance
by the thousands in the still sunshine. Suddenly anything
could happen to you. Your soul pulls towards the canyon
and then shines back through the white wings to be you again.

Thomas Berry's Intellectual Journey

by Mary Evelyn Tucker

From his academic beginning as a cultural historian, Thomas Berry has evolved over the last 30 years to become a historian of the earth. He sees himself not as a theologian but as a geologian. The movement from human history to cosmological history has been a necessary progression for Berry. In his own lifetime he has witnessed the emergence of a planetary civilization as cultures have come in contact around the globe, often for the first time. At the same time, the very resources for sustaining such a planetary civilization are being undermined by massive environmental destruction.

Thomas Berry began his academic career as a historian of Western intellectual history. His thesis at Catholic University on Giambattista Vico's philosophy of history was published in 1951. Vico (1668-1742) outlined his philosophy in *The New*

Science of the Nature of the Nations, which was first published in 1725 after some 20 years of research. Vico was trying to establish a science of the study of nations comparable to what others had done for the study of nature. Thus he hoped to make the study of history more "scientific" by focusing on the world of human institutions and causation.

Influenced by Vico, Berry has developed a comprehensive historical perspective in periodization, an understanding of the depths of contemporary barbarism, and the need for a new mythic wisdom to extract ourselves from our cultural pathology and deep alienation. Berry has described contemporary alienation as especially pervasive due to the power of the technological trance, the myth of progress, and our own autism in relation to nature.

When Berry set out for China in 1948, he met William Theodore de Bary on the boat leaving from San Francisco. De Bary was on his way to China as the first Fulbright scholar of Chinese studies. Berry intended to study language and Chinese philosophy in Beijing. Their time in China, while fruitful, was cut short by Mao's Communist victory in 1949. After they returned to the States they worked together to found the Asian Thought and Religion Seminar at Columbia. Berry's friendship with Ted and Fanny de Bary has lasted nearly 50 years.

Discussions with Ted spurred Berry's interest in Asian religions, especially Confucianism. Likewise, Fanny has supported Berry's ecological thought through her work with the American Teilhard Association of which Berry was President for the decade of the 1970s. Berry taught Asian religions at Seton Hall (1956-1960) and St. John's University (1960-1966) and eventually moved to Fordham University (1966-1979). Berry founded a PhD program in the History of Religions at Fordham, which was the only one of its kind at a Catholic university in the United States.

What distinguished Berry's approach to religion was his effort not only to discuss the historical unfolding of the traditions being studied, but also to articulate their spiritual dynamics and contemporary significance. This made his classes and his writings on Asian religions remarkably stimulating and memorable. Equally important in Berry's approach has been his balanced effort to highlight the distinctive contributions of both the western traditions and the Asian religions. In addition, he has shown a long-standing appreciation for the spirituality of indigenous traditions in both Asia and the Americas.

His concern for embracing pluralism and diversity of thought was eloquently expressed some 30 years ago: "Diversity is no longer something that we tolerate. It is something that we esteem as a necessary condition for a livable universe, as the source of Earth's highest perfection... To demand an undifferentiated unity would bring human thought and history itself to an end. The splendor of our multicultural world would be destroyed."

Berry has been able to appreciate the deep spiritual impulses and devastating human sorrows which have given rise to the world's religions. From this perspective he has discerned which spiritual resources are needed to create a comprehensive multicultural perspective within the Earth community. For Berry, tolerance of diversity of religious ideas is comparable to protecting diversity of species in the natural world; human diversity and biological diversity are two aspects of a vital ecological whole.

Confucianism has had special significance for Thomas because of its cosmological concerns, its interest in self-cultivation and education, and its commitment to improve the social and political order. With regard to Confucian cosmology, Berry has identified the important understanding of the human as a microcosm of the cosmos. Essential to this cosmology is a "continuity of being" and thus a "communion" between various levels of reality—cosmic, social, and personal.

Berry's appreciation for native traditions and for the richness of their mythic, symbolic, and ritual life has been enhanced by his encounters with the ideas of Carl Jung and Mircea Eliade. Jung's understanding of the collective unconscious, his reflections on the power of archetypal symbols, and his sensitivity to religious processes has made him an important influence on Berry's thinking. Moreover, Mircea Eliade's studies in the history of religions have been enormously useful in Berry's understanding of both Asian and native traditions.

Within this larger framework of interpretive categories, Berry is able to articulate the special feeling in native traditions for the sacredness of the land, the seasons, and the animal, bird, and fish life. For Berry, the Confucianism and Native American traditions are central to the creation of a new ecological spirituality for our times.

In formulating his idea of the New Story, Berry is much indebted to the thought of Pierre Teilhard de Chardin. In particular, Berry has derived from Teilhard (and from other writers such as Loren Eiseley) an enormous appreciation for developmental time. As Berry writes frequently, since Charles Darwin's *Origin of Species* (1859), we have become aware of the universe not simply as a static cosmos but as an unfolding cosmogenesis.

From Teilhard, Berry has also derived an understanding of the psychic-physical character of the unfolding universe. This implies that if there is consciousness in the human and if humans have evolved from the earth, then from the beginning some form of consciousness or interiority is present in the process of evolution. Matter, for both Teilhard and Berry, is not simply dead or inert, but a numinous reality consisting of both a physical and spiritual dimension. Consciousness, then, is an intrinsic part of reality and is the thread that links all life forms. There are various forms of consciousness and, in the human, self-consciousness or reflective thought arises. This implies for Berry that we are one species among others and as self-reflective beings we need to understand our particular responsibility for the continuation of the evolutionary process. We have reached a juncture where we are realizing that we will determine which life forms survive and which will become extinct. We have become co-creators as we have become conscious of our role in this extraordinary, irreversible developmental sequence of the emergence of life forms.

Berry's approach has been much more inclusive in terms of cultural history and religion, while Teilhard's has been remarkably comprehensive scientifically. These two approaches have come together in Berry's book, written with the mathematical cosmologist Brian Swimme, called *The Universe Story* (1992) Here for the first time is the narration of the story of the evolution of the solar system and the earth along with the story of the evolution of *Homo sapiens* and human societies and culture. While not claiming to be definitive or exhaustive, *The Universe Story* sets forth a model for the telling of a common creation story. It marks a new era of self-reflection for humans, one that Berry has described as the "ecological age" or the beginning of the "ecozoic age."

Berry's ideas on the New Story began in the early 1970s as he pondered the magnitude of the social, political, and economic problems we were facing in the human community. He notes how the old story was functional because "It shaped our emotional attitudes, provided us with life purpose, and energized action. It consecrated suffering, integrated knowledge, and guided education." This context of meaning provided by the old story is no longer operative. People are turning to New Age novelties or to religious fundamentalism for orientation and direction. However, neither of these directions will ultimately be satisfying. We are confronted with dysfunctionalism in both religious communities and in secular societies.

Berry proposes a new story of how things came to be, where we are now, and how our human future can be given some meaningful direction. In losing our direction we have lost our values and orientation for human action. This is what the New Story can provide.

Berry states that to communicate values within this new frame of reference of the earth story we need to identify the basic principles of the universe process itself. These are the primordial intentions of the universe towards differentiation, subjectivity, and communion.

Differentiation refers to the extraordinary variety and distinctiveness of everything in the universe. No two things are completely alike. Subjectivity or consciousness is the interior numinous component present in all reality. Communion is the ability to relate to other people and things due to the presence of subjectivity and difference. Together these create the grounds for the inner attraction of things for one another. These are principles which can become the basis of a more comprehensive ecological and social ethics that sees the human community as dependent upon and interactive with the earth community. Only such a perspective can result in the survival of both humans and the earth. As Berry has stated, humans and the earth will go into the future as one single multiform event or we will not go into the future at all.

This New Story is born out of Berry's own intellectual formation as a cultural historian of the West, turning toward Asian religions, examining indigenous traditions, and finally culminating in the study of the scientific story of the universe itself. It is a story of personal evolution against the background of cosmic evolution. It is the story of one person's intellectual journey in relation to Earth history. It is the story of all of our histories in conjunction with planetary history. It is a story awaiting new tellings, new chapters, and ever-deeper confidence in the beauty and mystery of its unfolding. It is this story which provides a comprehensive context for orienting human life toward the "Great Work" of our time. As Thomas suggests, history calls us in the late 20th century to create new, life sustaining human-earth relations. The life, beauty and diversity of the planet need to be preserved and enhanced for future generations. This is the Great Work to which we are each called by Thomas Berry.

The Meadow Across the Creek

by Thomas Berry

My understanding of the Great Work began when I was quite young. I was eleven years old. My family was moving to the edge of town where the new house was being built. The house, not yet finished, was situated on a slight incline. Down below was a small creek and there across the creek was a meadow. It was an early afternoon in May when I first wandered down the incline, crossed the creek and looked out over the scene.

The field was covered with white lilies rising above the thick grass. A magic moment, this experience gave to my life something that seems to explain my life at a more profound level than almost any other experience that I can remember. It was not only the lilies. It was the singing of the crickets and the woodlands in the distance and the clouds in a clear sky...

...Perhaps it was not simply this moment that made such a

deep impression upon me. Perhaps it was a sensitivity that was developed throughout my childhood. Yet as the years pass, this moment returns to me and whenever I think about my basic life attitude and the whole trend of my mind and the causes I have given my efforts to, I seem to come back to this moment and the impact it has had on my feeling for what is real and worthwhile in life.

This early experience, it seems, has become normative for me throughout the entire range of my thinking. Whatever preserves and enhances this meadow in the natural cycles of its transformation is good, what is opposed to this meadow or negates it is not good...

...That is good in economics that fosters the natural processes of this meadow... So in jurisprudence, law and political affairs —that is good which recognizes the rights of this meadow and the creek and the woodlands beyond to exist and flourish in their ever-renewing seasonal expression...

Religion too, it seems to me, takes its origin here in the deep mystery of this setting...It had none of the majesty or the power of the oceans, nor even the harsh magnificence of desert country; yet in this little meadow the magnificence of life as celebration is manifested in a manner as profound and as impressive as any other place I have known.

First Nations and the Future of the Earth

by Rebecca Adamson

It's crucial to understand that as a society, we can reorganize. We can reorganize socially, politically, and economically, and we can reorganize according to our values. In my own heritage within the Cherokee Nation, we always had a White Council, the women's council, which ruled during times of peace, and we had a Red Council, the men's council, which ruled during times of war. The goal was the balance, the harmony, the bringing together of both wisdoms and both energies for the good of the Nation. We absolutely have to begin that journey on a grand scale. We are running out of time.

I'd like to share several stories, starting with one about the San people (better known as the Bushmen) in Botswana and Namibia in southern Africa. If you have ever seen the movie, *The Gods Must Be Crazy*, those are the San people. Listening to these people, you hear the most incredible language. You hear pops and clicks. Up until 1963, it used to be legal to hunt them. You could go to the government in Botswana and Namibia and get a hunting permit and hunt them down.

Our organization, First Nations, began working with the Sans three years ago. We met with them on the Kalahari desert, which was essentially the very last of their ancestral territories. They had been driven and driven into one of the most harsh environments. They still adapted, and still were surviving. While we were there, they were notified by the government of Botswana that they were going to be removed at the end of the rainy season, and once again displaced from what was now the remaining little bit of their territorial lands.

In their generosity of spirit, they gifted us with a trance dance. A trance dance is a very ancient calling for guidance and understanding. As I listened to the singing, I'd close my eyes and I'd hear the snap of twigs. I'd hear the crack of branches, the rustle of grasses. I'd hear the wind, the whirring as a bird takes flight. And I realized what I was hearing were the very sounds of nature, that these people were a part of the sacred creation in every expression of their life. By most anthropological accounts, this was the most ancient language known to humankind. How else would we have learned to speak, if it wasn't through the sheer imitation of nature?

What's happening to the San people is happening to indigenous people around the world. There remain about 300 to 400 million indigenous people and we cover over 70 countries. We truly are the globalization issue, with face, heart, feeling, soul. We are the globalization issue. What defines an indigenous person is the fact that we predate any other groups in our territories, but also equally important is our spiritual link to the land, our connection that is deeply embedded with who we are in understanding and relating to the land.

If you could see a map of the world's remaining critical habitats and the indigenous people's territories, the overlap is evident. And it's not a coincidence. Alaska is a classic example of the critical habitat story as it unfolds for indigenous people. I went up there in 1992 on a fact finding mission because then-Governor Hinkel had banned fishing of chum salmon. Now, there are no grocery stores in the Alaska villages. You live off of what you gather, hunt, or fish. So the closing of chum salmon was basically a death sentence to many of the village people, and simply said, "Starve." At Port Graham they had already lost their sealing because of the Valdez oil spill, with 11 million gallons of oil absolutely destroying the marine ecosystem. They no longer could hunt caribou, moose, or mountain goat, and in one single year, the sports hunters had killed every single bear in their territory, taking the paws and the heads home as trophies. Two bears will carry a village through the winter.

Now they were being told they could no longer fish chum salmon. Native people's salmon fishing is only four percent of the total take, while 96 percent of the salmon take is done by commercial and sports fishing, in what is a very fragile and delicate ecosystem.

What is happening in Alaska is happening to us around the

world. Indigenous people are being robbed in so many other ways. Extensive knowledge of medicinal properties of plants, fungi, and insects within their territories have provided a sort of pharmacopoeia for indigenous peoples around the world. Many of the early synthetic drugs such as quinine and aspirin were derived from indigenous knowledge, and today this traditional knowledge is one of the principal sources for the rapidly growing pharmaceutical and genetic engineering industries.

The covert acquisition and commercial marketing of this knowledge (we call it bio-piracy) is undertaken by obscure university research departments to multinational pharmaceutical corporations. Once patented and trademarked, the knowledge is effectively expropriated from indigenous people.

Also occurring throughout these biodiverse regions, especially in Asia and in Latin America, is the industrialization of farming, where large tracts of land are opened up for commercial plantations. The goal of expanded food production is used to justify wholesale displacement of indigenous people. It is reported to be at the very root of ethnic cleansing taking place in Guatemala, Peru, Brazil, Bangladesh, Myanmar, Indonesia, Irianjaya, Timor, and Molaccas.

The multinationals have targeted extractive operations through the 21st century in indigenous lands, according to the United Nations multinational division. You cannot understand how the extractive frontier operates without studying the role that government plays. The Alberta government first opened the territories of the Lubicon Cree for oil exploration in the 1970s. The Cree fought for an injunction to stop it. Nothing was done. By 1984, 400 wells were drilled within 25 miles of the community. The Cree went to Geneva and filed a human rights complaint. Four years later, the DMI Corporation leased 11,000 square miles of Cree territory from the government to build a huge pulp mill. The Lubicon Cree barricaded the roads. The government offered 100 square miles and 45 million dollars as a settlement. One year after DMI had moved in, the UN did declare that the Lubicon Crees' human rights were violated. Yet nothing was done.

The Cree, with an organization called Friends of the

Lubicon, called for a consumer boycott of all DMI paper products. By 1995, 45,000 retail stores joined the boycott. So DMI sued the Cree. Justice McPherson awarded $1 million of damages to DMI, but he did allow the picketing to resume. Within two months, DMI pulled out from the territories. A year later, the actual legal costs were overturned. So in the end, the Lubicon Cree have protected their territories. They've protected the very sacredness of the forests in which they live.

However, many indigenous peoples have no recourse within their own countries. In Papua New Guinea, it is a criminal offense for any indigenous people to research, organize, or challenge any multinational operations in their country. British Petroleum got similar legislation passed in the Dominica. We are the stewards of the last remaining truly sacred territories, which are also the critical habitats and the biodiversity hotspots for all of us. Indigenous people won't stand a chance of surviving the 21st century without your help. The liberalization of trade and its corresponding acceleration of globalized markets threatens our survival more now than it ever has before. This is not just about indigenous people, nor is it just about the right thing to do. This scenario will destroy us all.

It is in gatherings such as the Bioneers or the Socially Responsible Investment Forum, or the World Trade Organization and IMF demonstrations, that a unity of voices is heard. Now, more than ever before, indigenous people need your alliance.

First Peoples worldwide, through First Nations, has begun a major Indigenous People's Rights Campaign. We have designed a new social investment screen which uses as criteria a distillation of all the rights that have been set forth by international treaties. We've come up with eight principles that go into screening any investment. What we have right now, through this investment screen, is the only international advocacy vehicle for indigenous people. When we went with the Sans, with the Cree, to the United Nations, or the International Labor Organization, or the World Bank, we were always told, "Sure, we'd really like to help you, but we have to be invited in by your country." Now, what country's going to say, "C'mon down! Watch us kill and displace indigenous people?" It doesn't happen. The investment screen gives us a forum that we can use to have the market protect our culture, not destroy it. In 1982, Calvert became one of the very first mutual funds to take a stand against apartheid, and back then many people said it couldn't be done. Yet we all saw an end to apartheid. This screen can become a powerful tool, and I ask you to use it.

In addition, together we need to build an international campaign to stop indigenous genocide. We know that we can kill all humankind with a single bomb. We can destroy the ozone, we can blow up the planet. This means the current rules of the game must change. These are not win or lose, power and control scenarios any longer. We all lose.

The interdependency of humankind, the relevance of relationship, the sacredness of creation is ancient, ancient wisdom. Economic development, more than any single issue, is the battle line between two competing world views. Tribal people's fundamental value was sustainability, and they conducted their livelihoods in ways that sustained resources and limited inequalities in their society. What made traditional economies so radically different and so very fundamentally dangerous to Western economies were the traditional principles of prosperity of Creation versus scarcity of resources, of sharing and distribution versus accumulation and greed, of kinship usage rights versus individual exclusive ownership rights, and of sustainability versus growth.

In the field of economic development, economists like to think Western economics is value-neutral, but in truth, it is not. Success is defined according to production units or monetary worth. The contrast with successful indigenous development is stark. For example, since they understand the environment to be a living being, the Northern Cheyenne have opposed coal strip mining on their reservation because it kills the water beings. There are no cost measurements of pollution, production, or other elements that can capture this kind of impact. There is an emerging recognition of the need for a spiritual base, not only in our individual lives, but also in our work and in our communities. Perfect harmony and balance with the laws of the universe means knowing that the way of life is found by protecting the water beings. The indigenous understanding has its basis of spirituality in a recognition of the interconnectedness and interdependence of all living things, a holistic and balanced view of the world. All things are bound together. All things connect. What happens to the Earth happens to the children of the earth. Humankind has not woven the web of life; we are but one thread. Whatever we do to the web, we do to ourselves.

The environment is perceived as a sensate, conscious entity suffused with spiritual powers through which human understanding is only realized in perfect humility before the sacred whole. Both the Hopi and the Clinkit hold this concept of being in harmony and perfect balance with the laws of nature. Modern science is just now beginning to catch up with such ancient wisdom. Clearly, Bell's theorem of quantum physics, Einstein's theory of relativity, and Heisenberg's uncertainty principle indicate that how and when we look at subatomic particles affects what we see. All particles of matter, property, position, and velocity are influenced by the intention or presence of all other particles. Atoms are aware of other atoms.

According to this law of nature, a people rooted in the land over time have exchanged their tears, their breath, their bones, all their elements (oxygen, carbon, nitrogen, hydrogen, phosphorus, sulfur, all of their elements) with their habitat many times over. In the words of Diné traditionalist Ruth Benaly, "Our history cannot be told without naming the cliffs and the mountains that have witnessed our people. Here nature knows us." The closest contemporary philosophy comes to understanding Earth-bound spirituality is the concept of Gaia. However, tribal people worship the sacredness of creation as a way of life, not as a philosophy or religion. In fact, none of the native languages have words or terms synonymous with religion. The closest expression of belief literally translates to "the way you live."

Human consciousness determines what we do and how we do it. Consciousness is given order through a belief system. The reality of any belief system is expressed through ideas and values, which give us practical guidance. Ideas work together with values in a consistent, mutually affirming system. Ideas such as love, truth, and justice work according to values of caring, honesty, and fairness. The wise to be wise must also be just. Every society organizes itself politically, socially, and economically according to its values. For tribal people, who see the world as a whole, the essence of our work is in its entirety. In a society where all are related, simple decisions require the approval of nearly everyone in that society. It is society as a whole, not merely a part of it, that must survive. This is the indigenous understanding. It is the understanding in a global sense. We are all indigenous people on this planet, and we have to reorganize to get along. I am here today because this gathering, the Bioneers, this community of leadership, believes in a sacred vision of humanity, and I was taught, "a vision is your life." In this case, it is our survival.

Wlomsen Mgaeso

by Joseph Bruchac

Driving to the house of a friend
our car turns, as if with a mind of its own,
towards the south where towers of smoke
now rise, replacing those of glass and steel.

We stare into a distance we cannot see
yet feel throbbing in our chests like a fist,
like the last pulse before breath joins the wind.

Then we turn back to go the other way
and see, circling low above the road,
the wide wings of a bird that we know.
Its tail is white, its head crested with snow.
It is an Eagle, not the bird of war, but
the one who brings from Ktsi Nwaskw,
the Great Mystery, a message of healing.

Though the heart may be broken
the spirit still knows how to fly.

Wlomsen Mgaeso means "Wind Eagle" in the Abenaki language.

The Spirituality of
Native African Culture

by Malidoma and Sobonfu Some

Malidoma, a member of Dagara tribe in Burkina Faso, West Africa, holds two PhDs—one from the Sorbonne in Paris and the other from Brandeis University. He and his wife Sobonfu are both initiated shamans of the Dagara tribe. They have been sent to the West by their tribal elders to promote healing of the planet by sharing the spiritual wisdom of their culture, which is being severely threatened by the invasion of Western technological ways.

Sobonfu and I come from a culture radically different from the modernism of the United States, a culture in which marriages are arranged and there is no divorce. A culture where everything is geared to the well-being of the community and the community is rooted in a lifestyle in harmony with nature. A culture where doors are never locked, where there are no guns or police.

About marriage based on "falling in love," our elders say, "Who is less able to make rational decisions about a lifemate and a lifelong commitment than two young people crazy in love?" In our society, the elders consider not how two people come together, but two souls come together, how two energies merge, and for what purpose these two energies must be brought together. Sobonfu says, "Getting married back home is not a one person thing; it is a whole village thing."

Before marriage, there is that which every young man and young woman goes through, called initiation. In this stressful six-week experience in the wilderness—primarily on your own but overseen at a distance by elders—you live with and off of nature, in touch with its spirituality, and you are helped to "re-member" the purpose for which you were sent into this life.

From the African shamanic perspective, a person who is not aligned with their spiritual self will never be fulfilled and will continue to look to others or to things for happiness. Initiation, a very difficult and dangerous process, aims to assist you to find out who you are, to introduce you to your spiritual self.

In the unique mission to which Sobonfu and I are called—sharing the spiritual wisdom of our culture in the West—we commonly talk about relationships, discord, and healing. A person not in relationship with him or herself, will have difficulty in being in relationship with anything. Regarding discord, we speak of divisions between a person's soul and mind. The mind must obey the dictates of the soul. It is the healing of this division which is the aim of initiation—understood as a process of remembering, bringing up to consciousness, getting in touch with the wisdom stored deep within.

Community, caring, and contact with the ways of nature are crucial to this process. The ways of Western society, of modernism—individualism, consumerism, isolation—are the extreme opposite of our culture's ways. In our experience, they contribute to extreme discord, inwardly and outwardly, and lead ultimately to chaos.

Modern culture lacks community, elders, and the deeply caring experience of initiation, an ongoing, lifelong process of getting in touch. Marriage, for instance, is an initiatory experience, in which two people's energies and life-mission are meshed together.

That's very important because without the other we can't grow; without a community we can't grow. My feeling is that each one of us is an incarnation of a spirit deeply rooted within the realm of nature and is here to give expression to that nature in a modern society which has been radically alienated from nature.

The more an indigenous person understands this modern culture, the more they are baffled by the direction it is heading—progressively destroying itself and, through its corrupting, materialistic power, dragging indigenous cultures around the world down with it.

In our assignment by our tribal elders, Sobonfu and I are excited to meet people such as you at this Earth and Spirit Conference. You are concerned about healing the planet, just as we are. You know that at root this means looking at your spirituality and that of your society. Gatherings such as this give us a brand new start in the battle to align ourselves with our own soul, so that our spirit can sing. In our sharing here, in our singing and drumming, in our dancing together, in our prayers to the Great Spirit, we are "getting in touch" and beginning to build a new tribe which is cohesive enough to withstand the pressures of Modernity. Our elders back home will rejoice to hear of this —allies in the West—who will join with us in a new spirituality which questions the ways of Modernity: man against nature, trust in technology, accumulation of material goods as the yardstick by which to measure happiness.

This very different kind of spirituality will be shaped by a clear listening to the voices reaching us at the depth of our consciousness, in that place we call our soul, that place which contains the patterns for life and relationships put there by the Creator over the ages of human evolution—the experiences of our collective past.

Out of this process of getting in touch with the depths of our being comes the healing and the vision and the power to move as a community to stop nature from being raped by Modernity, to challenge the compulsive denial, the arrogant paternalism, and the hollow pretense that have become viral infections endangering the future.

Goddess and the Garden: Interview with Starhawk

by Ruah Swennerfelt

The Goddess is first of all earth, the dark, nurturing mother who brings forth all life. She is the power of fertility and generation; the womb, and also the receptive tomb, the power of death. All proceeds from Her; all returns to Her. As earth, She is also plant life; trees, the herbs and grains that sustain life. She is the body, and the body is sacred.—Starhawk, *The Spiral Dance* (1979).

But most important, the Goddess is invoked in our awareness of our lived experience. So, I plant my garden, and I know Gaea in my hands and under my fingernails, I know Her as the seeds push up, the leaves unfold, the fruits swell and ripen. And because I have named this power, awakened to it, chanted for it, placed its images in my psyche, my experience of it is deepened and enriched.—Starhawk, *Dreaming the Dark: Magic, Sex and Politics* (1982).

In 1988, following time in jail for an act of civil disobedience, I participated in an eight-day spiritual retreat at a Jesuit center in eastern Massachusetts. Brigit, a fellow retreatant and one experienced at creating "feminist" rituals, offered an alternative to the daily Catholic liturgies. In those gatherings I experienced the divine in a new and profound way. I was impressed by the simplicity of the rituals and how we all had a role in shaping those rituals by our very presence and by what we shared. I wanted more, and Brigit suggested that I read The Spiral Dance, *Starhawk's first book. That began a journey which has enriched my life and given me great hope for the healing of the planet.*

Since then I have read all of Starhawk's books and participated in workshops about the Goddess and feminist (earth-centered) ritual led by her. She guides people into their deepest places and helps them feel their rootedness to the ground beneath them. As a Quaker, I have a profound respect for the expectant waiting and silent worship that awaits me each First Day in Meeting. My experiences with Starhawk have expanded and deepened my focus in Quaker worship. I see them as separate, but related.

Starhawk's vision of a just world for all its inhabitants, nonhuman as well as human, inspires me. She makes the relationship with Earth a primary connection. She makes the commitment to work for justice, at times risking arrest for her actions. Starhawk walks her talk.

Ruah Swennerfelt: I would like the readers to get a general idea of who you are. What first drew you to discovering the feminine divine?

Starhawk: My pull to the Goddess originally came from my feeling that in nature I truly had my sense of the sacred, my own ecstatic experience. When I was still very young, in my first year of college, I encountered people who called themselves witches, who spoke of nature as being sacred, and I said, "Wow, that's it." Seeing the divine, the sacred, in female form, was amazing coming from a Jewish background. Before this experience, God was formless and all figures of religious authority were male. That God was possibly female was a radical understanding and tremendously empowering to me as a young woman. I learned that I too can have a role in leadership and responsibility if that's what I'm called to. Our bodies are sacred. All things about the body are sacred—menstruation, childbirth—that's all sacred. After something like 30 years I find that in some ways the femaleness of it is less important to me. And the more I experience the Goddess directly as the earth, communication with real places on the earth, real energy, the Goddess is not an abstraction. I am conscious of the presence that we encounter when we're in nature.

Ruah Swennerfelt: I know that you live part time in San Francisco but spend as much time as possible on your small ranch farther up the coast, where you grow some of your own food. Is this desire to be in the garden a result of your experience of the Goddess as the earth, and how has that experience changed your daily life?

Starhawk: One day while meditating out in the garden I asked, "Why have a garden in a place that's already incredibly beautiful?" The garden said to me, "Grow food. If you eat the food you become part of the land." I began to think about it and knew that I had to make growing at least some of my own food a core part of my spiritual practice. All year round I can generally eat something I have grown myself on my land. The climate in California allows a year-round garden. It has been for me a very transformative experience. I had to learn about the earth in a much more direct and concrete way—from pruning trees to building fences. I have become a slave to fruit, planting, pruning, and canning. Last year was phenomenal; there were so many apples that I literally must have canned about 50 jars of apple butter, not to mention applesauce and apple pies. I gave away boxes of apples. I was lucky to have some established fruit trees—apples, plums, peaches, and nectarines—already on the land. Just today with the help of some friends I planted 20 olive trees. Eventually we hope to produce our own olive oil.

Ruah Swennerfelt: Planting trees is such a profound statement of faith. And that's related to something I've heard you speak of—permaculture. What does permaculture mean to you and how is it related to your faith?

Starhawk: Permaculture basically is a system of ecological design developed by an Australian, Bill Mollison. It's an approach to both agriculture and culture, designing systems that are sustainable and modeled on nature, where every system supports everything else. We look at how to form a garden that will become a self-perpetuating system, not take so much of our energy or fossil fuels, and sustain itself. It's a way of looking at the world. Let's first observe nature and then model what we do on nature. We try to design a system where each element serves more than one function. For example, planting the olive trees. We're planting them on the flat top of a very steep hill, where there has been a lot of slumping and erosion. Once a forest, it was later clear-cut and grazed. First we dug long ditches and berms on contours, which help infiltrate water into the land so that over time a higher water table is created. By infiltrating water at the top of the hill it keeps it from running down the hill and eroding. The olive trees can use the water now when they are young. After a few years we will be able to take them off the irrigation. Here we have an interesting climate, where we have no rain at all in the summer and from November to March we have an enormous amount of rain. We've had over 100 inches so far this year. Olive trees can survive the dry spells. We interplanted things that can grow in the same conditions and be mutually beneficial, such as herbs, spring bulbs, and clover to help feed the soil.

Ruah Swennerfelt: Do you see connections between your draw to the Goddess and your draw to the garden? The garden told you to grow food. Is this part of your spiritual practice?

Starhawk: The Goddess is not about some abstract idea; it's about realizing that all of us are completely dependent on nature, interacting with nature. We can't deny it, even living in the city. When you're in the country you are aware of the importance of things like rain. In contrast, when you buy fruits in the market you may be unaware that things like water and the earth are truly sacred. It's all very much integrated. My spiritual practice is about observing and working with nature. I'm fortunate to have a piece of land of my own to practice on. I'm trying to put into practice what I have learned from the land and teach it to other people. If we're going to live in a sustainable way we're going to have to learn something from the land. It's shocking that during thirteen years of education I never learned anything about soil, or about how to clean dirty water. These things are not that difficult to know about, but most of us don't have the background to understand it because our culture does not consider it vital. We have to make an effort to really ground ourselves, go out and start learning something from the earth.

Ruah Swennerfelt: You write and talk about magic and describe yourself practicing magic. Do you see magic in this relationship with the earth?

Starhawk: Magic is expanding our ability to hear the "great conversation" which is going on all the time, as my wonderful neighbor, Catherine Harrison, speaks of. It's always about communicating, at all different kinds of levels, from the chemical to the spiritual. It's opening our ears and beginning to hear that communication and beginning to understand it.

Ruah Swennerfelt: In the Fall 1996 issue of *EarthLight,* Jeremy Rifkin said that "eating is the ultimate political act." Since you've been involved in a lot of political actions and witnesses, what is your reaction to this statement?

Starhawk: For me, where eating can become political again is by taking responsibility for actually having some real relationship with the food we eat. It's amazing to me that with the American overabundance of food, we spend enormous amounts of energy deciding what we're *not* going to eat, while most of the world is starving. A more positive approach for me is to eat things I have a real relationship with—something I've gathered or something raised by someone I know. Even if you grow a pot of mint on your windowsill, it will teach you something about the cycles of life.

Ruah Swennerfelt: Is the food that you grow organic? Is that important?

Starhawk: It's a very important piece. It has to do with my relationship with the land. What I do has to benefit the land, build the soil, and leave the land in better shape than I found it. My service to the land, in return for the food I get, is to treat it right. Why would I want to put poison on the stuff I'm going to eat?

Ruah Swennerfelt: When you have to kill a slug or worm or caterpillar, what is your relationship to that creature?

Starhawk: Usually it's snails. They're not native. They're French food snails that escaped, and there are no natural predators. I send it a little blessing and dedicate it to Kali, to that aspect of the Goddess that's death. Everything lives by eating something else. Even plants live off the decay of other things that were once alive. Death and destruction are very much a part of the reality of what it means to be an animal. This is not something to fear, but is part of the cycle, something to honor. Without decay you can't have fertility.

Ruah Swennerfelt: Another aspect of your connection to Earth has been your involvement with the witnesses at the Headwaters redwood grove. Could you say something about that?

Starhawk: Headwaters is a 60,000-acre forest in Humboldt County, east of Eureka, California. It's the largest remaining stand of unprotected old-growth redwoods. It's owned by Maxxam Corporation, and there has been an ongoing struggle since the mid 1980s, when Maxxam took over from Pacific lumber. Maxxam wants to clear-cut. This redwood stand is vital for the survival of endangered species, including the spotted owl, the marbled murrelet, and the salmon. In September a group of us hiked into the actual groves that are at the center of the conflict.

This is an issue I've supported for years. I had petitioned and been arrested for the cause, but I had never actually seen what we were fighting for. Actually seeing the old growth forest was a life-changing experience. There is so much power in the trees and the land; it's so much alive. The trees have a spirit—that's not an abstraction. Their spirit spoke to me. I realized that that kind of presence, that power in the ecosystem itself, that sense of aliveness, used to be normal. It's what everyone used to experience. The world we live in is incredibly dead and devitalized. Old religions arose in a context of an earth that was alive and speaking loudly. People then created rituals based on what was evident around them. But they are only metaphors to us. We don't get it that our own birthright has been taken away from us. We have lost our connections to the fauna and systems that sustain us; to the basic life experience that people once had. For most of us that's completely out of our reach. Kids in the inner cities have never seen any kind of a living forest, one that hasn't been managed or created. The land I have is very beautiful, but very different from what it was. I don't even know what this place is supposed to look like. Hundreds of years of logging the biggest, fattest trees took the genetic cream of the crop, leaving the runts to reproduce. Even if we stopped the logging and clear-cutting it will never be what it was.

Ruah Swennerfelt: Last year I was at a ritual where you embodied and became the good green Earth. I experienced your transformation in that moment. Could you talk about that experience?

Starhawk: It's hard for me to talk about it. The more I work with the earth, the more I identify with it and the less difference I feel between my body and the earth. There is a direct connection between the health of the soil and health of me. Perhaps I identify too deeply. At a deep level we are all the good green Earth. The more we realize we can tune our consciousness to the actual earth around us, we can work with the powers of generation and healing. It is a feeling of ecstasy, of great love and compassion, wanting to reach out and enfold.

Ruah Swennerfelt: Is there more that you would like to share at this time?

Starhawk: The Goddess tradition merges the new science with the discovery that this planet is a living body, that it is self-regenerating. And as we get to understand that, we will change the way we treat the planet. We will throw out our poisons. Ritual is the way we as humans enact our relationship with the earth. We need to ground and honor the land, acknowledging that we and the land are partners. Rituals help build and create community. A favorite ritual I experienced last summer was one for fire protection that was held behind the volunteer fire department. Our summers are so dry that from one spark thousands of acres could be gone. Each person brought to the ritual something they had grown or picked and made a charm, and spoke of what it represented about their relationship to fire. We charged them with energy, sang, hung them up on a dead tree, and left them there all summer. It was a beautifully simple ritual. It was very fortunate that we didn't have any fires. In fact we had rain in August, which is highly unusual. We did a rain ritual in September. We cut the charms into pieces and people took them home and put them in their wood stoves to protect their homes, asking for rain to come intermittently and not in terrible floods. It hasn't flooded too badly up here this year either.

Ecology: An Islamic Perspective

by Iftekhar A. Hai

Al Ghazali, the most renowned Muslim scholar, philosopher, writer and teacher, who lived from year 1058 to 1111CE during the Muslim era in Spain and Portugal, said, "I can excel in rational knowledge (law, theology, philosophy and science) while remaining egotistical, self centered and arrogant. People can become masters in worldly knowledge with their inner self still impure."

Moses Maimonides, the most renowned Jewish scholar, philosopher, writer and teacher was greatly influenced by the writings of Al Ghazali. He lived from 1135 to 1204 CE, born in Cordoba during the Muslim era in Spain, said, "You cannot achieve excellence in thoughts, word and deeds without the purification of the heart with divine knowledge."

These two great people lived to influence multitudes of people from generations to generations. Their works are still held in high esteem. Even today, these two philosophers and thinkers are read and quoted for their wisdom. From all their writings it is evident that they not only respected and enhanced human rights by explaining the law, they also were firm believers in extending kindness and compassion to the animals. Both compared human beings as a refined species of the animal kingdom.

The difference between human being and animal life is the intellect—the intellectual power to decipher, analyze and compare, the intellectual power to judge, rationalize and act according to the dictates of the one's conscience.

The heart of the conscience has been maintained by the criteria of what is Right and what is Wrong, as contained in our respective Holy Scriptures. In this case, I shall refer to the Quran, the Muslim Holy Book and the Hadith, a collection of sayings and practices of the Prophet Mohammed (pbuh*), who lived

*The traditional phrase used by Muslims to honor prophets and messengers of God, often abbreviated as pbuh.

from 570 to 632 CE.

Since the central idea of this essay is to explain our sacred relationship with animals from an Islamic perspective, it is necessary to give examples from the life of Prophet Mohammed (pbuh), the guiding light to nearly 20 percent of the world population. The following are the examples relating to animals that are mentioned in the Quran and Hadith.

1) Life is created sacred. Do not kill anyone, except by way of Law and Justice (Quran 6:151). Here the scholars are unanimous in interpreting life as human life only. No human should be killed except when due process is exhausted through the democratic institutions of law and justice. However, Islamic jurisprudence called the Sharia (Islamic laws drawn from the Quran) says that animals are also considered God's creation, they also possess life. Do not kill any animal for fun, thrill or sport, except to sustain human life. This means cruelty that results from hunting for thrills and fun are not allowed. Hunting is permitted only under strict rules of survival. The hunted animal should not be subjected to any pain or torture. The animal should be immediately put to rest by dismembering its jugular vein. This act immediately puts a stop to the flow of blood to the brain, the central command where all pain is registered. Another Hadith of Prophet Mohammed (pbuh) is to razor sharpen the tool that you use to put down an animal, since a blunt knife or tool is more likely to give more pain during the process of euthanasia.

2) Prophet Mohammed (pbuh) loved cats. It was normal for his cat to purr and come close to Prophet Mohammed (pbuh). He always made sure that there was food and water for the cat. He also petted and loved his cat. This cat was one day taking a siesta next to Prophet Mohammed (pbuh) and it cuddled next to the Prophet's body in such a way that it was sleeping on a part of his gown. The Prophet woke up, by the call of prayer from the mosque and saw the cat in deep slumber on his gown. In order not to disturb the cat's sleep, Prophet Mohammed (pbuh) cut off that part of the gown with scissors on which the cat rested. He then went to pray in the mosque. This act of kindness became a hallmark for billions of Muslims around the world and is quoted frequently when instituting love and kindness for animals.

3) When news reached Prophet Mohammed (pbuh) that a stray cat had died because a person intentionally kept it locked in a room to prevent it from frequenting his abode in search of food, Prophet Mohammed (pbuh) admonished the man severely and asked him to atone for his sins. This man, he added, will receive punishment not only in this life but also in the Hereafter for his cruelty to the stray cat.

4) A women of ill repute quenched her thirst one hot afternoon and was ready to leave the well. Along came a thirsty dog sticking out his tongue for want of water, looking at her in a state of desperation. She was overwhelmed with kindness and sympathy for the dog. She immediately went to the well and with the water satisfied the dog's thirst. When Prophet Mohammed (pbuh) heard this he said, "Allah forgave her sins and admitted her to Paradise for that one act of kindness towards the animal." He further said, "There is compensation for every act of kindness to any animal."

5) The Muslim defense army was diverted and made to travel a different route at the time of the attack from the Crusaders so as not to trample the ant hill, next to trees that also contained beehives. The needless intrusion, noise and commotion were considered cruel and not in line with the sacred relationship that humans enjoy with the animals and insects as part of Allah's creation.

6) Horses and camels were always used in war, and as transport. Laws were made never to overload a camel on caravan routes, to stop for food and drinks at regular intervals and to see that the animals are well rested and fed. Any sick animal was taken out of service and treated for its sickness.

Recorded history says that when Caliph Omar bin Khattab, third Caliph after Prophet Mohammed (pbuh) passed away, was traveling to Jerusalem, he did not double piggy back on the camel with his companion. They both shared the camel alternatively so as not to overload the camel with the weight of two individuals.

In India, when Muslim Moguls ruled, pigeons, peacocks, ducks and all other animals were part and parcel of nature's beauty in the spacious royal gardens. The rose bushes and other nectar plants were cultivated in the Mogul gardens so as to maintain and cherish the special relationships and life cycles of other animals, especially the bees. They collected the nectar from various flowers and had a beehive in the royal palaces. The animal and human remains were recycled in such a way so as to maintain the delicate life cycles, honoring the sanctity of life and environmental concerns.

It is for this reason that the Quran says, "We (the people) are the Custodians or Vicegerents of Allah on Earth. We will be questioned on the Day of Judgment, which is sure to come, whether we held the Criteria of Right and Wrong on the Earth which Allah bestowed on us, with all the gifts of life."

Befriending the Earth:
A Theological Challenge

by Rex Ambler

Up till now we have been able to take the environment more or less for granted. We have had little reason to think seriously of its significance for us, or for the future of our children. But now we have an environmental crisis and we are having to think very seriously indeed. Unfortunately, we are not well prepared for the task. The crisis has wrong-footed us. Our attitude to the environment has been shaped by a long history of industrial development for which the environment has been little more than a material resource, and one that, it was supposed, we were fully entitled to exploit as much as our needs required.

What is worse, our religious tradition, which might have been expected to challenge this assumption, has in fact gone along with it and offered little by way of an alternative. Nature has hardly been the subject of religious concern. It has been left to secular interests to exploit it and secular science to understand and interpret it. Many recent theologians have even taken the view that religion has no business interpreting the world; although at one time it did so, with the help of philosophy. It has now relinquished (or should relinquish) that task to modern scientific research.

The problem is that over the course of time, religion in the West has progressively *narrowed* its concern to the point where it is focused almost exclusively on personal human needs. This is particularly true of Christianity, a point made by critics of Christianity who regard it as far too narrow in principle. Ludwig Feuerbach in the nineteenth century put it polemically: "Nature, the world, has no value, no interest for Christians. The Christian thinks only of himself and the salvation of his soul."

A number of ecologists have echoed that criticism, but with the added barb that Christianity can therefore be held responsible for the environmental crisis. Ian McHarg was one of the first to emphasize this at the beginning of the environmental movement twenty years ago: "Judaism and Christianity have long been concerned with justice and compassion for the acts of man to man, but [they] have traditionally assumed nature to be a mere backdrop for the human play."

In general this statement has to be accepted as true, and we can find plenty of evidence for it in the history of Christian theology. Martin Luther maintained that the Biblical account of creation in Genesis "plainly teaches that God created all these things in order to prepare a house and an inn, as it were, for the future man," whilst Emil Brunner, one of the leading Reformed theologians of our own time, can still maintain that the world of nature is "never anything more than the 'scenery' in which the history of mankind takes place." At a more popular level we can surely find people, and indeed whole religious movements, to whom the environment means virtually nothing because it does nothing for the salvation of their souls.

With a history like this, how can we respond creatively to the present crisis of the environment? The earth cries out for our concern—and not for its own sake alone. We can no longer care for ourselves if we do not also care for the earth on which we depend. How can we do this? I want to suggest three things we can do theologically. We can consider, first, whether Christian one-sidedness can be explained historically, whether, secondly, there are balancing ecological themes in tradition which could now be recovered, and thirdly, whether new insights, such as those from the Quaker tradition, have something special to contribute.

Historical Christianity and Indifference to the Earth

I have already suggested that, as well as having a natural tendency to concentrate on humans, Christianity has notably *narrowed* its concern over the course of time. If we cannot recognize this, we might well be persuaded to abandon Christianity as inherently ecologically blind and insensitive. It is therefore helpful to consider the pressures on Christianity which have constrained it during the course of its history.

It began with an affirmation of *human uniqueness*. The faith of Israel, from which the Christian faith arose, marked itself off from the faiths of its Middle Eastern neighbors by affirming that humans had a unique relation to God and a unique calling to share in his creative purposes. Of all the creatures, humans were created "in the image and likeness" of God. They were called to the task of becoming his people, and in this special role to act as kings over the earth, to "subdue" the earth and to "have dominion" over it (Genesis 1:26-28, RSV). In the context of its time we can recognize this affirmation as a liberation for human beings who were prone to see themselves as bound to nature and wholly at its mercy. In the context of a later time, and of our own time in particular, with greatly increased human numbers and technological power, we can see this affirmation as dangerously one-sided.

The early Christians inherited this belief in a special calling for human beings, but they were also faced with a crisis in their world, which led them to believe that the world was soon coming to an end. They responded to this by projecting their hopes onto another world altogether. That is why the New Testament is so little concerned with the affairs of the world, even with the affairs of everyday social life.

In this respect they were undoubtedly influenced by the "apocalyptic" writings of Judaism, which looked to a supernatural intervention by God to resolve the sufferings and injustices of the world. Within a century or so they also came under the influence of classical Greek philosophy, which carried a similarly despairing message about the present life on earth. In this case, however, the solution was thought to lie in a personal liberation from all earthly involvements, including, ultimately, our involvement with the body. Out of this heady mix came the typically Christian idea of heaven, as a place, the only place, where our deepest human longing could be fulfilled. Out of this too came the idea of the soul, as the truly valuable part of ourselves, in distinction from the body, which was to be held in suspicion and sometimes even despised. The old Jewish faith in God's will for his people on earth had now been narrowed down to a belief in the church as a community of souls waiting for salvation.

There was, however, some accommodation to the needs of the world as Christianity became more established as the predominant religion of the Roman Empire. It came to be felt that the church could, after all, have some tempering effect on government and society, and in this oblique way serve the interests of God's kingdom. But this did not fundamentally affect the dominant, dualistic way of thinking: the affairs of the spirit were still sharply distinguished from the affairs of the world. Indeed the church's involvement with the world became all too worldly, using the same weapons of control that characterized the empire itself.

At the time of the Reformation the distinction was formulated by Luther as a distinction between "two kingdoms," two modes of God's rule in the world, the one a spiritual mode focused on the church and the other a material mode focused on the state. There is no doubt that Luther and the other reformers hoped that the one kingdom would support the other, that the two kingdoms would be complementary. But what followed in fact was a steady process of secularization in which the institutions of society became alienated from the church and from any kind of religious identity. For that reason, the church had no option but to regard itself as the one focus of God's presence in the world.

In the meantime secular society developed a faith of its own, the very earthly faith in the possibility of human liberation through material progress. It developed a picture of this world that made this secular faith seem realistic and legitimate, namely the scientific picture of the world as essentially matter. A radical dualism had once again been established, at least for that diminishing number of people who could still regard life as having a spiritual significance. The church had to spend most of its energy on preserving that spiritual significance in the face of a very powerful secularism. It had little time or energy for the world itself—even for the human world of politics, let alone the wider world of nature. Its preoccupation has therefore been narrowed even more: to the personal concerns of individuals who, for one reason or another, find the secular world inadequate to their needs.

The Ecological Face of Christianity

The picture I have drawn so far is not to be taken as a balanced picture. It is an account only of the pressures that have led to narrowness. We can also recognize that sometimes those pressures have been resisted and another face of Christianity has emerged.

In the Biblical account of Creation, much has been made of the special status and role of human beings. But that account also tells the story of the creation of the earth. And at the end of each "day" of creation, according to the story, "God saw that it was good," implying that the earth and its creatures had value in the sight of God quite independently of their value to human beings. Later, in the ecological disaster of the flood, Noah is commanded to take into the ark "of every living thing of all flesh ... two of every sort ... to keep them alive with you; they shall be male and female" (Genesis 6:19). He is not to save only those that will be useful to him. When the flood subsides and they return to dry land, God says to Noah, "Behold, I establish my covenant with you, as many as came out of the ark... that never again shall all flesh be cut off by the waters of a flood" (Genesis 9:8-11).

It is not a strong theme in the Hebrew Bible, but it is there. The Psalms, for example, celebrate the life of nature and, as in Psalm 104, recognize God's care for animals: "These all look to thee, to give them their food in due season" (Psalm 104:27). The Book of Job describes the mysteries and intricacies of nature, which displays a wisdom far beyond the reach of Job's understanding, so that Job is made to feel small and insignificant (Job 38-40). "Where were you when I laid the foundation of the earth? Tell me, if you have understanding'"(Job 40:3,4). The Book of Isaiah is sensitive to nature's vulnerability; it predicts a time when "The earth shall be utterly laid waste and utterly despoiled" as a result of human misconduct.

The earth lies polluted under its inhabitants;
for they have transgressed the laws,
violated the statutes,
broken the everlasting covenant.

Therefore a curse devours the earth,
and its inhabitants suffer for their guilt;
therefore the inhabitants of the earth are scorched,
and few men are left. (Isaiah 24: 3-6. Cf. Hosea 4:1-3.)

In the teaching of Jesus, again, nature is said to teach us a lesson: "Do not be anxious about your life....Look at the birds of the air; they neither sow nor reap nor gather into barns, and yet your heavenly Father feeds them...."(Matthew 6:25-26). In nature there is an order of mutual care and provision which invites us to emulate it. Nature is not inferior to us; on the contrary, it sets an example.

The writings of St. Paul mark the beginning of the new concentration on spiritual human needs, and yet even here we find that the wider creation is involved. We come to know the source of our own being in God by recognizing a common, creative source of all being. What can be known about God is plain to them, because God has shown it to them. "Ever since the creation of the world his invisible nature, namely, his eternal power and deity, have been clearly perceived in the things that have been made" (Romans 1:19, 20). Later in the same letter he suggests that the creation will also be involved in the liberation of human beings in the hoped-for future. Like a woman in labor, he says, the creation has been "groaning, waiting 'with eager longing for the revealing of the sons of God" (Romans 8:9-23). What exactly he meant by this, and how exactly he imagined that "the creation itself will be set free from its bondage to decay" (Romans 8:21), is not clear. It is likely however that he was drawing on the old Jewish expectation of "a new heaven and a new earth" where human and other creations will live in harmony, "the wolf and the lamb shall feed together.... they shall not hurt or destroy in all my holy mountain" (Isaiah 65:25). It was of course entirely in keeping with the faith of Israel that human life should be expected to be fulfilled in "a land" fitted for them, just as, at the beginning, it had been formed in "a garden."

We have to wait for the great theologian of the fourth century, Augustine, before this theme is developed much further. It was no doubt his appointment as bishop of Hippo at a time of crisis for the Roman empire that led him to think more widely about the implications of faith for the world. As a young man he had been ready to settle for the narrow view of faith which we have seen to be characteristic of Christianity in general. "I desire to have knowledge of God and the soul. Of nothing else? No, of nothing else whatsoever." He had also been strongly influenced by the Manichees who despised nature, and the human body, as the source of evil in the world. When he came to write the magnificent *City of God*, however, he had set his mind wholly against such narrowness. In a passage which is obviously aimed at the Manichees he criticizes those who despise and reject the apparently evil aspects of nature, like fire and frost, and even animals like frogs.

> They do not consider how admirable these things are in their places, how excellent in their own natures, how beautifully adjusted to the rest of Creation, and how much grace they contribute to the universe by their own contribution, as to a commonwealth... divine providence admonishes us not foolishly to vituperate things, but to investigate their utility with care, and where our mental capacity or infirmity is at fault, to believe that there is a utility though hidden.

Nature is therefore not to be valued simply in terms of its usefulness to *us*. "It is not with respect to their convenience or discomfort, but with respect to their own nature, that creatures are glorifying to their Creator." They may indeed have a value quite beyond their immediate utility and quite beyond our limited understanding. We have to accept them as part of God's creation even while their significance is hidden from us, which means in effect that we have to accept them in faith. There is a "commonwealth" of creatures which has its own order and meaning. Our business is to understand it and to live in harmony with it.

More could be said about Christian visionaries and thinkers who followed Augustine, including Francis of Assisi who "befriended" the earth and Benedict who founded an order to work with it sympathetically, but we should be unlikely to find again such a sensitive understanding of its God-given ecology. It is a task that Christians have to take up again today.

The Implications of Some Quaker Insights

My own Quaker tradition sometimes sees itself as essentially Christian, sometimes as on the fringe of the Christian movement, but nonetheless has been subject to the same kind of pressures that have led to narrowness elsewhere, and has concerned itself almost exclusively with the needs of human beings.

There are, admittedly, some notable exceptions to this rule. George Fox, the founder of Quakerism, even as a young man was given to understand that

> I must not eat and drink to make myself wanton but for health, using the creatures in their service, as servants in their places, to the glory of him that created them; they being in their covenant, and I being brought up into the covenant, as sanctified by the Word which was in the beginning, by which all things are upheld; wherein is unity with all Creation.

And Quaker preacher John Woolman also had a practical sensitivity to creatures reminiscent of Francis of Assisi.

> I believe that where the love of God is verily perfected, and the true spirit of government watchfully attended to, a tenderness towards all creatures made subject to us will be experienced, and a care felt in us that we do not lessen that sweetness of life in the animal creation which the Great Creator intends for them under our government.

We can also find many examples of Friends' practical concern for the environment, from the care of farm animals to the study of botany. Yet we cannot say that these concerns have led us, in the past, to serious reflection on the ecology of the earth, the damage we are doing to it or the fundamental changes required in our attitude and behavior to ensure that we protect it.

Quakers do nevertheless have a special contribution to make to the wider Christian movement as it, too, tries to come to terms with the challenge. I would highlight five insights from the Quaker approach that could form the basis of a theological response.

The first insight is that we can be open to new leading from the Spirit, not bound to the formulations of a past revelation. We need not feel bound always to justify our views by reference to the Bible or some other authority. We recognize not only that we live in a very different situation from those of the past, but also that God can and does speak to us in this situation. In the distress of the earth we can hear the calling of God to care, just as in the past we have heard God in the sufferings of the poor. It can surely now be part of our worship in silence, as the Buddhist poet Thich Nhat Hanh says, "to hear within ourselves the sounds of the earth crying."

The second insight is that we can recognize God within Creation—starting with ourselves—rather than as being above or outside it. We can learn to sense God's reality by paying attention to what happens within us, by listening for a voice or becoming aware of a light that can lead us to what is ultimate for us because it is the source of all life and all being. But having sensed that and having learned to respond to it, we can then learn to sense it in other people, and in our other fellow creatures: in animals and plants, but also in mountains and seas and the whole vast universe.

What we sense here—when we are open enough in ourselves to do so—is not the voice or presence of an invisible person, but the mysterious reality, indescribable in itself, which sustains all life and all being as we know it. We may of course use personal images to refer to it—what else but images do we have at our disposal?—but if we take these literally we are in danger of obscuring one important truth they are meant to illuminate, that the ultimate source of all life is mysteriously present within life. (For this reason too we should be especially wary of those images of God, like "king" or "father," which portray God as a person who dominates or controls the world.)

In practice that means that we get closer to God as the source of our life by affirming "that of God" in all life that we encounter. John Woolman drew this implication with great clarity in an entry of his *Journal*:

I was early convinced in my mind that religion consisted in an inward life, wherein the heart doth love and reverence God the Creator and learn to exercise true justice and goodness, not only toward all men but also toward the brute creatures... that as by his breath the flame of life was kindled in all animal and sensitive creatures, to say we love God as unseen and at the same time exercise cruelty toward the least creature moving by his life... was a contradiction in itself.

Third, we can think of spirituality as an active transformation of life-making peace in the world—rather than as a passive acceptance of grace. There must of course be a moment of acceptance, when we recognize that we ourselves, for all our failures and confusions, are accepted by God. But this experience can acquire significance in our lives only as we then accept others, whatever *their* failures and confusions. This follows naturally from our perception that the ultimate basis of our lives is precisely what unites us with the lives of others; or, to put it the other way round, that the point at which we find unity and friendship with others is the point at which we find unity with the source of our own being.

That is the important link between our affirmation of "that of God in everyone" and our commitment to ensuring that everyone lives at peace with everyone else. We seek to realize in practice the deep bond that we can dimly perceive holding us all together. In the new situation of environmental crisis we can surely perceive another bond between ourselves and the earth. The life of the earth, because it is now vulnerable to our power, is part of our life. Our life therefore can be realized and fulfilled only if we commit ourselves to the care of the earth. Making peace with the earth is now, or should be, part of our spirituality.

Fourth, we can have hope for the world if we believe the kingdom of God can come through us, i.e. through our response to the light and truth that is given us. Quakers are, it is true, in danger of being utopian because we tend to play down the evil in the world. But we falsify our belief if we suppose that human beings are fundamentally good and are led to do wrong only unintentionally. The present abuse of the earth from blatant self-interest and greed is enough to bear witness to the power of evil in human life, but we do have confidence in the God-given capacity of human beings to respond to the light when it is shown them, and fundamentally to change their ways. It is a confidence precisely in God's working in them based on the experience of God's working in us, and often against the grain of self-will.

We need not therefore be devastated by the evidence of human destructiveness. We can still believe that human hearts are vulnerable, and we can believe this of everyone without exception since the God we believe in is precisely the God within creation. Because with Fox we have a sense of "the infinite love of God" we can also have "a sense of all conditions" through which God may work. We do not therefore need to build our hope on a fantasy of divine intervention in the future, despairing of ourselves and imagining that God will clean up after us when the party is over. Admittedly, the present outlook is particularly bleak, but it is bleak for everyone, and this fact alone can bring a light to bear on people's hearts as they seek to find a life with some hope and meaning.

And fifth, we can resist, by conviction and daily practice, all violence, material greed and the ethic of domination. Quakers initially developed the "testimonies" of peace, simplicity and equality in relation to the conflicts of European society. But it is significant that they now apply equally well to global society, and even more widely to the ecology of the earth. Our perception has been—and it still holds—that destructive conflicts and oppression arise from a narrow commitment to our own immediate welfare, without regard for the welfare of others, and from a mistaken reliance on purely material means for achieving this. The sufferings of the poor, the brutality of war and the humiliations of state oppression can all be traced back to this spiritual inadequacy.

These evils will be overcome only when people can be persuaded to seek their welfare in the "common-wealth" of society, and to employ means for achieving it that are really commensurate with the ends they seek, that is, nonviolent and peaceful. Our testimonies against war and inequality have therefore been aimed at persuading people—and reminding ourselves—as to where their wealth lies: in the discovery of a common identity and a common cause with other human beings. Those testimonies apply in the same way to our treatment of our natural environment which, as Augustine said, is itself like a "commonwealth," in which each creature in its own way serves the interests of the others. The difference now is that the commonwealth of people and the commonwealth of the earth have become inseparably interrelated and interdependent—have become in fact one new commonwealth of life. Our thinking about God and the world, and the way we live in relation to them, must now give recognition to that fact.

The Spark

by Chris Hoffman

Sometimes
when you round a bend
or come over a crest
the word you use for divinity
will wake in your heart and fly
through your mouth urgently
out into the universe.

This is the spark
that shows your own life
has struck against the great life
like flint on steel.

There will be a certain clarity
of space, with every mountain range,
every tree, every blade of grass,
every glistening water droplet or grain of sand
distinct
yet wedded at the core.

Don't cling to this experience.
Don't put your bread on the shelf
So you can admire it.
Eat it fresh.
Digest it.
Let it become who you are.

Mutual Learning

**We engage in mutual learning experiences as we create
an Earth community listening and speaking from the heart.**

**In so doing, we are informed
by one another's wisdom and compassion**

How do I engage with others to share knowledge and differences of opinion?

What important insights have I been given recently?

"A human being is part of the whole, called by us "Universe," a part limited in time and space. He experiences himself, his thoughts and feelings as something separated from the rest—a kind of optical delusion of his consciousness. This delusion is a kind of prison for us, restricting us to our personal desires and to affection for a few persons nearest to us. Our task must be to free ourselves from this prison by widening our circle of compassion to embrace all living creatures and the whole [of] nature in its beauty."
—*Albert Einstein, 1950*

"We commit ourselves, our energies and our hearts, to create and facilitate spaces for collective wisdom to arise. We are calling together, in spirit and action, guardians of that opening through which differences are honored as differences but also revealed as aspects of a larger knowing."
—*From* A Call to Collective Wisdom *published by the Fetzer Institute*

"Direct encounter with animals, meeting them eye to eye on their own ground, evokes a sudden wonder and respect. Their vivid life brings us alive to the source that creates and sustains all beings. Without such encounters, we risk losing that part of ourselves which most deeply resonates with nature."
—*Elizabeth Roberts and Elias Amidon*

"It were happy if we studied nature more in natural things, and acted according to nature, whose rules are few, plain and most reasonable.... The heavens, earth, and waters with their respective, various, and numerous inhabitants, their productions, nature, seasons, sympathies, and antipathies, their use, benefit and pleasure, would be better understood by us; and an eternal wisdom, power, majesty, and goodness very conspicuous to us through those sensible and passing forms, the world wearing the mark of its Maker, Whose stamp is everywhere visible and the characters very legible to the children of wisdom."
—*William Penn*

The Lucky Little Seaweed

by Mark McMenamin

Once upon a very long time ago (430 million years ago, to be more precise) there lived a sad little seaweed near the shore of a shallow sea. The little seaweed loved its warm and well-lit aquatic home, but the neighborhood was becoming more dangerous with each passing week. Big, fast-growing seaweeds were beginning to crowd the area and shade out the smaller, less aggressive forms. Voracious animals, who swam or crawled within the ocean, had developed a taste for seaweed salad. These animals were becoming more numerous every day and were even beginning to threaten the seaweeds that lived right next to shore in the saltiest water, a zone that used to be safe. The sad little seaweed was feeling the pinch of increased competition.

One dreary morning, in the shade of a newly grown patch of aggressive seaweed, the little seaweed met an aquatic fungus. "Excuse me," said the fungus, "but I am about to infect and eat you."

"Why would you want to do that?" asked the little seaweed.

"Well," replied the fungus, "it is getting harder and harder to make a living on this part of the sea floor. I normally prefer to eat dead organic matter—like old decayed parts of seaweeds—but voracious animals have been devouring my favorite foods before I get my share. With their fishy fins or crabby claws, these animals move faster than I can stretch my fungal fingers."

"You know," offered the little seaweed, "I have a similar problem. Beneath these big seaweeds, I can't find enough light to grow. They are shading me out, leaving me weak. The future looks bleak, so you might as well infect me and get it over with."

The fungus was happy to oblige. Fungal fingers, what scientists call hyphae, gently probed the little seaweed, entering here and there, beginning to suck away the living fluids, molecule by molecule. Just then there was a major earthquake. A portion of the seafloor heaved upward, becoming land, and the seawater drained away. The big seaweeds went tumbling back into the ocean, carried along by the ebbing water. But the little seaweed, anchored as it was to the fungus, was left stranded ashore.

"Now what?" asked the little seaweed in desperation.

"No problem for me" replied the fungus. "My hyphae can grow down, down into the mud, just as easily as I can grow deeper and deeper into you. I can grow my fungal fingers down as far as I need to. When they reach water, I just suck it up. So you see, I am in no danger of drying out." "But you are," the fungus continued, "and I suppose I ought to get as much out of you as I can before the sun bakes you to a crisp."

The fungus continued sucking out the living fluid from the little seaweed, molecule by molecule. But in the bright sun, the little seaweed was beginning to taste different. The fungus discovered that the living fluids it was feasting upon were becoming sweeter and sweeter.

"Say, you are a sweet little seaweed," said the fungus. "I would like to taste your sweetness forever. It seems a shame to kill you."

"I'm sweet because I am finally getting enough sunlight," the little seaweed explained. "When I get enough sunlight, I can create lots of sugar by photosynthesis."

"That is a most admirable talent," observed the fungus, with a hint of envy in its voice. Suddenly, the fungus had a bright idea: "Little seaweed, I have a proposal for you."

"I'm listening" replied the little seaweed.

The fungus continued with excitement, "You know, my hyphae can provide nutrition as well as take it away. That is my special talent—controlling the flow of water, nutrients, and such.

The interesting thing is that I can just as easily send you fluids as suck them out of you."

The little seaweed felt a glimmer of hope shimmer through its bright green gelatinous skin. "Tell me more," the little seaweed begged.

"Well, if I provide you with water and mineral nutrients, can you guarantee me a continuous supply of sugar?"

"Oh yes!" replied the little seaweed. "In this bright sunlight I can produce much more sugar than I could possibly use all by myself. I am afraid of drying out, however, but you appear to have already solved that problem."

"I think we have a deal," said the fungus.

Thus began the most "fruitful" collaboration of all time—the coming together of seaweed and fungus to form an entirely new kind of life on Earth: land plants. So now, every time you admire a great oak tree, run across a lovely green lawn, or munch on a salad, remember the little seaweed and this tale of teamwork at the ocean's edge.

What We Bless, Blesses Us

by J. Ruth Gendler

I didn't know there was another me in the world. It seems like every time I smell a flower I see myself.
—Jill, age 10, from *When Thought is Young* by Richard Lewis

We live in a reciprocal conversation with the world. There are so many ways to say this. The poet Ghalib declared, "It is the rose unfolding that creates the desire to see." Winston Churchill said, "We shape our buildings and then they shape us." And in *Anatomy of a Rose,* Sharman Apt Russell writes, "Flowers smell so good because insects smell so well," going on to describe how a honeybee might visit 500 flowers in one foraging trip.

Pay attention. Whatever we work on (music, creek restoration, teaching, gardening, cooking) works on us. It is all a dialogue, a conversation between the cook and the vegetables, the gardener and the plants, the artist and her materials, the bee and the flower, the body and the soul.

Call it mutual use or symbiosis, the golden rule or common sense. An ad for juice says, "Do unto your body as you wish it would do onto you." I prefer to think of it as reciprocity, a kind of ardent exchange. We could also call it respect, reverence, the path of beauty. What we bless, blesses us.

So much is speaking in and around us if we let ourselves be open to the exchange. The soul blesses the body, the body blesses the soul. The dance of reciprocity between the body and soul is echoed in the dance between the self and the world. The Kogi say, "We are always making offerings to the sun and to the mountains and to the stars. That is why we live here." The Bal Shem Tov, the founder of Hasidim, expressed it this way: "We are here to sanctify the world." Yeats like this: "How but in custom and in ceremony/are innocence and beauty born?" What a beautiful sense of purpose. Your presence is requested here, now, to be a small mirror to this great beauty.

We can nurture a sense of reciprocity by being quiet and patient, by listening and opening our senses, by letting ourselves receive the world with curiosity and respect. The more we are alive to, the more the world comes alive in us. For some, this opens up into a kind of mysticism; for some, a more activist engagement. Both responses are important. Living with awareness of reciprocity amplifies wonder and allows us to live in the world with more grace; it decreases our self-importance as it increases a sense of belonging. Reawakening a sense of the interrelationships that are at the center enlarges our hearts and expands our vision.

Cultivating the quality of reciprocity reminds us to be grateful for the many gifts and exchanges that sustain our lives.

Relational Intelligence

A speech given at the Bioneers Conference
October 2004

by Nina Simons

I want to speak with you this morning about what lies at the heart of many of the toughest issues that we face, both as a culture and as a species. As crucial as they are to illuminate a future landscape of hope, innovative environmental solutions and strategic social models alone won't be enough to alter our collective course. What's ultimately required is a change of heart, a shift in how we relate to each other and to the whole of the living Earth. The root source of our gravest challenges—both socially and environmentally—is a crisis of relationship.

The tear in our relational fabric is apparent in every area of our lives. The evidence surrounds us—from the corporate invasion of our schools to the profusion of divorce and domestic violence; from toxic factory farming to the loss of civil liberties; and from deforestation and global warming to people making war on each other all over the world.

We've got a lot to learn about how to be in relationship in a way that is not only enduring, but can help us to heal our personal and societal wounds. And, "in times of drastic change," the social philosopher Eric Hoffer said: "It is the learners who inherit the future. The learned usually find themselves equipped to live in a world that no longer exists."

How, then, can we enhance and accelerate our learning about conscious kinship?

First, it might help to stop idolizing rational intelligence to the exclusion of our other capacities. As Candace Pert says: "We have bodies for other reasons than to transport our heads around." A wealth of additional information might be available to us, if we also valued the abundant physical, emotional, and intuitive cues we receive.

Western culture has long overemphasized the importance of mental intelligence, or IQ. For most of us, this means that reorienting ourselves toward a broader focus that integrates emotional or relational intelligence means swimming against the tide.

For many centuries throughout our history, the value of feeling and relationship has been vastly underrated, derided, or even scorned. Most often it's been relegated to the disrespected world of "intuition" or sentimentality, and left to the women and children.

Our other ways of knowing, through our hearts, hands, and spirits, have become weakened from disuse, as we've become distracted by an emphasis on getting more stuff. In the Cherokee language, there's no word for the love of an inanimate thing—love is only possible between two sentient beings. Anyone who loves a thing is considered insane.

And, both personally and politically, we've paid a very high price for the commodification of nearly everything in our culture, for, as Jeremy Rifkin says, valuing "belongings more than belonging."

Fortunately, there are some encouraging signs of change, on a societal level. The European Union is an inspiring example of healing relationships on an immense scale between peoples who not so long ago fought the bloodiest wars in the history of our planet. Over the past few decades, Europeans have created a truly transnational vision and are beginning to adopt a new global consciousness.

Currently with 25 member nations, with a population 50% larger than the US on a land mass only half its size, the EU is now the world's largest economy, with far less wealth inequality between rich and poor than we have in the US. In terms of their quality of life, they have more physicians per capita; longer average life-spans; lower crime; far fewer prisoners and less violence than we do.

Citizens of the EU tend to think of themselves as working to live, whereas in the US, they say, we live to work. Their annual vacation time is more than double what ours is here.

Jeremy Rifkin, in his new book *The European Dream*, notes

that the two cultures have now developed diametrically opposed ideas about freedom and security. For Americans, freedom is associated with autonomy and independence. For many young Europeans, however, he says, "freedom is now found in embeddedness, in having access to many interdependent relationships. The more communities one has access to, they believe, the more options one has for a full and meaningful life."

A more relational orientation is peeking over the horizon, in a wide range of domains and disciplines. Increasingly, research is revealing the value of whole body learning, proving that our entire neural networks and our emotions are profoundly involved in all thought and in how we relate to the world and create meaning. Increasingly, our sciences are evolving less linear, more holistic models of how things work.

New communications disciplines can offer a helpful framework through which to revisit our relational musculature. The emerging field of nonviolent communication, for example, suggests that, in situations of conflict, we track the emotions that lay beneath the content of the words.

By responding receptively to the emotional message—and not the verbal one—embattled moments can become swiftly and enduringly defused, creating a real opening for people to question their previous positions.

Promising relational social technologies are emerging in many fields. Thanks in large part to Candace Pert's work on the "molecules of emotion," the study of emotional intelligence, or EQ, is expanding rapidly. People who have a higher "EQ" tend to have happier, more productive and fulfilling lives. EQ is defined as "the ability to perceive emotions, to access and generate emotions to assist thought, to understand emotions, and to reflectively regulate emotions so as to promote emotional and intellectual growth." Cultivating our capacity to step outside of our emotional reactions, noting them more dispassionately, might offer the time and space needed to assess a number of possible responses to select the one that's most relationally attuned.

With a history of relations that have reinforced hierarchy, domination, and disrespect as the norm, we have a lot of unlearning to do. To alter our orientation to one of partnership and reciprocity will require real commitment, practice and patience. But I believe that our biological orientation toward relationship, and what biologist E.O. Wilson calls "biophilia"— that innate affinity that life has for life—strengthens our likelihood of success.

As human beings, we're built for relationship. Our young remain dependent far longer than most other creatures, and our neural systems and limbic brains are hard-wired for empathy, compassion, and connection. Furthermore, as naturalist Janine Benyus has noted, we're a highly adaptable species, and truly excel as mimics.

Fortunately, we have an abundance of relational intelligence to learn from, if only we can humbly accept its tutelage. The natural world is resplendent with symbiotic long-term reciprocal relationship, between blossom and pollinator, moisture and mycelium, plants and herbivores. In nature, no one lives in isolation, and the sense of balanced interdependence is palpable in any thriving ecosystem. We can opt to be mentored by its mastery, if we can quiet ourselves long enough to hear, smell, feel, and learn from it. I believe our survival, as well as our joy, may depend on our making this shift, bringing a practice of relational learning to the center of our attention.

As the renowned biologist Humberto Maturana once said: "Love, allowing the other to be a legitimate other, is the only emotion that expands intelligence."

And, since this is Sunday morning, this is my prayer for us in this pivotal time:

> May we all attend to reuniting our heads, hearts and hands, taking some time to be receptive, suspend judgment, and wait patiently for the information that arrives, unbidden.

> May we practice being still and really listening—to our selves, to each other, and to the gentle whispers of the living intelligences of the natural world.

> To navigate the wild changes ahead, decrease the violence of this tumultuous time, and shift our civilization's direction, we will need to invest the same authority and value in our relational intelligence and learning as we've previously

given to our intellectual development.

If we can do that, we will build a contagious energy that will ultimately lead to real healing and restoration—the restoration of our wholeness, as a global community—of our deep and fundamental interdependence with each other, other species, and the whole interwoven web of Creation.

As the Lakota people say, in ending every prayer: O Mitakuye Oyasin—to all our relations.

Ah-men, ah-women, and aho.

Watering the Seeds of the Future: Interview with Michael Meade

by K. Lauren de Boer

Michael Meade is a master storyteller and scholar of mythology. When it comes to bringing storytelling to bear on one of the most pressing difficulties of our time—the disillusionment and violence to which our youth are prey—he is one of our most creative thinkers. He is the founder of the Mosaic Multicultural Foundation, which is currently focused on youth at risk, "genius based" mentoring, and developing the "arts of community" in diverse organizations and groups. For over seven years, Michael has worked bringing the arts of poetry and myth to gang youth, college students, artists, and into prisons and other settings. He is the author of Men and the Water of Life, *and co-editor of* The Rag and Bone Shop of the Heart *and* Crossroads: Quest for Contemporary Rites of Passage. *Four years ago, at a conference in San Francisco with Michael Meade, Robert Bly and James Hillman, I encountered, in Michael's work, the powerful role storytelling can play in the work of change. In the following interview, Michael converses about myth, cosmology, eldering and youth, trees, mentoring, finding our work in the world, and more. Enjoy the feast.*

K. Lauren de Boer: Something you said a few years ago at a conference struck me: "Ecology without mythology will be defeated." It seems that this has something powerful to say to anyone concerned for Earth or ecology. Would you elaborate?

Michael Meade: I was working with an old idea that there are two great creations in the world. One we call nature, the infinite production of this elaborate, amazing green garment. The other great creation of the world is the endless creation of stories. "Myth" come from *mythos*, a Greek word which means "stories", but also "the telling of the stories." I would say it also means the living out of the stories. Two great worlds—the garment of nature and the array of stories—endlessly intersecting in meaningful ways.

K. Lauren de Boer: Would you say there is an ecology of story?

Michael Meade: Yes. And ecology is a story. You can write a history of modern ecology. But then, you can take the word itself and find many meanings and stories inside it. To me, the world is all stories, because I approach it from the perspective of myth. Nature is its own story with its own language, its own lexicon— the trees, animals, rivers. Our way of connecting to it has to be woven into story. If someone wants to save a particular forest, they may have to risk life and limb. But, they also have to explain what they're doing and why it's happening right there. That begins the story of it, and if the story is strong enough, that's when the saving happens.

K. Lauren de Boer: Cultural historian Thomas Berry states that it's all a question of story. Being without a functional cosmology, a story that meets the needs of our time, is at the base of all our difficulties. The story of evolutionary cosmology, a gift that science has given us, has the potential for helping us create a new myth. Would you agree?

Michael Meade: I agree with parts of it. I agree that we're bereft of a living cosmology. We're also at a loss for a living mythology. To me, cosmology is literature. I love cosmology. The stories of cosmos, how it came to be and how it stays around are also the creation myths of the world.

Cosmology, means the stories we keep making up about the world we find ourselves in, the literature of living in the world. Often, it gets captured by science or by religion. My sense is that it's closer to literature, to storytelling. Certainly, there are provable facts and interesting artifacts that can tell an evolutionary story, an ongoing revelatory story. On the other side, religious folks tend to grab hold of cosmology. They make a certain story out of, interestingly enough, revelation as they see it. I would go another way and say that *mythos*, or mythology, tries to stay with the storied nature of cosmology. I'm looking for a third place that's betwixt and between science and religion.

K. Lauren de Boer: What do you mean by "storied nature"?

Michael Meade: Our nature is to tell stories in order to find the meaning of our own lives. It's what I call our "second nature," what's second nature to us, humans as part of nature. I don't accept the idea that there is nature, and then us. In our second nature, you find that we are woven with greater nature. That weaving, its surprises and cycles, are what we call stories. Meanwhile, nature is feeding back to us its bio-version of the cosmic story. Nature is talking to us; we are responding with stories.

I grew up in New York City. I got to know the sky as slivers and sections suspended between tall buildings. I never saw enough trees. Maybe that's why I'm surrounded by trees now. But even at that time, it seemed to me that certain parts of nature were talking to me. Now, it's become more evident. When I go for a walk, I get this odd feeling that that little rock over there is trying to tell me something. I've tried to become more alert to that.

Where I sit and write in the morning is exactly where I can watch the birds coming and going in the big apple tree with seven trunks. They love to go in and out of that tree. It's hard for me not to notice that the only separation between the images and thoughts going back and forth in my mind, and the birds going back and forth in that tree, is the pane of glass that's between us. So, I've learned to see nature as a storied thing, subtly weaving in and out of our lives.

If it's talking to us, it's something we can learn from, or use as guidance for our lives.

And converse with. I've wondered over the year why I stay here. It's because I haven't finished the story I'm getting from the tree.

K. Lauren de Boer: You haven't finished the conversation.

Michael Meade: Conversation is an old word that means "to turn about with." I think we're "turning about" with nature all the time. It's speaking to us in very dramatic and very subtle ways. These things that we do to harm nature and the Earth cause the conversation to shift and become full of argument. An argument that begins where we reject what is 'second nature' to us.

It turns to more superficial conversation. As we diminish diversity, we diminish the richness of the language.

As we diminish the diversity of nature's great story, which speaks with so many voices, and at the same time move toward global networking, we are causing a reduction of language. Studies are finding that for people to speak in broader terms across the globe, a simpler language is required. And modern language is already simpler than tribal languages, simpler in nuance.

K. Lauren de Boer: It's making things more monolithic?

Michael Meade: Storied nature, the implication of nature's abundance of stories that it wants to tell with every plant, tree, seed, fruit is paralleled by a similar potential explosion within people. It comes out in language, as if we're spitting seeds and fruits and little broken twigs as we speak to each other.

K. Lauren de Boer: This reminds me of the story you tell of the banana tree and the moon, where the gods give a choice to the first couple about death.

Michael Meade: It's one of our cosmological stories, from Madagascar. The story says that we've chosen this business of living and dying like the trees. We are like trees that produce fruit and seed; our living and dying fructify the world around us whether we know it or not. We have made, and keep making choices, that are related to the trees around us.

An interesting thing for me about that story is that it ties together the coming into the world of children and death. It seems to me it's a story about learning generosity toward future generations by making the choice of dying to our own lives, but spreading seeds that go on.

When the idea comes up that we can make a new myth, I have to quibble over the words and some of the implications. I think, like the trees, we keep re-growing the same shape and similar forms. Yes it's a new tree, but it's also the same apple tree that started all that trouble back in that other garden. We keep encountering the Tree of Knowledge of Good and Evil, keep missing the Tree of Life.

It's the second week of January now and right in front of where I sit and write, there's one apple left hanging on the tree. All around it, the bare branches, within it the seeds of time. That apple has in it the story of the original garden, but also the story of all other apple possibilities. There it hangs, both fruit and seed, impervious to winter and the flooding rains we've had. There's something persistent about cosmology and about myth, just the way there's something persistent about nature. A new myth is really the old myth telling itself in a way that engages us once again, taking us back to origins. Originality, so highly prized in the Western world, means "a return to origins."

It's like the trees and the seeds from the trees. We're handling old seeds and assisting new growth. Is it a new myth in the sense that it's another telling of the story?

Yes. Is it an old myth in the sense that the story's telling itself again? Yes. Going back to the story from Madagascar, we participate in the ongoing creation by being and by saying that in order to be conscious of what we're doing, we must accept that we will die. We're going to continue this choice made by the original parents—to die and leave progeny, leave living seeds in the world. When that choice is made, we change the conversation from being about "me and my need" and "my culture and its hunger" to being about continuing the story in a way beyond oneself. Which is part of the sense of cosmology as something that goes beyond oneself, of myth as telling the bigger story and of nature as life continuing its many forms.

K. Lauren de Boer: To future generations.

Michael Meade: Including future generations of thought and of imagination. The seed opens up to mean everything from people to the seeds of thought.

If a new myth is about retelling the old stories in a way that's needed, then it seems to me that youth are one of our primary sources of what's needed.

Youth are the edge of the story that the culture's telling itself. Youth are where the past and the future meet—the story is both being told and being found. It's like the making of a poem. It's a creation, but also a found experience. Youth live at that edge. They are strangers at the threshold of culture and at the threshold of nature, stumbling and striving into the story of their own nature, the nature around them, and the culture around them as well. Strangers at the threshold, they're an explosive act of nature, in flux and flood and growth. They're also the explosion of the culture. They're the past of the culture speaking its story in a new way, and the potential and future of the culture as well.

K. Lauren de Boer: Are they a symptom of what needs to be healed, or what needs attention?

Michael Meade: A culture gets the youth it deserves, the youth it has made. They are always symptomatic, and a place where healing can begin. I've said to ecological groups that if you can get meaningful numbers of youth working at the story of ecology, change will occur more rapidly, more surprisingly, more beautifully.

K. Lauren de Boer: You've said, in "Throw Yourself Like Seed," that stories are about change and that ritual is the art of change. How can story and mythology help?

Michael Meade: Someone once described mythology as "the lie that reveals the truth." Mythology's modern connotation means "something false." But the word itself has to do with emerging truth. Something people usually see as fiction is actually carrying meaning and truth in the depths. Young people are just like that. People say, "They just want attention," and I say, "What's your point?" Attention is required for them to find themselves. "Themselves" is something that's a deeper story in them that modern culture would deny, reject, overlook.

People often send kids to camps in nature. It's a smart idea. They fit in with nature because they're exploring their own nature. I work with all kinds of young people. At fourteen, young people are having the seed ideas of their life. What we call middle school, early high school, is the time when the seed, the core imagination and seed ideas of their life are bursting within them and are seeking what I call the "waters of attention," the blessing, blessed waters from the culture around them that will allow those seed imaginations to grow.

K. Lauren de Boer: What happens if they're not shown the recognition of that seed?

Michael Meade: Now, we're back to death. William Blake said that the garden of the soul is already planted and is waiting for the water of life. Call it the water of attention. There are innate ideas, dreams, stories, buried in people. When we don't water those seeds, culture loses ideas. It loses imagination. It loses the capacity to dream itself forward. I mean that literally.

K. Lauren de Boer: What happens to someone whose innate core cannot grow?

Michael Meade: The 'second nature' of a person (the innate capacities) needs two kinds of attention. The person has to attend to it themselves. It also needs the other kind of attention which used to be called a blessing—the attention, especially from someone who's respected, someone who says, "I saw that. I heard that. I see the seed of life you're coming from." If these two kinds of attention don't happen, a kind of death is occurring, a withering.

K. Lauren de Boer: The gift atrophies.

Michael Meade: Atrophy occurs and we it call depression and suicidal tendencies. For some, there's too much fire in the seed to simply atrophy and those burst into violence. Each young person is like an extreme story compelled into this world. Because of the intensity of life each person carries, there are two big tendencies, one toward suicide, one toward homicide. Either atrophy, withdrawal, and implosion or the explosion in which the seeds are cracked, blown, and strewn about to become the kind of seeds that don't find an earth in which to grow. There's violence that comes from the lack of attention to one's seed. How does that relate to the violence from outside?

K. Lauren de Boer: What happens if we don't deal with the reverberations of violence from September 11th with young people?

Michael Meade: September 11th was a horrible thing, incomprehensible in many ways. At the same time, I was doing work in South Central Los Angeles. When I'm there, I see terrorism every day. We have an internal terrorism in this culture. You can look in both directions—the outer terrorist and the homegrown, inner terror—both come from seeds of life so consistently rejected over generations or an extended period of time, that they can't grow in a meaningful way. They can become dead seeds and seeds of death.

To my eye, a terrorist is someone who's already dead. That's why they're so hard to deal with. None of the things that normally apply to human psychology, apply to them. They found a suicide note in the car that a terrorist left in the Boston airport. It had been written two years before the attack. He was carrying his death note for two years…he was already dead. Terrorists are in the world of the dead, trying to drag other people there.

I've been with fifteen- and sixteen-year-old kids holding a gun, planning to go shoot someone based on some neighborhood revenge drama, and they intend to be shot while doing it. If you say, to them, "What about your future?", they'll say, "I don't have one." If you say, "Isn't there anything you want out of life," they say "I won't get anything out of this life." It's a tragic, grievous thing—to sit with someone of that age and realize not just that this person is about to kill and be killed, but that this person might already be dead.

K. Lauren de Boer: They haven't had that inner seed recognized.

Michael Meade: And something has happened that's caused that to seem impossible. I don't know if it's ever completely removed. I would say there's always the possibility of bringing that seed to life. But, seeing the terrorists made me realize they were in the same condition. Their story has stopped, and they want to take everyone to the land where their stories are frozen or dead.

K. Lauren de Boer: We don't recognize the terrorist in our own youth.

Michael Meade: Even more seriously, we don't recognize the terror we've visited upon our youth. Someone planning major destruction, including destroying their own life, has made a suicide pact. I've seen it with kids who shoot at cops. They usually don't even hit very well. What they're doing is trying to get the cops to shoot them. It's a suicide plot. A lot of gang killing is actually mutual suicide. There are many things that a culture does that stops the story of some of its people. That's a form of terrorism.

Beyond a Culture of Fear

by K. Lauren de Boer

Fear is the cheapest
room in the house. I'd like to see you
in better living conditions.
—*Hafiz*

Give us a happy ending and we write a new disaster story.
—*Barry Glassner*

"It's a campaign of fear and consumption," states rock star Marilyn Manson, "Keep people afraid and they'll consume." This lucid insight into the connection between our mass media news diet, the incitement of fear, and consumerism emerged in an interview with Manson in the recent film, *Bowling for Columbine.* Manson was the brunt of criticism by many community members and the media for somehow inciting the kind of violence that led to the tragic 1999 incident in Littleton, Colorado where two Columbine High School students killed twelve students and a teacher using handguns.

Why direct blame toward Manson? Because of the rock lyrics he writes. And yet, asks Manson, who has more influence on violent behavior, [former] President Clinton, who was shooting bombs overseas, or himself, just a guy singing some rock and roll songs?

On the same day of the shootings at Columbine, the film's maker Michael Moore points out in his interview with Manson, President Clinton ordered the heaviest bombing assault yet in Kosovo.

"What would you say to the kids who did the shooting at Columbine?" asks Moore. Manson responds: "I wouldn't say a thing. I'd listen to what they have to say. That's what no one did."

Bowling for Columbine is a gutsy, often disturbing probe into the absurd cycle of fear prevalent in American culture today. Our obsession with guns, suggests the film, is the same irrational obsession driving the US war economy. Our violent, fear-filled society is one marked, not coincidentally, by addictive over-consumption. Not long after September 11, George W. Bush evoked the fear of terrorism and the virtues of being a good consumer practically in the same breath.

The phenomenon of misplaced fear in American culture is not uncommon, asserts sociologist Barry Glassner, author of *The Culture of Fear: Why Americans Are Afraid of the Wrong Things*. From overblown crime statistics to exaggerated germ scares to plane wrecks, a wide array of groups–including businesses, advocacy organizations, religious sects, and political parties–benefit and profit from promoting fear. Glassner's book, at its essence, raises important questions about how misbegotten fears find their way into the public psyche through a process driven by power and money. He writes:

> Samuel Taylor Coleridge was right when he claimed, "In politics, what begins in fear usually ends up in folly." Political activists are more inclined, though, to heed an observation from Richard Nixon: "People react to fear, not love. They don't teach that in Sunday School, but it's true." That principle, which guided the late president's political strategy throughout his career, is the *sine qua non* of contemporary political campaigning. Marketers of products and services ranging from car alarms to TV news programs have taken it to heart as well.

Glassner's book continues with an exploration of how the "vendors of fear tap into our moral insecurities and supply us with symbolic substitutes."[1]

The kind of insecurity and fear exploited by the current US administration may be good for business in the short run, but it's bad policy in the long run. Human energy, when manipulated by fear, can become distorted and destructive. Fear can incapacitate and paralyze us, keeping our energy in check. But when the energy does assert itself, it can do so in horrendous ways. Addictive consumerism, adherence to narrow beliefs about the nature of reality, and desperate clinging to what deadens us are some of those. Conformity to fabricated and obsolete worldviews, such as one that sanctions the bombing of other countries to protect our hegemony over resources like oil, is another. Giving in to despair is yet another.

Heroes and Villains

The heroes we choose and those we vilify can define us in powerful ways. We live in a country where Al Qaeda and Saddam Hussein have taken on mythic proportions as villains, and where violent characters like Rambo and Dirty Harry are the touted heroes of presidents. In a revealing essay from *Mennonite Life* (December, 2001) entitled "The Original Peacemakers: Native America," author James C. Juhnke points out that US history textbooks highlight the warriors, not the peacemakers of the original Americans, despite the fact that, like all human communities, Native Americans were people of both peace and war."The notable Indians in the master narrative of American history are the military heroes—men such as Pontiac, Tecumseh, Geronimo, Crazy Horse, and Sitting Bull," writes Junhke. "Sherman Alexie, popular Native American novelist and poet, put a cogent question in the mouth of one of his characters: 'When are the Indians ever going to have heroes who don't hurt people? Why do all of our heroes have to carry guns?'" White Americans, the article points out, build historical monuments for the Indian warriors, not for the peacemakers. [2]

In some respects the emergence of a character such as good child-wizard Harry Potter as a hero in these times seems like a good sign. By depicting a world where good triumphs over evil, one recent Op-Ed states, the Harry Potter books give us strength to face real enemies.

Yes, maybe. However, a story motif of good triumphing over evil can as easily justify a campaign to invade Iraq as it can inspire one to do battle with a carefully discerned internal demon or, say, the destructive impact of voter apathy on democratic society. A tale doesn't automatically impart wisdom simply because it depicts the triumph of good. In fact, many traditional myths depict not the decimation of evil, but its transformation. Good and evil are interconnected forces in the cosmos; their encounter is part of a dialectic that ultimately brings about the overall restoration of the whole.

The True Face of Evil

Not surprisingly, one such story comes from Native Americans, the original peacemakers and arguably the earliest practitioners of participatory democracy on the planet. Part of an epic Iroquois legend, the story of the Great Peacemaker, speaks powerfully to our current situation, both in terms of the disturbing fervor for war and the need for hope in people with a conscience of peace. Furthermore, the legend has added power and relevance in that it looks to our past as a nation, to the influence of the Iroquois Confederacy on its founders.

Philosopher Jacob Needleman provides a stirring rendition of the legend in his recent book *The American Soul: Rediscovering the Wisdom of the Founders*. The following passage is a condensation of Needleman's account, which draws on an unpublished retelling of the Onandaga story of creation by Maril Rianna Blanchard.

The part of the legend we are most concerned with begins at a time when human beings cannot live in peace. There is strife and contention between nations. In Needleman's words, "There is no place, no structure, no condition within which the forces of Earth and of the human can confront each other in a way that allows a harmonizing, uniting, and peacemaking force to act from within."

The Creator sends the Great Peacemaker to aid the human beings. The Great Peacemaker sets out on a quest to end violence among human beings with the message of "peace that is power." He is said to bring a "New Mind" to the nations. This is something they readily accept, Needleman elucidates, because they "glimpse something infinitely more honorable than war...the field of life in all its vibrancy, a call to serve what is far greater than oneself."

But there is one very powerful chief, Atotarho, who does not accept the message. Atotarho is an intimidating figure who "eats human beings," whose body is crooked in seven places, and who has snakes in his hair. He utters a great bloodcurdling cry: *Hwe-do-ne-e-e-e-e-eh–!*, which means "When will this be? It has not come yet!"

"The actual identity of Atotarho," writes Needleman, "and the story of the struggle with him throw astonishing light on the meaning of the democracy created by the Iroquois Confederacy and on the mystical pragmatism that lies at the root of our own American democracy."

Atotarho represents a concept of evil that the Western mind is at odds with, one which speaks, not to the age-old battle between good and evil, but to the human propensity to defeat peace by giving into despair. "Atotarho is not the figure of evil who simply opposes out of an irredeemable black heart," writes Needleman, "[He] is evil as inability–incapacity to hope, incapacity to try.... When he is defeated, he is defeated by being awakened to his own power of love and wisdom.... Human evil is goodness acting under a wrong thought; human evil is love acting under a wrong fear, a wrong striving; human evil is the power of the spirit under the yoke of a despairing master."

True to the matrilineal nature of Iroquois society and to their Constitution, the delivery into the world of the Great Peacemaker's message is mediated by a woman. Women have equal participation in Iroquois governance. And it is the women—the clan mothers—who appoint the chiefs of the nations and who have the power to depose them. Because the woman is the first to accept and understand the message of the "peace that is power," the Great Peacemaker gives her a new name: Jigonhasasee, meaning "New Face." "It is in your countenance," he tells her, "that the New Mind is manifest."

Having the blessing of Jigonhasasee, the Great Peacemaker then goes to none other than Hiawatha, perhaps the most well-known figure of Iroquois legend. Hiawatha is a "weak and degraded figure" when he finds him. Like Atotarho, he eats human beings. Hiawatha is given a "New Mind," as the nation chief, when he looks at his own reflection in a kettle of water and sees the Great Peacemaker instead. Hiawatha sees his own greater potential in the Great Peacemaker, and commits himself to bringing the message of peace to Earth. Eventually, Hiawatha and the Great Peacemaker go to confront Atotarho, who continues to utter the great cry of despair. Atotarho alone stands in the way of the Great Peace.

Hiawatha, whose name means He Who Combs, must comb the snakes from Atotarho's hair. Atotarho, who has been consistently cynical, hears the words of the Great Peacemaker when he says that peace, justice, and health will only come when humans are ready to accept them. Hiawatha, with the aid of the Great Peacemaker, is able to break through Atotarho's considerable resistance as they deliver to the evil chief the Great Law of Peace. They are able to awaken within Atotarho his own sense of power and wisdom. Hiawatha combs the snakes from Atotarho's hair and his mind is made straight; despair has been defeated.

The Great Peacemaker plants the Great Tree of Peace, a white pine, whose roots extend throughout the world. All the nations bury their weapons of war beneath it. Peace reigns when Atotarho, now with a New Mind, goes on to become the great chief of all five Iroquois nations. [3]

Now Is Not the Time to Give up

Ultimately, the Great Peacemaker legend provides a basis for faith, for moving us past despair. To give into despair is to succumb to fear, the ultimate source of all human violence. Evil is the incapacity to hope or to try, we learn from the story, and so the question becomes: Do we continue to utter Atotarho's cry of despair or do we use the energy of dark times to renew our inner commitment to a peace for all life, to inner peace, to peace in all directions, as the roots of the Great Tree of Peace depict? How we bring about peace in our own lives, how we choose to be exemplars of a planetary sustainable peace is the "radical" (from Latin, *radicalis,* for "root") action which lays the foundation for a transformation of collective consciousness.

In our time when we are at war with the planet itself, the tale of Hiawatha, Atotarho, and the Great Peacemaker has meaning not just as a tale of peace between nations, but for peace with the Earth. We are "cannibalizing the Earth" through our over-consumption and resource extraction and require a "new mind" to bring about *Pax Gaia.*

New Mind refers not just to calm passivity, but to "peace as power," which means we are in right relationship not only to our inner nature, but to the energies of Earth and Cosmos, even to their more troubling aspects of chaos and uncertainty. This requires faith of a kind that can only come to us from a desire for justice for the entire Earth Community.

Coming from such a place of power, how might we move beyond a culture of fear in dark times?

• A vibrant and functional democracy depends on the honest dissemination of information. The corporate media, in its rightward drift and easy compliance to political power, is failing the general populace. Citizens groups might start running interference and holding the corporate media responsible for perpetrating violence and consumerism under the guise of news and entertainment. We can start by being conscious of just what they are serving up as our media diet. We can boycott toxic news and demand that they stop creating a culture of fear.

• Don't let consumption define who we are. True peace is to see ourselves as citizens, not simply consumers. We are human beings in a communion of Earth's subjects.

• Develop our powers of listening—to young people, to Earth, and to our inner sense of peace. We also need to believe in the wisdom of our young people. In *The Soul of Politics*, Jim Wallis tells the remarkably hopeful story of the Gang Summit in Kansas City in 1993, where warring barrio gang members came together on their own initiative, listened to each other, and not only worked out a truce, but talked about "transformation and rebuilding." "New visions will require new visionaries," writes Wallis, "and they will most likely come from ordinary people who are willing to become a part of the changes they seek for the very ordinary circumstances of their lives and their society. And that will be the extraordinary thing." [4]

All lasting change begins with people talking to each other, with public square diplomacy, with community.

• Have faith that alternatives to the corporate political parties are not only possible, but that the time is right. Paul Ray, in a paper entitled "A New Political Compass," states that there are a group of "new progressives" constituting 36 percent of the population who are not yet truly represented by a political party. Dennis Kucinich, while a Democrat, is one Washington politician who represents the "political north." Ray characterizes the political north as the Wisdom Culture Paradigm.

• Practice a spiritual ecology of peace. This practice gives us the basis for moving beyond a world of fear, violence, and war because it is a practice based in the embrace of all life and an acceptance of the forces of ecology at work in our lives. This includes chaos, uncertainty, and surprise. Spiritual ecology, through a practice of quieting and attuning our mind to rhythms outside language brings peace because we are in accord with the present moment. Fear of the future falls away.

• We need stories. The Peacemaker legend is one story of a particular people which has some potential for our time. However, telling our sacred Universe Story, seeing ourselves in a meaningful role within that unfolding, is a powerful force for peace within. We are the heroes of that story, the source for peace in the world. Accessing that source and creating in ourselves a New Mind is the Great Work of our time.

Martin Luther King, Jr. wrote: "Those who make peaceful change impossible make violent revolution inevitable." If we commit ourselves to creating peaceful change by not giving into despair and a culture of fear, we practice the spiritual ecology of peace. We take the step of faith that will make violence and war obsolete as solutions to conflict.

Endnotes

1. Barry Glassner, *The Culture of Fear: Why Americans Are Afraid of the Wrong Things*, (Basic Books, 1999), p. xxviii.

2. James C. Juhnke, "The Original Peacemakers: Native America," (*Mennonite Life*, December 2001), vol. 56 no. 4.

3. Jacob Needleman, *The American Soul: Rediscovering the Wisdom of the Founders*, (Tarcher/Putnam, 2002), pp. 215-236.

4. Jim Wallis, *The Soul of Politics: Beyond the "Secular Left" and the "Religious Right,"* (Harcourt Brace & Co., 1995), p. 295.

Clan of One-Breasted Women

by Terry Tempest Williams

At a Bioneers conference held in San Rafael, California in October 1999, Utah writer and naturalist Terry Tempest Williams chose to share parts of the epilogue from her 1991 book, Refuge: An Unnatural History of Family and Place. *The book is a powerful personal account of the life experience of a Mormon woman and her family in dealing with the consequences of radioactive fallout from the Nevada nuclear test site.*

The test site was illegally created on the ancestral lands of the Shoshoni people. The lands were stolen by the US government in violation of the 1863 Treaty of Ruby Valley. The intent of the signed treaty was to guarantee the sovereignty of the Shoshoni people over their traditional homeland, Newe Segobia-ratitor.

As a prologue to her talk, Williams told conference participants that she chose to read her essay to remind us all how necessary it is to keep telling the stories of the US military industrial complex, over and over again—to never forget the great burden of environmental poison it forces us all to carry. Deploring the stubbornness of politicians who continue to reject the Comprehensive Test Ban Treaty, Williams asked: How do we sacrifice humanity in the name of personal vendettas? Why do we tolerate such blatant arrogance?

Here is her address at the Bioneers conference in October 1999:

I belong to a Clan of One-Breasted Women. My mother, my grandmothers, and six aunts have all had mastectomies. Seven are dead. The two who survive have just completed rounds of chemotherapy and radiation.

I've had my own problems: two biopsies for breast cancer and a small tumor removed between my ribs diagnosed as "a borderline malignancy." This is my family history.

Most statistics tell us breast cancer is genetic, hereditary, with rising percentages attached to fatty diets, childlessness, or becoming pregnant after 30. What they don't say is living in Utah may be the greatest hazard of all.

We are a Mormon family with roots in Utah since 1847. The Word of Wisdom, a religious doctrine of health, kept the women in my family aligned with good foods: no coffee, tea, tobacco, or alcohol. For the most part, these women were finished having babies by the time they were 30. And only one faced breast cancer prior to 1960. Traditionally, as a group of people, Mormons have a low rate of cancer.

Is our family a cultural anomaly? The truth is, we didn't think about it. Those who did, usually the men, simply said, "bad genes." The women's attitude was stoic. Cancer was a part of life. On February 16, 1971, the eve before my mother's surgery, I accidentally picked up the telephone and overheard her ask my grandmother what she could expect.

"Diane, it is one of the most spiritual experiences you will ever encounter."

I quietly put down the receiver.

Two days later, my father took my three brothers and me to the hospital to visit her. She met us in the lobby in a wheelchair. No bandages were visible. I'll never forget her radiance, the way she held herself in a purple velour robe and how she gathered us around her.

"Children, I am fine. I want you to know I felt the arms of God around me." We believed her. My father cried. Our mother, his wife, was 38 years old.

A little over a year after my mother's death from cancer, my father and I were having dinner together. He had just returned from St. George, where his construction company was putting in natural gas lines for towns in southern Utah. He spoke of his love for the country: the sandstone landscape, bare-boned and beautiful. He had just finished hiking the Kolob trail in Zion National Park. We got caught up in reminiscing, recalling with fondness our walk up Angels Landing on his fiftieth birthday and the years our family had vacationed there. This was a remembered landscape where we had been raised.

Over dessert, I shared a recurring dream of mine. I told my

father that for years, as long as I could remember, I saw this flash of light in the night in the desert. That this image had so permeated my being, I could not venture south without seeing it again, on the horizon, illuminating buttes and mesas.

"You did see it," he said.

"Saw what?"

"The bomb. The cloud. We were driving home from Riverside, California. You were sitting on Diane's lap. She was pregnant. In fact, I remember the date, September 7, 1957. We had just gotten out of the Service. We were driving north, past Las Vegas. It was an hour or so before dawn, when this explosion went off. We not only heard it, but felt it. I thought the oil tanker in front of us had blown up. We pulled over and suddenly, rising from the desert floor, we saw it clearly, this golden-stemmed cloud, the mushroom. The sky seemed to vibrate with an eerie pink glow. Within a few minutes, a light ash was raining on the car."

I stared at my father.

"I thought you knew that," my father said. "It was a common occurrence in the fifties."

It was at that moment I realized the deceit I had been living under. Children growing up in the American Southwest, drinking contaminated milk from contaminated cows, even from the contaminated breasts of their mothers, my mother—members, years later, of the Clan of One-Breasted Women.

When the Atomic Energy Commission described the country north of the Nevada Test Site as virtually uninhabited desert terrain, my family members were some of the "virtual uninhabitants."

One night, I dreamed women from all over the world were circling a blazing fire in the desert. They spoke of change, of how they hold the moon in their bellies and wax and wane with its phases. They mocked at the presumption of even-tempered beings and made promises that they would never fear the witch inside themselves. The women danced wildly as sparks broke away from the flames and entered the night sky as stars.

And they sang a song given to them by Shoshoni grandmothers:

Ah ne nah, nah—Consider the rabbits—
nin nah nah—How gently they walk on the earth—
Ah ne nah, nah—Consider the rabbits—
nin nah nah—How gently they walk on the earth—
Nyaga mutzi—We remember them—
oh ne nay—We can walk gently also—
Nyaga mutzi—We remember them—
oh ne nay— We can walk gently also—

The women danced and drummed and sang for weeks, preparing themselves for what was to come. They would reclaim the desert for the sake of their children, for the sake of the land.

A few miles downwind from the fire circle, bombs were being tested. Rabbits felt the tremors. Their soft leather pads on paws and feet recognized the shaking sands while the roots of mesquite and sage were smoldering. Rocks were hot from the inside out and dust devils hummed unnaturally. And each time there was another nuclear test, ravens watched the desert heave. Stretch marks appeared. The land was losing its muscle.

The women couldn't bear it any longer. They were mothers. They had suffered labor pains, but always under the promise of birth. The red-hot pains beneath the desert promised death only, as each bomb became stillborn. A contract was being drawn by the women who understood the fate of the Earth as their own.

Under the cover of darkness, ten women slipped under the barbed-wire fence and entered the contaminated country. They were trespassing. They walked toward the town of Mercury in moonlight, taking their cues from coyote, kit fox, antelope, ground squirrel, and quail. They moved quietly and deliberately through the maze of Joshua trees. When a hint of daylight appeared they rested, drinking tea and sharing their rations of food. The women closed their eyes. The time had come to protest with the heart, that to deny one's genealogy with the Earth was to commit treason against one's soul.

At dawn, the women draped themselves in Mylar, wrapping long streamers of silver plastic around their arms to blow in the breeze. They wore clear masks that became the faces of humanity. And when they arrived on the edge of Mercury, they carried all the butterflies of a summer day in their wombs. They paused to allow their courage to settle.

The town, which forbids pregnant women and children to enter because of radiation risks to their health, was asleep. The women moved through the streets as winged messengers, twirling around each other in slow motion, peeking inside homes and watching the easy sleep of men and women. They were astonished by such stillness and periodically would utter a shrill note or low cry just to verify life.

The residents finally awoke to what appeared as strange apparitions. Some simply stared. Others called authorities, and in time, the women were apprehended by wary soldiers dressed in desert fatigues. They were taken to a white building on the other edge of Mercury. When asked who they were and why they were there, the women replied, "We are mothers and we have come to reclaim the desert for our children."

The soldiers arrested them. As the ten women were blindfolded and handcuffed, they began singing:

You can't forbid us everything
You can't forbid us to think—
You can't forbid our tears to flow
And you can't stop the songs that we sing.

The women continued to sing louder and louder, until they heard the voices of their sisters moving across the mesa.

Ah nenah, nah
nin nah nah—
Ah ne nah, nah
nin nah nah—
Nyaga mutzi
oh ne nay—
Nyaga mutzi
oh ne nay—

"Call for reinforcements," one soldier said.

"We have," interrupted one woman. "We have—and you have no idea of our numbers."

On March 18, 1988, I crossed the line at the Nevada Test Site and was arrested with nine other Utahans for trespassing on military lands. They are still conducting nuclear tests in the desert. Ours was an act of civil disobedience. But as I walked toward the town of Mercury, it was more than a gesture of peace. It was a gesture on behalf of the Clan of One-Breasted Women.

As one officer cinched the handcuffs around my wrists, another frisked my body. She found a pen and a pad of paper tucked inside my left boot.

"And these?" she asked sternly.

"Weapons," I replied.

Our eyes met. I smiled. She pulled the leg of my trousers back over my boot. "Step forward, please," she said as she took my arm.

We were booked under an afternoon sun and bused to Tonopah, Nevada. It was a two-hour ride. This was familiar country to me. The Joshua trees standing their ground had been named by my ancestors who believed they looked like prophets pointing west to the Promised Land. These were the same trees that bloomed each spring, flowers appearing like white flames in the Mojave. And I recalled a full moon in May when my mother and I had walked among them, flushing out mourning doves and owls.

The bus stopped short of town. We were released. The officials thought it was a cruel joke to leave us stranded in the desert with no way to get home. What they didn't realize is that we were home, soul-centered and strong, women who recognized the sweet smell of sage as fuel for our spirits.

Native Medicine
and the Inner Healer

by Alan Strain

I was a child in a small town in southern Idaho. One summer day when I was eight, I was walking home from Vacation Bible School and passed a neighbor's Irish Setter sleeping on the sidewalk. On a mischievous impulse I stamped my foot as I went by. The dog awoke, grabbed my left leg in his teeth and bit deeply into my calf muscle. Nearly two weeks later the dog was discovered to have rabies, which had recently killed other dogs in our area. It was almost the end of the incubation period when the Pasteur treatment should be given. Perhaps it was too late, but next day, serum was flown from Boise into an alfalfa field near our house and greatly-accelerated twice-daily shots were begun.

During weeks of confinement in a darkened room I often talked with my mother about what was happening to me, and I became aware that I might soon die. But ever since those talks, I have never had the slightest fear of death, a testimony to my mother's deep respect and faith in me and the great, enfolding spirit beyond.

My Sacred Place

Two years later we moved to southern California and I continued my recuperation from my close encounter with death, which had left me with a serious heart murmur. I soon rebelled at the advice of a young family doctor who told me that it was likely I would die before thirty unless I gave up all sports and physical activity. When I was 14, I bought a bicycle, got a 12-mile morning paper route, and began spending my weekends riding into the San Gabriel Mountains, just to the north.

Three miles up an abandoned, dusty dirt toll road to the Mount Wilson observatory, I discovered a small oasis, called Henniger's Flats. For the next five or six years, this became my sacred place. I often rode there Friday afternoon, and returned home for supper on Saturday.

My oasis had grown up around a crystal-clear bubbling spring that flowed all year. There were a few pines, several aspen, some poison oak, mountain lilac and other small plants and herbs. There was soft, level ground to spread my bedroll. During the years I went there, I never once saw another human being in that lovely, strangely remote place; though there were frequent visits from other of my relations that shared our spring.

Here in this special place, most of the controlling beliefs of my later life were shaped. I read Gandhi's autobiography which led me to Thoreau's essays on non-violent disobedience and other topics. and to the essays of Emerson, Thoreau's mentor. Emerson's "Self Reliance" became my first creed.

Most important, perhaps, it was here I first knew an intensely personal relation with the world of Nature and knew myself as integral with it. To this day, the sound of wind moving through pines makes me tingle. Here I first knew a personal connection with mountain lilac and with the deer, and coyote, and raccoon who came to the spring, and with the water that drew them. But above all, I knew this as a place to heal and become whole again.

Plant Spirit Medicine

In 1961 I was the 8th grade teacher at Peninsula School in Menlo Park, California. That spring, I drove with my students to the Hopi villages in Arizona. While there, we had some remarkable walks and talks with villagers, including some elders, both men and women.

On our walks with our Hopi guides near New Oraibi (now known by its Hopi name, Kyakotsmovi), we marveled at the dry farming for which the Hopi are well-known.

Years later I knew a man who, it is clear to me, communicates directly with plants and their spirits. He is a professor of art in a university and has an arboretum attached to his studio. It was clear to me when I first visited him there, that he was personally in touch with Nature and with spirit in ways I was not. The plants in his studio were personal friends, accorded the respect given wise and respected elders. But when we talked about their awareness and feelings, he sensed my skepticism.

He walked over and sat down next to a plant, a delicate fern, as

I recall, and he settled into silent meditation for some minutes, eyes closed. After several minutes, the plant began to shrivel and collapse before my unbelieving eyes. Some sound must have escaped me, for he opened his eyes, made a soft sound of anguish, motioned me to silence, and returned to his meditation, this time for many minutes. The stricken plant rejuvenated visibly, but my friend was sad that its full vitality had not returned by the time we parted. Happily, when I saw it later, it looked in excellent health.

While I have not entered into a mystical connection with plants as my friend has, I have felt close to particular plants since I was a small child. Once, lying in a field of fresh clover in Idaho, watching a bee gather nectar several inches away, I became so involved with both bee and blossom that all sense of "the other" disappeared. The memory of that moment has lingered all my life.

A large English lilac overhung the back door of the first house I remember calling home, and I still can imagine bathing in its fragrance and feeling the same personal closeness I felt with the comparatively scent-free mountain lilacs near the spring at Heninger's Flats.

All my life I have felt a close relationship with certain trees: the poplars around our house in Idaho, the pungent pepper trees around my first school in California, and the pine trees at Idyllwild Pines, a conference grounds where I worked summers during high school.

Recently I encountered a remarkable book, *Plant Spirit Medicine,* by Eliot Cowan, a shaman who turns to plant spirits for assistance in health, often with remarkable results. He believes that plant spirits are everywhere and can be contacted by anyone who invites their companionship and help. It includes fascinating stories and interviews with a wide variety of healers who use plants in their healing. Knowing that I have approached having mystical encounters with plants in the past. Cowan's book inspires me to seek at-one-ness with more of "all my relations."

I lived in the middle of what once was land of the Banock-Shoshone Indians. When I was eight, a neighbor my age and I were exploring a lava-tube cave under the sagebrush-covered volcanic plateau beyond our house at the edge of town. Inside we found more than we bargained for—an Indian burial on a ledge overlooking a deep chamber. Ever since that awesome discovery, Indian people have appeared repeatedly in my life. Now for over 30 years much of my work as a teacher has involved me with Indian people, Native American studies, and Indian Country.

Only recently, however, did I discover the delightful and important books of Carl Hammerschlag, about his many years of work as a doctor among native peoples of the Southwest, where he learned to be a healer in spite of himself.

In 1965, as a young doctor from the East Coast, Hammerschlag joined the Indian Health Service and was assigned to work in the Santa Fe Indian Hospital serving the Pueblo people along the Rio Grande. "I thought," he wrote, "I could bring healing to plain people who would welcome my expertness. I was ready to save the world—people needed me. I didn't know I was going to the Southwest to be healed myself."

He was unprepared for the crowded conditions he found in the hospital and the poverty in their villages. But his patients set about working patiently to make him a healer.

Among his many teachers was Santiago, a Pueblo priest and clan chief, who had been hospitalized with congestive heart failure. On Carl's first visit to his bedside, Santiago quizzed him about where he had learned to heal, then asked with a beatific smile, "Do you know how to dance?"

Carl continues:

> Touched by whimsey at the old man's query, I answered that sure, I liked to dance; and I shuffled a little at his bedside. Santiago chuckled, got out of bed, and, short of breath, began to show me his dance.
>
> "You must be able to dance if you are to heal people," he said.
>
> "'And will you teach me your steps?" I asked, indulging the aging priest.
>
> Santiago nodded. "Yes, I can teach you my steps, but you will have to hear your own music."
>
> The young doctor, amused, discounted Santiago as "another mystical holy man slightly removed from the realities I had to deal with."

But a seed had been planted, a friendship begun, and I later visited him many times in his home. The seeds that Santiago had planted within my psyche would not sprout until I returned East so that I might go to Yale and study psychiatry.

This first meeting between Santiago and the young Doctor Carl inspired the title of his first book, *The Dancing Healers: A Doctor's Journey of Healing with Native Americans.* It is a book of stories by a superb storyteller about the author's life and those of his Indian patients and friends over his 20 years working as a doctor and psychiatrist in the Southwest. His own journey is woven into the stories he tells of patients he works with as he learns to become a *healer,* not only a "well trained" Western doctor. Perhaps the central thing he learns is that "the spirit plays as big a role in our wellness and sickness as the mind and body do."

Hammerschlag's second book, *The Theft of the Spirit: a Journey to Spiritual Healing with Native Americans,* vividly portrays through powerful, poignant stories what the Hopi are experiencing today as a microcosm of the modern world.

"Since more than half of all the artifacts and art objects that the Hopi consider sacred have been stolen," writes Hammerschlag, "religious leaders cannot pass on the knowledge of ceremonies, and there will be no qualified successors. These losses are equivalent to the destruction of the Wailing Wall, the burning of the True Cross, and the leveling of Mecca."

"Thefts of sacred objects will continue if we allow reverence for life to be replaced in our hearts and our shared experience by desire for money, possessions, and technology. Multiplication has taken precedence over sanctification. Truth is less respected than wealth and what is good is respected less that what is easy. The result is that the portion of ourselves that is imbued with spirit becomes faint and sick. When history is written, let it not be said that we floundered because we allowed the theft of our spirit. There is still time."

Ten Caterpillars Yawning: Interview with Carolyn Toben at Timberlake Farm

by Cindy Spring

The Center for Education, Imagination and the Natural World is located at Timberlake Farm Earth Sanctuary in Whitsett, North Carolina. Timberlake is a unique place of beauty with wildflower meadows, four miles of gentle trails, small streams and tall hardwoods and pines. Fourteen resident deer find refuge there. Fish, ducks, frogs, and turtles thrive on two lakes. Wooden foot bridges and benches blend into the natural landscape and invite exploration and contemplation. It is a place dedicated to communion with the natural world. In 2001, the 165 acres of Timberlake were placed under an easement with the Conservation Trust of North Carolina.

Since Carolyn Toben co-founded the Center in 2000, it has been "a wildlife and child preserve" for not only children, but also teachers, parents and many visitors. Its programs were completely filled this past school year. The Center offers nature camps, teacher retreats, and provides "Special Design" programs for nearby schools and universities. In addition to organic gardening, recycling, and composting they have a lunch program that encourages children to live lightly on the Earth.

Cindy Spring: What prompted you and co-director Peggy Whalen-Levitt to begin the Center?

Carolyn Toben: We feel that a great deal is being lost for children today—a sense of wonder and a bond of intimacy with the natural world. We see a trend in the culture where nature is seen as an abstraction. Children know about global warming and ozone depletion. But they don't know the smell of the spring rain or the sound of a bullfrog. Most children today lack a sense of celebration of the dawn, the sunset, the moonrise, a reverence for life and growth and the cycles and seasons. We hope that we are offering what is missing.

[Ecophilosopher] Thomas Berry plays a major role in our thinking; he's been a mentor, advisor, and friend for 28 years.

Cindy Spring: How do you link imagination and the natural world?

Carolyn Toben: What Peggy and I know is that children are born with these deep inner faculties of imagination and intuition. Those faculties have to be brought forth through the life cycle. The neglect of this development in education leads to a deficit in the child and in the natural world and in the culture at large. Children have to be given an opportunity to develop, to respond with intimacy in the natural world, and to experience it through their senses and imagination.

For example, in one of our nature camps, we did a session of listening in the woods. We had thirteen children ranging in age from 5 to 7. We asked them to listen outwardly to hear what sounds they heard. They did that for a while and then told us what they heard and we wrote it down. Then we asked them to listen inwardly and not outwardly at all. And we wrote those down. In the second part, one little boy named Alex said: "I heard ancient fires crackling." A little girl named Sharon said: "I heard ten caterpillars yawning." We went back to our tree house which is the epicenter of the land. They quietly took their watercolors and created pictures of what they heard. So we had these extraordinary phrases along with their watercolor drawings. This is an important part of the process of nurturing the human being, to help them create their own images out of their own experience. We acknowledge the potential of their inner life and seek to allow it to unfold.

Cindy Spring: I wonder if the average adult could distinguish between listening outwardly and listening inwardly. Do you give them any guidance in listening inwardly?

Carolyn Toben: No. I don't give them any help in tuning inward.

They'll tell us what they hear inside themselves or what pictures they see.

Cindy Spring: How do you approach spirituality as a topic? Do you use the word "God?"

Carolyn Toben: Spirituality isn't approached as a topic separate from our daily lives here, but it's central and implicit in all we do. Thomas Berry has given us a new language to speak. He talks about the trees and the flowers and the sun being modes of divine presence. There's no need to use the word God. What we need now is to recover the foundations that lead to a sense of beauty, wonder, and intimacy. All religions are founded on these attributes.

Our intention is to create a bond of intimacy between children and nature. For example, through the seasons, we talk about the cycles of growth and the seed within the plant. Then we look at the plant and talk about the children's growth. We make those correspondences as often as possible. We talk about how you plant something and how you nurture it. We ask how they've been nurtured and cared for. In our Special Design programs, children come out through the seasons. They adopt a tree and then they come back and see how it's changed and grown and we talk about how they've changed and grown and how they see things differently by the end of the year.

One of the exercises I do on our earthwalks is to have them stop and pay attention to what is moving. And this is all in silence. So they notice the ripples on the pond, then the way the wind moves and stops, the way the leaves dance. One little girl said she noticed the beating of her own heart.

Then I say to them: "If we came back here tomorrow and stood exactly in the same place, would it be exactly as it is now?" Even the littlest children say, "No." And I say, "Why not?" And they say, "Because everything's always changing." Then I say: "Are you always changing?" And they say "Yes." It's a cosmological way of knowing. Nobody is taught that directly. They know it within themselves.

Cindy Spring: How has the landscape shaped you?

Carolyn Toben: As my family shaped this land, it was actually shaping us. The presence of the hardwoods, the cedars, the lakes, the creatures—they all live within us in what Thomas Berry terms "fulfillment." It's a relationship of giving and receiving. This is not a center in which the natural world is a backdrop for our human endeavors. It is the central focus. It's a very rich, abundant environment. Everything right now (August) is blooming. It's quite generative and verdant. If I go to a desert, I have an appreciation for the amazing variety there, but I long for the green of North Carolina. The Earth is constantly burgeoning forth and releasing new life. My imagination and generativity have flourished here because of all the wonderful organic forms.

Cindy Spring: Can you give me more examples of how you create that bond of intimacy between children and the natural world?

Carolyn Toben: In our nature camps, we use the Council of All Beings (created by Joanna Macy and John Seed) where the children make masks of animals they love. On the last day they come into the fire circle and they speak from the perspective of that animal, about how they feel as a member of that species and what they want to say to people. One day, the eagle said he couldn't fly as high anymore because the air was polluted. The grasshopper was sad because he wasn't appreciated, and the lizard was tracked down and wasn't paid attention to. It gave the children a chance for symbolic expression of their feelings. I've discovered that children are very concerned about what's going on. They can tell you stories about trees that they love that are being torn down or about housing developments coming in. They need ways to express these things.

We also have Magical Moments. It's a matter of stopping and taking in a moment as deeply as you can. You take in the movement, color, internal feelings, smells, listen deeply to the sounds. When I do this, I always give children the date, for example: "This is June 30, 2005, and we're here with one another and this is a very special moment." I invite them to close their eyes and remember what they have seen inwardly. At the end of the day together, we re-invoke those moments in a sharing circle.

At the Earth sanctuary, we have a Wishing Rock. It's large and fairly flat and under a maple tree that hangs over the lake. Children go individually out on the rock and make a wish and while they're wishing, all the other children wish that that child's wish comes true. So they get a lot of help with their wishes. I think the success of the Council of All Beings, Magical Moments and the Wishing Rock speaks to the need of children to ritualize their own experiences in a culture that isn't paying attention to that need. Children have a deep need for ritual and connection.

For more information, see the Center's website: www.beholdnature.org.

All the Time in the World

by Anthony Manousos

It takes all the time in the world
to enter the water and the wind wholly,
to let fall the imaginary boundaries
and return to the source and the destination.

It takes infinite patience to be the forest,
to cry with the chickadees and crawl with the ants,
to stalk with the cat, and forage with the bear,
to let the slow, timeless sap flow through your branches,
and feel roots and tubers pierce you like a lover...

Nothing begins or ends here: there is only the circle,
widening, calling back its own.
When you walk the path, you must be the path.
Do not be proud. Even the centipede knows this.

Everything that you touch changes
and changing, changes you.
Everything you think fills the air with its smell.

As you build you tipi or your city,
remember that knowledge and skills cannot save you.

When night falls, you must be the night.
When day breaks, you too must be broken.

Conscious Choice

We recognize that our daily choices, even the small and habitual ones, have an impact on Earth's species in both beneficial and destructive ways. We seek to promote lifestyles that lead to social justice, sustainability, and ecological security for all life on Earth.

In so doing, we live with conscious intent.

If the persuasive voice of advertising fell silent, what would I really want?

Do I make lifestyle choices consistent with my beliefs? Do I walk my talk?

We, the human species—whether we think so or not—whether we like it or not—are active participants in the creation of the world and the Universe. We are writer-actors on the stage of change; we are editing, writing, and rewriting the course of Nature's history…the historic intrusions of our human activity into the world of Nature are as significant in the ongoing process of Creation as a volcanic eruption, a great flood, or a catastrophic fire."
—C*hris Maser in* Forest Primeval

"When you need to cut down a tree or remove a plant from your garden, you can reflect on this prayer: 'We know we all are children of the same Mother Earth, of our Father Sun. But we also know that one life must sometime give way to another, so that the one great life of all may continue unbroken. So we ask your permission, we obtain your consent to this killing.'"
—*Frank Waters*

"The very least you can do in your life is to figure out what you hope for. The most you can do is live inside that hope. Not admire it from a distance, but live right in it, under its roof."
—*Barbara Kingsolver*

"We are all here on this planet, as it were, as tourists. None of us can live here forever. The longest we might live is a hundred years. So while we are here we should try to have a good heart and to make something positive and useful of our lives. Whether we live just a few years or a whole century, it would be truly regrettable and sad if we were to spend that time aggravating the problems that afflict other people, animals, and the environment. The most important thing is to be a good human being."
—*Dalai Lama*

"The commercials on television tell you the oven cleaner will just clean your oven. You spray the chemical on and everything you don't like disappears. But it doesn't disappear when you flush it down the drain. It moves toward the ocean and it kills."
—*David Brower*

Conscious Living

by Cindy Spring

How can I be a moral person when I live in such an immoral situation? I have discovered that I share with many people the experience of a painful paradox: developing heightened spiritual and political consciousness while living in America. How do we answer the peoples and other species of the world who often suffer mightily to bring Americans our gasoline, coffee, running shoes, silk shirts, and Chicken McNuggets?

How do we reconcile a passion for spiritual connection with the knowledge that we live an extremely privileged existence as compared to other members of the web of life? How do we justify our outrage at "those corporations" that pollute, exploit, and even enslave others, while still buying their products?

None of us claims to understand the "why's" of our existence. Why can I stop by a gas station instead of being an Ogoni tribesperson in Nigeria whose devastated land is covered with pools of oil from drilling? Why does a 12-year-old worker in Vietnam receive 18 cents from the $89.95 I just paid for my Nike walking shoes?

The examples could go on and on. I have more. You know others that I don't. I want to grapple with making conscious choices and understanding their remote consequences. I want to live my life according to moral principles that promote social harmony, justice, and a sustainable planet. But in so many ways each day, I violate my conscience, turn it off, or simply get paralyzed by the pain of the paradox. Since I am fortunate enough to have choices, I want to proceed. There's no turning back to an "unconscious" life.

I think the place to begin is with a reality check, by acknowledging the paradox: living two sides of a contradiction at once. And unless you are one of those admirable folks who have moved off the (electricity) grid and are growing your own vegetables, the paradox is a staple of daily life. A tension of opposites pulls us to live a moral life and also to carry on in the so-called normal world.

Years ago I read the following quote in *The Farther Reaches of Human Nature* by psychologist Abraham Maslow, and it has become a guidepost for me: "...let us think of life as a process of choices, one after another. At each point there is a progressive choice and a regressive choice. There may be movement toward defense, toward safety, toward being afraid, but over on the other side, there is the growth choice. To make the growth choice instead of the fear choice a dozen times a day is to move a dozen times a day toward self-actualization."

I like to extend that challenge to include the choices I make that I know have remote consequences, sometimes on the other side of the world. So I experience guilt in the grocery store, frustration with the time it takes to research detergent choices (do they test on animals?), chagrin at the extra expense of eco-friendly products, anger at clothing companies that will simply not stop using sweatshop labor (some of my favorite labels).

And it's not only consumer choices. What about all the water that runs down the drain rinsing those organic vegetables? Do I get out a lethal insect bomb when all my cornstarch efforts fail to stop thousands of ants from covering every can and box in my pantry? How many trees did they say it takes to produce a Sunday *New York Times*? Add your own laments to the list.

This could get crazy-making, which doesn't help anyone. Neither does the existential guilt that can come with the recognition that the Earth is a huge killing field. We kill animals so as to obtain their life energies to perpetuate our own. Since I choose to be basically a vegetarian, I slay a lot of plant life. Are you one of those "tweeners" like me who will only eat free-range chicken but not one from those poultry concentration camps?

If the questions I've raised are ones that you're also grappling with, I invite you to join me in wrestling with the paradox. Let's attempt to do the reality check that Buddhist teacher Joanna Macy put so cogently: "We have to learn to look at things as they are, painful and overwhelming as that may be for no healing can begin until we are fully present to our world, until we learn to sustain the gaze."

Ecozoic Activism: Embodying the Future, Here and Now

by Michael Dowd and Connie Barlow

Thomas Berry envisions the Ecozoic Era as a time when humanity is present to the Earth Community in a mutually-enhancing manner. Crucially, he presents this vision as the emerging Ecozoic Era. Roots and tendrils of a transformed human presence are evident right here and now.

Few, if any, of us live with this mindset consistently in the foreground. Nevertheless, we have viscerally experienced, if only fleetingly, its draw. We sense its capacity to open our hearts, to guide and empower action, to bring forth our own greatness as we step into the Great Work. We feel called to contribute in our own unique way.

The call is so new and fresh among us that there is no clear path, no time-tested set of practices that distinguish Ecozoic activism from earlier forms of environmental and social engagement. Surely, Ecozoic activism will embrace the best that has come before. It will build upon the successes of the past, while offering up emergent novelty as we shift from an exclusive focus on the human (or the divine and human connection) to the more-than-human realm.

Ecozoic activism will manifest in forms as diverse as any other expression of the life force. Yet beneath the diversity of doing will reside a shared core of being. The stronger the core, the more natural, compelling, and fruitful the response. To distinguish and nurture such core ways of being, such attitudes of the heart, is thus crucial to the emerging Ecozoic Era.

The following four attitudes of the heart are, in our estimation, the cultural coding necessary to effectively herald, embody, and usher in the Ecozoic Era. They could also be described as The Four Pillars of Ecozoic Activism.

1. Allurement

The dream drives the action.
—Thomas Berry

The foundation of Ecozoic activism is, of course, The Great Story—the epic of evolution. The Great Story is everybody's story; it is the overarching story of every thing and all times. Crucially, it is a creation story still in process. The Great Story thus embraces our visions of the future as well as the scientifically familiar record of the past. Ecozoic joins Paleozoic, Mesozoic, and Cenozoic in the pantheon of eras of complex life that have a tangible and honored presence in shaping the lives we lead today.

One of the things we learn from The Great Story is that reality is made of nested wholes—atoms within molecules, within cells, within organisms, within ecosystems, within bioregions. Wholes within wholes (holons)—each integral to itself yet also part of larger wholes, with no part able to fully comprehend the goings on of the larger wholes within which it is embedded. Within this nested holarchy of being, we observe that the larger wholes influence the activities of smaller wholes they encompass by way of signals that are experienced bodily. Discomfort or pain signals something to be avoided. We seek that which fascinates or gives pleasure. All this occurs within a context that Teilhard de Chardin characterized as "groping": feeling one's way into the future without knowing what lies ahead.

To move in the direction of fascination is *allurement*. In the human, we all have experienced allurement at the level of spirit as well as body. Ethical allurements color our dreams of the future. Actions that push our joy buttons, that light up our lives, signify paths of Ecozoic activism. To act within a state of allurement is thus at the heart of Ecozoic transformation. As Joseph Campbell was fond of saying, "Follow your bliss." In the midst of our actions we will be modeling the very end we are advocating.

There will always be actions to take as good citizens; there will always be problems to fix in the moment. But for the long-term, for soul sustenance and for confidence that our choices are, in fact, choices made not by our small selves but by that portion of the Great Self residing in each of us, we can trust our allurements as ultimate guides. We can trust that our share of the Great Work lies where our own great joy intersects with Earth's great need.

And then, the dream will indeed drive the action.

2. Trust

The Universe can be trusted.
—Michael Dowd

Ecozoic activism is driven by allurement, not by anger or fear. Yet in the face of grave disappointments, during those inevitable times when we come to doubt our self worth or the viability of our species, what gives us the strength to carry on? For eons, the religious answer to this question has been simple: faith.

A metareligious, spiritual movement grounded in and inspired by The Great Story will, by definition, be an inclusive, evolutionary spirituality. As a community of Jews, Christians, Pagans, Hindus, Buddhists, secular humanists, atheists, pantheists, panentheists, and so on, we honor the full breadth of our traditions, which continue to feed us in many ways. Those of us called to Ecozoic activism can unite in our trust in a self-organizing, time-developmental Universe—whatever our particular conceptions of Ultimate Mystery may be. Such trust will become increasingly supportive as the pain of this transition, this collective rite of passage into maturity as true *Homo sapiens sapiens* (doubly-wise humans) greets us again and again.

Trust in the Universe by no means translates into passivity. Rather, we are empowered to act in the face of the most formidable obstacles, in grave uncertainty, because we do trust.

Trusting the Universe means trusting that "everything is right on schedule." But it also means trusting that the anguish we feel over what is happening to others and to the natural world, and the yearnings we have for a just, humane, and sustainable society, are part of the Universe too, and right on schedule as well. We trust our allurements as the allurements of the Universe. We trust our sense of urgency as the urgency of the Universe. And we trust our own missteps as the untidy gropings of the Universe.

We trust, too, that the human venture does not represent a grave mistake, the one time in which Earth and the Universe somehow got it wrong. That would be the epitome of arrogance. In a time-developmental Universe, to judge earlier stages as bad or wrong from the vantage of one's own stage is unhelpful. Rather, those stages are accepted as simply what was so for their particular times. When we accept the past, rather than judge it, a combination of creative tinkering and stunning transformation becomes available. As Ken Wilber writes in a recent book, *A Theory of Everything*: "I have one major rule: everybody is right. More specifically, everybody—including me—has some important pieces of truth, and all of those pieces need to be honored, cherished, and included in a more gracious, spacious, and compassionate embrace, a genuine Theory of Everything."

Of course, to say that the Universe can be trusted is not to say that the Universe must be trusted. These are statements of meaning, not of empirical fact. Yet they are drawn from an understanding of The Great Story as offered to us by science. The Great Story is the ground of our trust, as it is of our allurement. In its embrace, we choose to stand in trust; we are empowered to act in trust.

"From a pragmatic point of view," wrote William James of our relationship with the Universe, "the difference between living against a background of foreignness and one of intimacy means the difference between a general habit of wariness and one of trust." Another way of saying this, and a statement that can serve as a powerful affirmation in times of doubt (and which we recommend in daily practice), is simply this: The Universe can be trusted.

3. Compassion

Comprehensive compassion is unfurling in the human species.
—Brian Swimme

Ecozoic activism drawn by allurement and grounded in

trust is an activism in which compassion unfurls naturally. Ultimately, such compassion becomes comprehensive— encompassing humans, the more-than-human realm, and, quite remarkably, beings with whom one has never come into contact and generations a thousand years hence. It will entail not only the empathic experience of others' suffering, but also the empathic experience of others' joy.

Comprehensive compassion is nurtured by how we speak. Who among us has not had our perception profoundly shifted by an encounter with Thomas Berry's expanded use of the word children? This, from the dedication page of his book, The Great Work: "To the children; to all the children; to the children who swim beneath the waves of the sea, to those who live in the soils of the Earth, to the children of the flowers in the meadows and the trees in the forest..."

Far more difficult than nurturing interspecies compassion will be nurturing compassion toward those humans here and now who seemingly stand in the way of mutually enhancing human-Earth relations. Buddhist monk Thich Nhat Hanh, in his poem "Please Call Me By My True Names," challenges us deeply: "I am the 12-year-old girl, refugee on a small boat, who throws herself into the ocean after being raped by a sea pirate, and I am the pirate, my heart not yet capable of seeing and loving." He closes, "Please call me by my true names, so I can wake up, and so the door of my heart can be left open, the door of compassion."

Such expansive compassion is not only an ideal but also, at times, a necessity. Julia Butterfly Hill speaks movingly of how she would not have been unable to persist in her perch in the redwood tree had she not broken through her rage against the loggers. How else could she survive day upon day of the roar of helicopters, the sneer of chainsaws, and the sad thunder of toppling trees?

Finally, there is the challenge of compassion for oneself. Compassion toward the pirates of the planet may be a powerful platform for Ecozoic activism, but we can count on ourselves to often feel and express the obverse: rage. We will fall short of our ideals, again and again. We will thus need to nurture an ongoing compassion for ourselves. As activists, we will judge and condemn others to the degree that we judge and condemn ourselves. As activists, we will trust the Universe to the degree that we trust that our own shortcomings serve a purpose and are gifts for our own and others' growth.

As with the Ecozoic Era, shimmering into existence in fits and starts, comprehensive compassion is unfurling in the human species, flickering in one heart, then in another and another.

4. Gratitude

If the only prayer you say in your whole life is, "thank you," that would suffice.
—Meister Eckhart

Ecozoic activism starts and ends with gratitude as gratitude is both an outcome and a source of the three previous attitudes of the heart. Cultivating gratitude opens us to allurement, strengthens our trust, and expands our compassion. Gratitude heightens our effectiveness as activists, for it holds anger, judgment, fear, and overwhelm at bay. As M.J. Ryan says, "Gratitude is the mother of joy."

Gratitude manifests in the midst of our everyday living when we pause to take account of how much we ourselves have been given. We are present to the wonder of the simplest gifts: a glass of water, a spoonful of food, a breath of air. At such times, our hearts are full.

Thomas Berry has movingly written that, while we humans contribute to the cosmos by discerning and telling the Great Story, it is ultimately our role, our calling, to become "celebrants" of this story. Affirmations of gratitude we speak as individuals in our own reflective moments are one form of celebration. So, too, are our comings together in community to celebrate a solstice, a life passage, or the memory of a moment of transformation in the immense journey of life. Celebrating life is an essential part of Ecozoic activism. In fact, dancing may be one of the more important things you can do to help usher in the Ecozoic Era.

So where does this bring us? In summary, we might say

that whatever else Ecozoic activism may come to entail, it will surely embody these four attitudes of the heart: allurement, trust, compassion, and gratitude.

These are the four pillars upon which the Ecozoic will be built.

Redwood Seder:
An Interview with Rabbi Arthur Waskow

by Richard Sheinen

Theology in Action
Introduction

In Judaism, a tree isn't just a tree. The Torah—the Hebrew scriptures—is known as the Tree of Life. So, too, is God, who is seen as continually growing and unfolding through creation. Even when a tree is, well, a tree, matters still aren't simple. For trees are sacred symbols of the abundance of God's creation, and they require protection. Which is why author and Rabbi Arthur Waskow joined a group of "redwood rabbis" and 250 ecologically-minded Jews on Sunday, January 26, 1996, for a Seder, or ritual meal, in the ancient redwoods forests of Humboldt County, California. They were celebrating Tu B'Shvat, the annual New Year for the Trees of the Jewish calendar. They were also protesting the logging of old-growth forests by Maxxam Corporation, whose chairman, Charles Hurwitz, is Jewish. At the end of the meal, 90 people walked onto Maxxam-owned land— the company and local police had been warned ahead of time—and planted redwood seedlings. They weren't kicked out by company police; they weren't arrested. Waskow hopes Hurwitz heard their message.
—Cheryl Lander.

Richard Sheinin: So what was it like to have this ritual meal in the middle of the forest?

Arthur Waskow: Totally extraordinary. Five hundred years ago, the Kabbalists, the mystics, created this amazing ceremonial meal that's built totally around fruits, nuts, and wine. Which means that to eat it you don't have to kill any living creature, even a vegetable. Fruits and nuts are given in profusion by trees, far more than they need for the next generation. And so it doesn't require the death of anything.

So this meal is really the meal of the Garden of Eden, the meal of peace between human beings and the Earth.

Richard Sheinin: You've got 250 people sitting at tables under the redwoods?

Arthur Waskow: Yes. But first, ahead of time, we also learned about the forest—how it's intertwined the species, the owls and the salmon and how they all intertwine with the redwood trees. And then somebody had talked to us about non-violence and civil disobedience because we were planning to end with an act of civil disobedience.

OK, so then we went to one of the redwood groves, where there are these trees that are 200 feet tall. One of the people there said something totally amazing, overwhelming to me. She said, "You know, a Torah scroll is wrapped around two wooden poles. And they're called *eytzim*," which is also the word for trees. And she said, "What would a sefer Torah, a Torah scroll, be like if these redwood trees were its *eytzim*? Imagine if the scrolls were wrapped around these trees."

And then she looked at us and said, "If there were a Torah scroll so big, we, each of us would be just big enough to be a letter in the scroll. And the question is whether we're prepared to be letters in the great Torah scroll." Then the Seder itself has four different courses, built around four different cups of wine. One white, one white with a drop of red, one red with a little white, and then one all red. And there's a whole sense that these four courses are about the four different worlds that the Kabbalists talked about. The world of spirit or being; the world of knowing; the world of feeling; and the world of doing. And the universe is made up of God's unfolding into those four worlds of reality.

So the four courses of the Seder are built around those four worlds. And you eat different kinds of nuts and fruit for the different worlds. And you sing; there are dances. This whole practice—it's only about 500 years old, which in Jewish terms is pretty new. So it's very open and fluid for people to shape in each generation.

Richard Sheinin: This whole practice of what?

Arthur Waskow: Of the Seder. Even *Tu B'Shvat* itself. The 15th day of the month of *Shevat* is the new year of trees—it's when the "fiscal year" begins for tithing the fruits of trees. Because the rabbis said that was when the juice, the sap, began to rise again in the trees in midwinter. So it just stayed like that for 1,500 years, until a bunch of mystics settled in northern Israel about 500 years ago. And they took this day and said, "This is not just the day of ordinary trees, but of the tree," meaning the Tree of Life, which by that time the mystics understood as the unfolding of God.

The second thing they said was, "What is tithing about? Tithing is about abundance coming only if you share it. And God's abundance, the whole flow of all the abundance of the world, only keeps coming if we understand how to share it with the poor. So we're going to take this day and do a whole series of things that evoke sharing."

Then a century ago, the Zionist movement said, "Look, we actually need to begin planting trees and reconnecting with the Earth. It's not enough to have a Seder and say prayers. We actually have to do the task of connecting with the Earth." But that was with the Earth of the land of Israel. And then 25 years ago, American Jews began to say, "Look, all the trees of the planet are in danger and the Earth is in danger." So Tu B'Shvat has now become a kind of Jewish Earth Day.

Richard Sheinin: The Redwood rabbis sent out a press release that refers to Hurwitz as being in violation of "the deepest precepts of Jewish ethics."

Arthur Waskow: There is a passage in the Torah in Deuteronomy which says, even if you're at war against the city, you can't destroy the fruit trees of the city, or near the city. Even if you're at war! The rabbis then said, "Look, if that's true, then you can't possibly destroy trees casually, for no good reason, when you're at peace." And then they broadened it to the protection of all nature. This became a whole principle of rabbinic Judaism, that you had to protect the Earth. I've read the Maxxam Corporation's annual reports, and they say it's good business to use wood from old redwoods, the ancient redwoods, the ones that are 500 or 1,000 years old. Why? Because they don't have knots in them. And so you can sell their wood for paneling to wealthy people for much higher prices than you can for, you know, 30-year-old trees. For the sake of the higher profit involved, in being able to sell this ancient wood, they have been willing to destroy what many of us view as sacred places.

These trees were around when the rabbis created Tu B'Shvat in the first place. But Hurwitz is clearly more responsive to approaches built around the Torah than he is, as far as we can tell, to anything else.

Richard Sheinin: What has he said?

Arthur Waskow: Well, he said, "I don't agree." But he keeps answering letters, which he hasn't done with a lot of the secular environmental groups.

At the end of the Seder about 90 people out of the 250 went to the edge of the Pacific Lumber Company—Maxxam property where they're doing logging. There we walked onto the property in order to plant new redwood seedlings in an area that's been denuded. And the redwood rabbis had written Hurwitz, saying we intended to plant trees and we would like you to affirm that it's OK. And he wrote back saying, "No, there's another place you can plant trees." To which the redwood rabbis said, "Thank you very much." It turned out it was a tree farm which was not the point.

So we arrive. And in fact there's a car with the company's own police, and we walk onto the land and we do the planting, and they don't in fact call the cops. And we ended up dancing and singing on a piece of the Pacific Lumber-Maxxam land, which, as the locals said, previously had been a place where people had been handcuffed and beaten by the cops and what have you. But at this time, something different happened. We had an amazing, miraculous moment.

The Entire Universe in a Piece of Bread

by Thich Nhat Hanh

This food is the gift of the whole Universe—
the Earth, the sky, and much hard work.
May we eat in mindfulness so as to be worthy to receive it.
May we transform our unskillful states of mind and learn to eat
with moderation.
May we take only foods that nourish us and prevent illness.
We accept this food to realize the path of understanding and love.

from *Plum Village Chanting and Recitation Book*, compiled by Thich Nhat Hanh and the monks and nuns of Plum Village, 2000.

A few years ago, I asked some children, "What is the purpose of eating breakfast?"

One boy replied, "To get energy for the day." Another said, "The purpose of eating breakfast is to eat breakfast." I think the second child is more correct. The purpose of eating is to eat.

Eating a meal in mindfulness is an important practice. We turn off the TV, put down our newspaper, and work together for five or ten minutes, setting the table and finishing whatever needs to be done. During these few minutes, we can be very happy. When the food is on the table and everyone is seated, we practice breathing: "Breathing in, I calm my body. Breathing out, I smile," three times. We can recover ourselves completely after three breaths like this.

Then, we look at each person as we breathe in and out in order to be in touch with ourselves and everyone at the table. We don't need two hours in order to see another person. If we are really settled within ourselves, we only need to look for one or two seconds, and that is enough to see our friend. I think that if a family has five members, only about five or ten seconds is needed to practice this "looking and seeing."

After breathing, we smile. Sitting at the table with other people, we have a chance to offer an authentic smile of friendship and understanding. It is very easy, but not many people do it. To me, this is the most important practice. We look at each person and smile at him or her. Breathing and smiling together are very important practices. If the people in a family cannot smile at each other, the situation is a very dangerous one.

After breathing and smiling, we look down at the food in a way that allows the food to become real. This food reveals our connection with the Earth. Each bite contains the life of the sun and the Earth. The extent to which our food reveals itself depends on us. We can see and taste the whole Universe in a piece of bread! Contemplating our food for a few seconds before eating, and eating in mindfulness, can bring us much happiness. Having the opportunity to sit with our family and friends and enjoy wonderful food is something precious, something not everyone has. Many people in the world are hungry. When I hold a bowl of rice or a piece of bread, I know that I am fortunate, and I feel compassion for all those who have no food to eat and are without friends or family. This is a very deep practice. We do not need to go to a temple or a church in order to practice this. We can practice it right at our dinner table. Mindful eating can cultivate seeds of compassion and understanding that will strengthen us to do something to help hungry and lonely people be nourished.

In order to aid mindfulness during meals, you may like to eat silently from time to time. Your first silent meal may cause you to feel a little uncomfortable, but once you become used to it, you will realize that meals in silence bring much peace and happiness. It is like turning off the TV before eating. We "turn off" the talking in order to enjoy the food and the presence of one another.

I propose that during eating, you refrain from discussing subjects which can destroy the awareness of the family and the food. But you should feel free to say things that can nourish awareness and happiness. For instance, if there is a dish that you like very much, you can see if other people are also enjoying it, and if one of them is not, you can help him or her appreciate the wonderful dish prepared with loving care. If someone is thinking about something other than the good food on the table, such as his difficulties in the office or with friends, it means he is losing the present moment, and the food. You can say, "This dish is wonderful, don't you agree?" When you say something like this, you will draw him out of his thinking and worries, and bring him back to the here and now, enjoying you, enjoying the wonderful dish. You become a bodhisattva, helping a living being become enlightened. Children, in particular, are very capable of practicing mindfulness and reminding others to do the same.

The verse which follows can help us practice mindfulness while eating.

In this food,
I see clearly the presence
of the entire Universe
supporting my existence.

This verse helps us see the principle of dependent co-arising, as we see that our life and the lives of all species are interrelated.

Eating for Peace

by Thich Nhat Hanh

All things need food to be alive and to grow, including our love or our hate. Love is a living thing, hate is a living thing. If you do not nourish your love, it will die. If you cut the source of nutriment for your violence, your violence will also die. That is why the path shown by the Buddha is the path of mindful consumption.

The Buddha told the following story. There was a couple who wanted to cross the desert to go to another country in order to seek freedom. They brought with them their little boy and a quantity of food and water. But they did not calculate well, and that is why halfway through the desert they ran out of food, and they knew that they were going to die. So after a lot of anguish, they decided to eat the little boy so that they could survive and go to the other country, and that's what they did. And every time they ate a piece of flesh from their son, they cried.

The Buddha asked his monks, "My dear friends: Do you think that the couple enjoyed eating the flesh of their son?" The Buddha said, "It is impossible to enjoy eating the flesh of your son. If you do not eat mindfully, you are eating the flesh of your son and daughter, you are eating the flesh of your parent."

If we look deeply, we will see that eating can be extremely violent. UNESCO tells us that every day, forty thousand children in the world die because of a lack of nutrition, of food. Every day, forty thousand children. And the amount of grain that we grow in the West is mostly used to feed our cattle. Eighty percent of the corn grown in this country is to feed the cattle to make meat. Ninety-five percent of the oats produced in this country is not for us to eat, but for the animals raised for food. According to a recent report that we received, of all the agricultural land in the US, eighty-seven percent is used to raise animals for food.

Mindful eating can help maintain compassion within our heart. A person without compassion cannot be happy, cannot relate to other human beings or to other living beings. And eating the flesh of our own son is what is going on in the world, because we do not practice mindful eating.

The Buddha spoke about the second kind of food that we consume every day—sense impressions—the kind of food that we take in by the way of the eyes, the ears, the tongue, the body, and the mind. When we read a magazine, we consume. When you watch television, you consume. When you listen to a conversation, you consume. And these items can be highly toxic. There may be a lot of poisons, like craving, like violence, like anger, and despair. We allow ourselves to be intoxicated by what we consume in terms of sense impressions. We allow our children to intoxicate themselves because of these products. That is why it is very important to look deeply into our ill-being, into the nature of our ill-being, in order to recognize the sources of nutriment we have used to bring it into us and into our society.

The Buddha had this to say: "What has come to be—if you know how to look deeply into its nature and identify its source of nutriment, you are already on the path of emancipation." What has come to be is our illness, our ill-being, our suffering, our violence, our despair. And if you practice looking deeply, meditation, you'll be able to identify the sources of nutriments, of food, that have brought it into us.

Therefore the whole nation has to practice looking deeply into the nature of what we consume every day. And consuming mindfully is the only way to protect our nation, ourselves, and our society. We have to learn how to consume mindfully as a family, as a city, as a nation. We have to learn what to produce and what not to produce in order to provide our people with only the items that are nourishing and healing. We have to refrain from producing the kinds of items that bring war and despair into our body, into our consciousness, and into the collective body and consciousness of our nation, our society. And Congress has to practice that. We have elected members of the Congress. We expect them to practice deeply, listening to the suffering of the people, to the real causes of that suffering, and to make the kind of laws that can protect us from self-destruction. And America is great. I have the conviction that you can do it and help the world. You can offer the world wisdom, mindfulness, and compassion.

These comments are excerpted from a public talk given at the Riverside Church, New York City, September 25, 2001. The entire talk appears on his website www.plumvillage.org/TNH/embracing_anger.htm

Wonders of the Watershed: A Bioregional View

by Gary Snyder

Watershed is a marvelous thing to consider: this process of rain falling, streams flowing, and oceans evaporating causes every molecule of water on earth to make the complete trip once every two million years. The surface is carved into watersheds—a kind of familial branching, a chart of relationship, and a definition of place. The watershed is the first and last nation, whose boundaries, though subtly shifting, are unarguable. Races of birds, subspecies of trees, and types of hats or raingear go by the watershed. The watershed gives us a home and a place to go upstream, downstream, or across in.

The water cycle is our springs and wells, our Sierra snowpack, our irrigation canals, our carwash, and the spring salmon run. It's the spring peeper in the pond and the acorn woodpecker chattering in the snag. It's where our friends live, it is our friends. The watershed is beyond the dichotomies of orderly/disorderly, for its forms are free, but somehow inevitable. And the life that comes to flourish within it constitutes the first kind of community.

The agenda of the watershed council starts in a modest way: like saying "Let's try and rehabilitate our river to the point that wild salmon can successfully spawn here again." In pursuit of this local agenda, a community might find itself combating clearcut timber sales upstream, water-selling grabs downstream, Taiwanese drift net practices out in the North Pacific, and a host of other national and international threats to the health of salmon. A small but significant number of watershed councils are already in existence, fully awake and conscious, with some strong views about what should be done. These include the Friends of the Los Angeles River, the Putah Creek Council, the Yuba Watershed Institute, the Greenwood Watershed Association, the Redwood Coast Watershed Alliance, and the

Mattole Restoration Council.

They are ready and willing to play ball with the California Bureau of Land Management, the state, the Pacific Southwest Region office of the Forest Service, and the others who signed the 1991 Agreement for a "co-ordinated regional strategy for saving biological diversity in California." If a wide range of people will join in on this effort—people from timber and tourism, settled ranchers and farmers, fly-fishing retirees, the businesses and the forest-dwelling new settlers—something might come of it. But if this joint agreement were to be implemented as a top-down prescription it would go nowhere. Only a grassroots engagement with longterm land issues can provide the political and social stability it will take to keep the biological richness of California's regions intact.

All public land ownership is ultimately written in sand. The boundaries and the management categories were created by Congress, and Congress can take them away. The only "jurisdiction" that will last in the world of nature is the watershed, and even that changes over time. If public lands come under greater and greater pressure to be opened for exploitation and use in the 21st century, it will be the local people, the watershed people, who will prove to be the last and possibly most effective line of defense. Let us hope it never comes to that.

In an exposition of what he terms Cultural Bioregionalism, Gary Snyder turns his attention next to the practical promise of such ideas as a commitment to place and "staying put." He envisions a "non-nationalistic idea of community" where "anyone of any race, language, religion or origin is welcome, as long as they live well on the land." Using a Native American term for the North American continent, Turtle Island, he imagines a culture where citizenship is empowered by the organizing principle of inhabiting a single place over time—a citizenship which includes non-human and human alike in cities and suburbs, farms and wilderness.

This sort of future culture is available to whomever makes the choice, regardless of background. It need not require that a person drop his or her Buddhist, Jewish, or Muslim beliefs but simply add to their faith or philosophy a sincere nod in the direction of the deep value of the natural world, and the subjecthood of non-human beings. A culture of place will be created that will include the "United States," and go beyond that to an affirmation of the continent, the land itself, Turtle Island. We could be showing Southwest Asian and South American newcomers the patterns of the rivers, the distant hills, saying, "It's not only that you are now living in the United States. You are living in this great landscape. Please get to know these rivers and mountains, and be welcome in here." Euro-Americans, Asian Americans, African Americans, can, if they wish, become "born again" natives of Turtle Island. In doing so we also might even (eventually) win some respect from our Native American predecessors, who are still here and still trying to teach where we are.

Watershed consciousness and bioregionalism is not just environmentalism, not just a means toward resolution of social and economic problems, but a move towards resolving both nature and society with the practice of a profound citizenship in both the natural and the social worlds. If the ground can be our common ground, we can begin to talk to each other (human and non-human) once again.

Animal Grace

by Mary Lou Randour

As many times as I heard the word "grace" used in the Episcopal Church in which I was raised, I never really quite understood what it meant. I knew I longed for it; like many others I was seeking a direct, felt experience with an intangible, unknowable, but sought after, "Other." Some may call that "Other" God; or may refer to it as a creative process, or as emptiness. All I knew was that despite my yearning to find grace, it always seemed beyond my ken.

As I recount in my book, *Animal Grace*, I unexpectedly grasped the meaning of grace shortly after I became an animal activist. One evening as I was walking our two dogs with my husband after a day spent engaged in a number of animal protection activities, I noticed a sense of calm stillness within me; a serenity infused my being. At the same time, I felt powerful, resolute, and vital. In an "Aha!" moment of recognition, I turned to my husband saying, "Now I know what grace is; I am experiencing it at this moment."

Grace, the very personal experience of being filled with life-giving energy that draws us closer to the numinous, can lead to a rapid shift in our perspective and redirect our lives. It certainly did with me. After I opened my mind and heart to the animal lives all around us, I benefited spiritually. I resumed my spiritual search, which I had neglected, with a newfound vigor and commitment. Paradoxically, I discovered what I had been looking for once I let go of my need to find it and instead turned to helping others—to doing what I could to protect and cherish that "great and mysterious and mute nation"[1]—the animal nation.

The countless animals I encountered once I opened myself to their world—suffering in factory farms, caught in the jaws of leghold traps so their skins could be used for some fur ornament, being forced against their will to entertain us in circuses, rodeos, and roadside zoos, terrified and isolated in cages of laboratories where their bodies are used as "tools" to test our products—taught me an important spiritual lesson. They taught me not to be afraid of suffering and how opening ourselves to others' pain can release us from the limitations of our own egos and lead to living our lives more joyously and more responsibly. Animals had given me the gift of grace.

As I began this new life of service to animals, I learned the requisite of any spiritual path: the development of awareness and compassion. In *Animal Grace*, I describe awareness and compassion as two pillars of spiritual development. Awareness is not about something happening to us or something we may achieve after many disciplined hours of meditating or praying; it is about opening, learning, deciding, and acting. Carol Adams, a feminist writer and activist who writes about animal care, ecology, and ethics asserts that it is "attention to suffering [that] makes us ethically responsible."[2] I agree. Attention to suffering exercises our moral and spiritual imagination. Our spiritual concerns must be linked to an ethical perspective. Spirituality without ethics is like a sculpture without an armature—it can collapse into itself. And ethics without spirituality runs the danger of becoming dry, lifeless, or self-righteous.

Awareness, then, is not an end in itself; it also is the source of compassion. Compassion, like awareness, is an action, a response to suffering. It not only is essential to our spiritual development, but to the formation of our character. We are what we do. Reciprocally, compassion is necessary to complete awareness. The movement between awareness and compassion is a dynamic interplay between increased awareness and compassionate action. Through our commitment to increased awareness and compassion we are guided down the path toward grace.

Because animals surround us and intersect our lives in so many ways, they offer us countless opportunities every day to exercise awareness and compassion. We simply have to take spiritual advantage of their presence. For example, we perform many tasks daily—washing our faces, brushing our teeth, using various household products. In each case, we can decide to use a soap, or toothpaste, or detergent that has not been tested on animals. The first step is to recognize that almost all personal cosmetic and household products are tested on animals, unless otherwise indicated. (Animal testing of these products is not mandatory; companies believe testing on animals gives them some protection from lawsuits.) Then we need to take in what "animal testing" entails, which means to allow ourselves to unflinchingly understand and feel the experience of the animals who are being used in this way. When we do we may experience many painful feelings—sorrow, rage, grief—as we enter the animals' worlds and feel their anxiety, fear, and agony. We can gain the courage to enter into this kind of empathic identification with animal suffering by realizing that the movement toward spiritual wholeness often begins by answering the invitation to become aware of suffering.

There are some circumstances when we may become aware of suffering but it is hard to respond compassionately in a way that will have any direct effect. We may care about the homeless and be able to volunteer to work in a shelter, or lobby our legislators for policies that will help them, but may at times feel discouraged about making any real difference.

With animals, we can have a very direct effect as soon as we take a compassionate action. We can buy products not tested on animals, by both reading the labels and only buying those products that say, "no animal testing" and "no animal ingredient." For help in doing this, we can write organizations such as the American Anti-Vivisection Society and ask them for their *Compassionate Shopper's Guide*.[3]

Every time we purchase a product that is not tested on animals, we have spared an animal of suffering and death. By doing this we can turn an ordinary shopping experience from a chore into a spiritual activity. As we decide to purchase products not tested on animals we commit ourselves to a respect for creation and life; we take an action that respects the integrity of creation and honors the interdependent web of existence.

We can repeat this spiritual exercise of honoring and protecting the animals around us many times a day, every day.

After learning about the lives of farmed animals, understanding their desire to live, to participate in social relationships with their kin, and to pursue their interests, we may decide not to eat them. Recognizing and respecting the integrity of their lives, we may choose a plant-based diet. Again, when we buy our food and then cook it, we can transform these mundane actions into spiritual moments in which we honor the unity of existence. We can choose the clothes we wear with care so that no animals have suffered on our account; we can choose forms of entertainment that do not rely on the exploitation of other animals, avoiding circuses, many zoos, "sea world" enterprises, and rodeos. As we commit ourselves to an awareness of the animal lives surrounding us, and as we respond compassionately to their plight, we open ourselves to the sacredness of creation. Acknowledging our kinship with all life opens the door to the divine process. And, as we participate in what I feel are these holy activities of honoring animal lives, we do not have to diminish our commitments to other worthy social concerns. Every action I have mentioned that can reduce animal suffering are activities that we already are engaging in every day—personal care, eating, and choosing entertainment.

Throughout history animals have been our companions. They have been linked with supernatural forces, acted as guardians and shamans, and appeared in images of an afterlife. In modern times, we have documented the many ways in which animals can heal our physical and psychological illnesses, help us cope with death, teach us to love, and expand our consciousness. The invitation of animal grace is to reciprocate the many gifts that animals have given us by transcending the species barrier. When we overcome the species barrier, which historically has been one that has separated human animals from the rest of nature, we exercise a spiritual muscle. We can apply this wisdom to other relationships as well, finding a union with other humans, regardless of race, sex, national origin, or any other category. Animal grace enables us to fathom the arbitrariness of distinctions, the illusion of difference, and allows us to realize the continuity of existence. And when we do, we indeed find "an old joy returns in holy presence."

Endnotes

[1] Joy Williams, "The Inhumanity of the Animal People?" *Harpers* (August 1997), p. 60.

[2] Carol J. Adams, "Caring about Suffering: A Feminist Exploration," *Beyond Animal Rights: A Feminist Ethic for the Treatment of Animals.* Joseph Donovan and Carol J. Adams, eds. (New York: Continuum, 1996), p. 193.

[3] American Anti-Vivisection Society, 801 Old York Road, #204, Jenkintown, Pa. 19046-1685; (215) 887-0816; aavsonline@aol.com or www.aavs.org.

Jim Corbett,
Goatwalker Cowbalist

by David Ray

In the Sonoran Desert near Cascabel, Arizona, along the San Pedro River, my wife Judy and I tried to keep up with Jim Corbett, trying not to brush springy cactus and heaving and puffing as he scrambled ahead of us, agile as a goat. We felt privileged on that hike, for we knew we were in the company of a major philosopher and friend of the earth. We were following a man we regarded as a hero for his role in leading refugees to safety as they fled deadly violence in Central America during past decades. We knew that Jim was known for other achievements, "speaking truth to power" and doing everything he could to sponsor low-impact or even redemptive land usage, reclaiming rivers and wilderness from human damage.

In his book *Goatwalking: A Guide to Wildland Living, a Quest for the Peaceable Kingdom*, Jim Corbett used his experience in ranching as a springboard for reflections reminiscent of Thoreau and the mystical wisdom of both Christian and Hebrew traditions. Though a Christian for sure in practice, Jim referred to himself sometimes as a pagan, in the root sense of the word, and at other times as a "Judeo-Quaker." Clearly he did not want to be labeled.

The word Christian is too often appropriated by those who may talk the talk but not walk the walk as Jesus and Jim Corbett did. Jim walked quietly and carried a big faith.

As a Quaker he knew that stereotypical labels obscure and oversimplify the complexities of faith. His widow Pat Corbett recalls that the closest thing he would say when asked to describe his beliefs was "a follower of Rabbi Jesus of Nazareth." He could as easily, I think, have claimed Buddha as his guide.

Jim Corbett left behind an impressive new manuscript with the working title of *Cowbalah*, a work of such reach and diversity that it defies categorization. Mystical, ecological, theological, expansive, brainstorming, the book has no boundaries other than what Daniel Baker, a devoted student and advocate of Corbett's work, describes as "about the expansion of peace and love into the world."

The mark of a great book is whether it changes lives. *Walden*, *The Jungle*, *Crime and Punishment*, *Huckleberry Finn*—one cannot experience these books and emerge as the unenlightened reader who began on page one. It would be hard to find a reader who does not feel more enlightened and informed after living with a major work of literature, whether true or not. The same can be said of *Cowbalah*. One cannot be the same after reading it.

As my wife and I traipsed behind Jim Corbett on that hot afternoon a year or two before his death, we were filled with gratitude that we were not depending on him, as so many refugees from Central America had, to lead us to sanctuary. But we could easily see why he thought of himself as a goatwalker. At a distance he might have been mistaken for one, maneuvering through brush and mesquite. We knew he often slept outside, with only a poncho between him and the sky, a lifestyle hardly recommended for the severe arthritis that had twisted his hands and feet. We wondered what had fired this man's dedication, his intensity, his sacrifices. Few of any faith follow the good Samaritan's example with such literalness. Why had Jim Corbett insisted on being a good Samaritan despite the law that discourages any action in regard to undocumented entrants other than turning them over to the Border Patrol? He had assisted the refugees in their legal efforts, and seen them again and again frustrated and denied, as if rejection were rigid policy. He knew that some of those peremptorily sent back faced certain death. Dealing with President Ronald Reagan's America, which seemed to have lost the capacity for compassion and lawful behavior, Jim had exhausted every means to help, then became a goatwalker out of frustration, defying the bellicose threats of the Reagan administration as he hiked across the perilous desert, leading groups and individuals to safety.

Thus Jim Corbett earned unsought fame by obeying humanitarian principles and US and international laws that transcend a particular government or administration. He saw that the US government had flouted those laws that would have at least given the refugees a fair chance. And for these acts of what he insistently called "civil initiative," Jim and several others of the Sanctuary movement were threatened with prison and put on trial. President Reagan referred to Central American death squads as his Freedom Fighters and enthusiastically funded murderers even of nuns and children.

One of the men Jim Corbett helped across the border had witnessed the murder of Archbishop Romero in El Salvador. This man fled soon afterwards when his best friend's head was rolled up against his doorstep. "What can we do?" asked a friend who perceived this man's post-traumatic agony. "Cry," Jim said, "there's nothing else we can do. I cry all the time." But he also helped the man. Jim was not a politician, a ranter, or a radical. He was simply a follower of Rabbi Jesus of Nazareth who took his religion literally. He suffered as though from an allergy to the tyranny and lies of the State as well as the desecration of the earth. I should add, by the way, that when a great person leaves, his friends and admirers do not always have the same memories. Some think Jim was so stoic he never cried, and it is possible that he meant something more profound than mere tears when he said all we could do was cry.

As the Sanctuary movement grew, Quaker Meetings and other churches were infiltrated by agents and provocateurs. It was not hard to spot these visitors, with their new Birkenstock sandals and garb reflecting their seeming belief that Quakers were not much different than hippies. The spies came to hear conspiracy, dissent, and strategy conferences of radicals, but their recorders probably picked up little more than the meaningful silence of Jim Corbett and others endowed with the rocky strength of their faith. It was the US Government that was engaged in conspiracies.

In the trial of the Sanctuary leaders in 1985 on "charges of conspiring to smuggle Central Americans into the United States," prosecutors were flummoxed by Jim Corbett, for it is hard to draw a bead on a man of few words. Though eight were convicted while two of Jim's co-defendants had charges dropped and one pleaded no contest, it seems that the waste of taxpayer money proved only that intimidation, harassment, break-ins, surveillance, covert operations and imprisonment were not about to deter people who compared the underground railroad for Central American refugees with earlier routes for escaping slaves.

Two decades later, the Sonoran Desert has been turned into a killing zone and the US has—in the judgment of many observers—become more bitterly polarized than at any time since the Civil War. Jim Corbett's voice is missing and his compassion and wisdom are not available to challenge those whose passions are limited to xenophobia and military options. Others are carrying on his work, but in the face of ever more heartless crackdowns and roundups and ever more sophisticated technology (night vision instruments, helicopters, heat-seeking devices, etc.) ever harsher measures are seen as the solution to the border crisis.

In *Cowbalah*, Jim Corbett expands his philosophic embrace to far more than the human, to the earth itself and all the animals on it, for they too have rights and needs and to deny them, as Jim clearly saw, is to stunt our own hearts and souls. The land's rights have been violated. The rivers and air are fouled. Community teeters toward anarchy, and it—*communitas* with the intensity of communion—is a need limited to no species or group. I had never previously heard of such an ambition as "redemptive" land use, but I was inspired on hearing Jim describe it when he gave a talk to our Quaker Meeting. My wife and I had just come from a presentation by a conventional developer, the kind that starts with a bulldozer and winds up with depleted nature and with houses that share a significant portion of indoor space with cars, as if autos have taken the place of cows that used to share European dwellings. The contrast with Jim's ideas about human habitat respectful of ecological and spiritual considerations was dramatic.

Jim Corbett's philosophy offers us wisdom for our personal and spiritual crises as well as the beginning of a solution for global issues. The local and global are one, and any reader who enters into a dialogue with the man speaking through his book will engage with the Corbett solution, which begins with prayer and compassion. Jim Corbett as activist was heroic, but as philosopher in his two books, he emerges as an author in the same league with Thoreau and Emerson.

It is hard to keep up with a goatwalker, but Jim Corbett invites us to try. And I have no doubt that, even more than refugees who needed this Samaritan to lead them across the desert, our planet and civilization in crisis desperately need the ideas he made such an effort to leave as legacy. I am tempted to use as metaphor a curious fact I found out recently about a small town in New Mexico that Judy and I visit. One's cell phone works only on top of the hill, in the cemetery. Sometimes the dead speak to us more clearly than the living. I'll leave it at that.

EXCERPTS FROM *COWBALAH*

Cease to eat anything defiled by violence; make your table the high altar of your daily religion; serve nothing that is produced by harming the land and its life or by any kind of cruelty; then the rest follows.

I avoid eating anyone I haven't known and cherished.

High wisdom is rooted in wildland stillness. One must cease searching for human guidance and listen to the earth. If ungrounded in eremitic wisdom, even altruistic love disorients, guiding its practitioner toward an ethic of self-sacrifice that denatures co-creativity. If ungrounded in wisdom and lovingkindness, a nature-centered ethic also disorients, degenerating into adversarial politics. And politics, if ungrounded in wisdom, lovingkindness, and a Nature-affirming morality, degenerates into a violent struggle to take directive control.

If our bedrock reality is all-inclusive communion, then God is Nature, but not the object nature invented to relegate the sacred to an imagined realm out beyond the sky. If communion is reality's bedrock, then God is also Love, but not just the nurturing love of a mother. Natural communion includes the devouring love of the wolf.

I don't intend to argue here against personal, political, or cultural efforts to reduce the violence, but I do want to emphasize that active allegiance to the Peaceable Kingdom begins with land redemption that lays the foundation for a covenant community's practice of true justice. In exile where we belong to no wildland community, we remain inextricably entangled in technocratic civilization's global war of conquest, which means we can only choose to reduce the damage. No amount of resistance to our war-making way of living will institute and cultivate a way to live peacefully, in community with untamed life. The fundamental obligation of the community that gives its allegiance to the Peaceable Kingdom is to redeem a home in the land where it can walk the covenanted way.

The task at hand is not to abandon or deconstruct civil society but to establish our civilization on a foundation of justice.

Whatever our addictions and enslavements, there's still hope for humanity, not because we're likely to become self-sacrificing saints but because our greatest joy and fullest liberty comes from co-creativity. As active communion, power redeems.

Prophetic revelation always moves toward redemptive transformation, not an idealistic expurgation or a dualistic extermination of evil.

The ability to live by fitting into Nature rather than a human hierarchy is still the foundation of freedom, because freedom is personal co-creativity that is born of harmonious wholeness.

For me, personally, allegiance to the Peaceable Kingdom is guided by Torah that is written on the heart and is enacted as co-creative communion that includes everyone, regardless of religion or even species.

One's life is the offering (which inner wisdom knows as the real meaning of prayer).

[T]he restoration of the earth as a human homeland, not the mystic's escape to heavenly bliss... requires that humanity learn to see "that of God" in every other.

Instead of wanting to go to heaven, the practical mystic wants heaven to come down to earth.

Whether wildland-nurtured communion is best centered for us by a cow, goat, buffalo, mescal, or mesquite is a matter of exploration rather than argument—and unideologically inclusive, in any case.

Inclusivity

We embrace the challenges and joys of truly diverse
viewpoints and values in all areas of life in order to more fully
accept and understand the depth of each other's experience.
We value Earth's diversity of life and respect the rights of each
species to flourish in its unique expression.

In so doing, we foster and encourage the unique gifts
in one another and in all life.

*Do I strive to be inclusive in my relationship, reaching out to those
with whom I have disagreements, or who have hurt me?*

*Have I done anything today that has taken me away from the
experience of love or the experience of God?*

*What barriers keep me from responding openly and lovingly to others?
Do I practice the art of listening deeply, even beyond words?*

"Perhaps one of the most precious and powerful gifts we can give another person is to really listen to them with quiet, fascinated attention, with our whole being, fully present."
—*Kay Lindahl,* The Sacred Art of Listening

"He who experiences the unity of life sees his own Self in all beings..."
—*Buddha*

"Who is wise? One who learns from all: 'From all my teachers I gained insight' (Psalm 119:99)."
—*Ben Zoma, quoted by Rabbi Rami M. Shapiro in* Wisdom of the Jewish Sages

"We all should know that diversity makes for a rich tapestry, and we must understand that all the threads of the tapestry are equal in value no matter what their color."
—*Maya Angelou*

"All ethics so far evolved rest upon a single premise: that the individual is a member of a community of interdependent parts. His instincts prompt him to compete for his place in the community, but his ethics prompt him also to cooperate. The land ethic simply enlarges the boundaries of the community to include soils, waters, plants, and animals, or collectively, the land."
—*Aldo Leopold*

Tao gives them life;
Virtue nourishes them;
Reality shapes them;
Chance completes them.
Thus the ten thousand things
All worship Tao and esteem virtue.
No one commands them
To worship Tao and esteem virtue.
They do it of themselves.
—*From the* Tao Te Ching, *51, translated by Herrymon Mauer*

On the Pulse of the Morning

by Maya Angelou

delivered at the inauguration of President Bill Clinton January 1993.

A Rock, A River, A Tree
Hosts to species long since departed,
Marked the mastodon,
The dinosaur, who left dried tokens
Of their sojourn here
On our planet floor,
Any broad alarm of their hastening doom
Is lost in the gloom of dust and ages.

But today, the Rock cries out to us, clearly, forcefully,
Come, you may stand upon my
Back and face your distant destiny,
But seek no haven in my shadow.
I will give you no hiding place down here.

You, created only a little lower than
The angels, have crouched too long in
The bruising darkness
Have lain too long
Face down in ignorance.
Your mouths spilling words

Armed for slaughter.
The Rock cries out to us today, you may stand upon me,
But do not hide your face.

Across the wall of the world,
A River sings a beautiful song. It says,

Come, rest here by my side.
Each of you, a bordered country,
Delicate and strangely made proud,
Yet thrusting perpetually under siege.
Your armed struggles for profit
Have left collars of waste upon
My shore, currents of debris upon my breast.
Yet today I call you to my riverside,
If you will study war no more. Come,
Clad in peace, and I will sing the songs
The Creator gave to me when I and the
Tree and the rock were one.
Before cynicism was a bloody sear across your
Brow and when you yet knew you still
Knew nothing.
The River sang and sings on.

There is a true yearning to respond to
The singing River and the wise Rock.
So say the Asian, the Hispanic, the Jew
The African, the Native American, the Sioux,
The Catholic, the Muslim, the French, the Greek
The Irish, the Rabbi, the Priest, the Sheik,
The Gay, the Straight, the Preacher,
The privileged, the homeless, the Teacher.
They hear. They all hear
The speaking of the Tree.

They hear the first and last of every Tree
Speak to humankind today. Come to me, here beside the River.
Plant yourself beside the River.

Each of you, descendant of some passed
On traveler, has been paid for.
You, who gave me my first name, you,
Pawnee, Apache, Seneca, you
Cherokee Nation, who rested with me, then
Forced on bloody feet,

Left me to the employment of
Other seekers — desperate for gain,
Starving for gold.
You, the Turk, the Arab, the Swede, the German, the Eskimo,
the Scot,
You the Ashanti, the Yoruba, the Kru, bought,
Sold, stolen, arriving on the nightmare
Praying for a dream.
Here, root yourselves beside me.
I am that Tree planted by the River,
Which will not be moved.
I, the Rock, I the River, I the Tree
I am yours — your passages have been paid.
Lift up your faces, you have a piercing need
For this bright morning dawning for you.
History, despite its wrenching pain
Cannot be unlived, but if faced
With courage, need not be lived again.

Lift up your eyes upon
This day breaking for you.
Give birth again
To the dream.

Women, children, men,
Take it into the palms of your hands,
Mold it into the shape of your most
Private need. Sculpt it into
The image of your most public self.
Lift up your hearts
Each new hour holds new chances
For a new beginning.
Do not be wedded forever
To fear, yoked eternally
To brutishness.

The horizon leans forward,
Offering you space to place new steps of change.

Here, on the pulse of this fine day
You may have the courage
To look up and out and upon me, the
Rock, the River, the Tree, your country.
No less to Midas than the mendicant.
No less to you now than the mastodon then.

Here, on the pulse of this new day
You may have the grace to look up and out
And into your sister's eyes, and into
Your brother's face, your country
And say simply
Very simply
With hope—
Good morning.

Spirituality in Place-based Community

by Freeman House

In all of northwestern California, the largest and most elaborate social event of the year before 1848 is said to have been the building of the fish dam at Kepel, near the confluence of the Klamath and Trinity Rivers. This highly formalized event occupied a hundred or more men (of the Yurok tribe) and their families for ten days exactly, and thousands of ritualized person hours went into the construction of the weir across the river each year. Once completed, the structure was fished for just ten more days, regardless of the size of the run or the number of fish caught, and then it was opened up and abandoned, to be built anew the next year.

Each step of the process—the cutting of the poles, their placement in the river, the ceremonies required before fishing began – was informed by such complex ritual content that the role of remembering the exact procedures and supervising the event each year was invested in one man, called a formulist by the anthropologists. It required his total attention for as much as 4 months of each year. After the structures were abandoned at the end of ten August days, he and his assistants remained in a hut above the dam site to be sure that it was washed away by early winter storms, so as not to interfere with later runs of other stocks of salmon.

This communal practice would not, by itself, have assured the continuity of salmon runs over the centuries. Yurok territory stretches from the estuary of the Klamath River upstream some 60 miles to its confluence with the Trinity. Further upstream and along the Trinity River, live the Hupa. Further upstream yet and along another large tributary, the Salmon River, the Karuk live. While the Kepel dam may have been the largest event in the salmon year, it was only one event embedded in an annual cycle of ritual self-regulation that was shared by the several tribes, and determined the timing and distribution of fishing practices. From one end of the vast river system to another, people were restrained from casual consumption of the fish until certain ceremonial practices were performed at specific locations.

The specifics of the "first salmon" ceremonies varied from place to place, and people to people, but they had several characteristics in common. They induced restraint through the means of powerful taboos: According to ethnobotanist Erna Gunther, "fresh salmon could not be consumed by any member of the community until the first spring salmon ritual took place. Supernaturally induced illness or death would occur if the taboo surrounding the capture of salmon were broken." Consumption of fresh fish was delayed until the first fish had been prepared and eaten ceremonially, after which a communal feast often took place, with assurances that all get fed. By now each delectable morsel of roasted salmon contains more than meat for the protein-starved; it contains the message of the full importance of the relationship between humans and their sources of provision.

After the initial first salmon ceremony was performed at the Yurok village of Welkwau, near the mouth of the river, strong young runners took the message upstream to the Hupa people. There, near the present town of Hoopa, ten days of ceremony and prayer were conducted before the people were allowed to fish. The Karuk conducted their first salmon observances, near present day Somes Bar. Here the community at large, perhaps hungrier because they had waited longer, removed themselves to the hills surrounding while the sacred first fish was taken and ritually eaten by spiritual leaders. When the people returned to the village, fishing and feasting began.

Widely accepted models of human nature as driven by greed and self-interest would lead us to expect one people warring against another over the salmon runs of the Klamath basin until one group dominates the resource, or the resource is destroyed. The earliest anthropologists, however, discovered an entirely different picture. They found a largely trilingual people with elaborate trail systems between their homelands used to coordinate ceremony with the movement of the salmon. Those trails were used by young runners to keep the peoples abreast of the movement of the salmon and relay the news that appropriate rituals had been performed that signaled that the fish could be taken. Collective ritual practices were built around the life of the river rather than on conflict between user groups and this was accomplished without sacrificing the diversity of unique tribal identities. The anthropologists found a shared tradition of intertribal ritual self-regulation that seems to have arisen right out of the river.

Free Range Salmon

by Cindy Spring

Do I relate to Earth as a bounty of resources primarily for human benefit, or am I committed to a sustainable global society founded on respect for all species? Or both? Nowhere do I sense this paradox more clearly than in the stories of the Salmon People...

I am Salmon. Born in a gravel bed in a clear flowing stream, passing a year or so until I can break free of home and keep my date with ocean. I arrive exhausted in a salty world and shape shift to explore the farther reaches of my nature. To a girl from Idaho, Juneau is the big city, and Japan the exotic west. Several years of journeying is enough. The siren song of home calls me back to the same river mouth, the same stream, the same mothering stretch of pebbles. My final act: I turn my body into a shovel, create a new redd, and frenetically dance out my eggs to be fertilized by a hardy partner who has also seen the world. Scraped raw and fatigued by the effort, I die within a day. I offer up my body, muscled by ocean life and the final upstream swim, to continue the life of my community: bear, eagle, otter and human.

I am Salmon. Bred in a batch of identical first cousins in a hatchery, I am one of the lucky ones, taken to a rearing pond, carefully placed at a young age in a foster home. Another trip, another release, this time into a stream tended by caring humans who have tried to remove the logging debris, stop the farm and ranch runoff pollution, and fight for enough water not to be diverted so I can swim to the ocean. I must avoid the turbines of the dams, if I survive the brackish slackwater behind them. In the ocean, trawlers' nets abound. Just like my wild kin, I hear a call to return. Chances are slim but I have no choice. Only the Olympic among us make it up the "fish stairs" alongside the dams. Because I have not lived well, I do not die well. I offer my body anyway.

I am "farmed" Salmon. Born in a tank ten feet wide and three feet deep. After a year or so, I'm released to a gigantic net pen in coastal waters, a hundred feet on a side and 60 feet deep. This is my home, covered with netting so I cannot jump out and birds cannot dive in. Confined in an area befouled with the waste of thousands of trapped salmon, the density is maddening. Antibiotics are pumped in regularly to make sure I don't die of infection. Epidemics happen often. Since my flesh will not turn pink in this prison, my feed is dyed. It's over in a couple of years. My only consolation in this woeful life is that my body feeds people who might otherwise starve. I do not sacrifice freely; I am sacrificed.

Sadness is my first response to the laments of the hatched and farmed salmon. And after that, a determination to support the shift back to letting creeks and rivers run free for migrating salmon. In the Pacific Northwest, small groups of intrepid individuals, like the Mattole Restoration Council in northern California, have been working for over 20 years to reclaim salmon habitat. A success here and there keeps everyone going in the face of continued logging which often undercuts the whole effort. I also support removing dams wherever possible. Since the four dams of the Snake River came on line in the late 1970's, all coho salmon dependent on that migratory corridor through Idaho, Oregon and Washington have become extinct.

If we could somehow end all salmon aquaculture, how do we answer the peoples of the world who depend on those fish? Answer: the same way we are ending the use of fossil fuels and the logging of old growth trees - with a vision of a sustainable and just world and the day-to-day work to make it so. Swimming upstream feels like such an apt analogy to the effort being made to turn commodity mania into community kinship. The difference is so perfectly captured for me in the current court battle to remove a dozen varieties of salmon from the endangered species list because "there are plenty raised in farms." At this point in human evolution, we're all swimming upstream.

I owe my understanding of salmon lives to two books: *Totem Salmon, Life Lessons from Another Species* by Freeman House (Beacon, 1999), and *My Story as Told By Water* by David James Duncan (Sierra Club Books, 2001).

Our Father,
which art in Birds and Fish

by Jordan Fisher Smith

If you think about it, it's easy to see how God and His miracles suffer as badly as men, women, and dogs do from being kept indoors too much and how badly God's creatures have fared during His long captivity in churches.

Several winters ago now a glowing image appeared on the inside wall of St. Dominic's Catholic church in the little town of Colfax, in the red-clay foothills along the west rim of the canyon of the American River's North Fork, where I was working as a park ranger at the time. If you squinted a bit, people said, the luminous apparition bore a resemblance to the Virgin Mary, and within a few days hundreds of the curious and faithful lined up outside the church in the cold waiting to see it. Before long, remote broadcast trucks from television stations showed up and trained their satellite dishes on the heavens, and once the visitation made the evening news, the line of people waiting to get into the church stretched out for blocks, and people brought sleeping bags and lawn chairs and camped on the sidewalk overnight to see it.

After a couple of weeks, a professor of physics from California State University Sacramento appeared to investigate the phenomenon at St. Dominic's. After inspecting the premises and interviewing the priest, the physicist announced his findings to the assembled press. It seems that a light fixture had been moved during recent repairs in the church, he said, and it was now arranged in such a way that it caught the morning sun shining through the stained glass windows and refracted the colored light onto a nearby wall. There had been an unseasonable spell of clear weather at the time, and the professor predicted that on the next cloudy day the Virgin would fail to appear. Sure enough, a couple of days later a big storm blew up into the mountains and made a lot of people feel foolish.

For my part, I admire those people for expecting miracles. But in my opinion a great wrong has been perpetrated on those who are convinced that God or the Blessed Virgin is more likely to show up at a church than somewhere else. I never got around to seeing the pretty light on the wall in Colfax, because at the time I was busy watching other events unfolding a few miles to the northwest. No one lined up around the block to see these things, so they were denied the legitimacy a crowd and a few television cameras can lend to any scene.

Paddling my canoe on the lower Yuba River, I saw winter run salmon returning to spawn. They ripped the surface of the water all around the boat with their shiny backs, surging up over the cobble bottom in the shallows where the water was barely deep enough to cover them, then stopping with their gills sucking and heaving, then bursting forward again.

I eased the canoe into an eddy and wondered how Pacific salmon, who hatch from eggs in some obscure stream and swim down to roam their adult lives over thousands of miles of ocean, navigate back to their home stream years later to lay their eggs and die. It is supposed that they can distinguish the flavor of their natal waters from all other tributaries they encounter as they swim upstream. But at the mouth of San Francisco Bay where these fish leave the ocean, the smell of their home tributary is watered down and mixed with hundreds of other streams, effluent from municipal sewage treatment, surface drainage from our towns and streets, and the bottom paint of ships in the Bay and in the Sacramento River. How salmon manage this feat is a miracle that will never tarnish in the face of an expert's explanation. But healthy salmon runs are getting harder to find.

Not long after the salmon ran, I saw a flock of about two thousand snow geese flying south for the winter. They covered the western sky in a huge white sheet, shimmering with individual wingbeats and "V" formations forming, breaking up and reforming. Snow geese spend the summer breeding on the Arctic tundra of Alaska among creatures such as musk oxen, caribou and grizzly bears. They had flown about 2,400 miles south when I saw them. How their bodies endure a flight this long with only a few stops to peck at the post-harvest leavings in frozen fields is beyond my comprehension, yet similar feats are repeated annually by a multitude of other species, most of them smaller and frailer than snow geese. It doesn't seem possible that there is that much energy in a bird. This is God, no doubt, in the form of bird. If you were God, wouldn't you show up in some common aerial form so you could keep an eye on things from above? Why not a thousand snow goose eyes for a thousand generations, looking down lovingly from the cold heights along the Pacific Flyway at our houses, roads, mountains, fields, and rivers?

There is great danger in not seeing God's hand and eyes in these things. Human destructiveness is blind, and the blindness is chewing through God's creation at a prodigious rate, finding a better use for almost everything than the use originally assigned to it. And for this reason the list of things that no longer share this earthly paradise with us grows daily.

So I'd like to suggest that we go out on Sunday (or any other day), alone or in congregations, and attend such events as fish runs and bird migrations as if we were attending church. No doubt some of us have already been doing so for years. Migrations in particular are the sort of miracles that tie the world's places together in your mind, making it hard to separate some of them out for condemnation to usefulness. Whether we like it or not, the lines between religious and secular affairs are now being blurred all over the world. Given this extension of spiritual authority into the houses of government and other formerly secular realms, might religion be presumed also to have something to say about how we conduct ourselves outdoors? Perhaps land and waters should not be exempted as purely materialist regions. The regard for the holiness of wild things that is discernible in the cave paintings of Pleistocene people has been losing ground for three millennia, a development that has paralleled the disappearances of wild things themselves. This might be a good time in history to reverse that trend. Surely people who are in favor of extending religion into secular life will be pleased at the prospect of conducting their daily affairs in a sacramental place. There will of course be some complications: If God is allowed to escape from church into the great outdoors, the line between expediency and sacrilege will have to be walked more carefully. This might slow things down for a while. Then again, slowing things down may prove an entirely practical thing to do.

In the meantime, on any night when the wind blows hard across the ridges in the mountains east of St. Dominic's Church, you can hear the world's greatest organist perform a requiem for all the kinds of things that no longer walk, crawl, swim, or grow on earth, using the branches of pine, cedar and fir and the rocky notches and pinnacles of the Sierra Nevada as a great instrument. However you conceive God to be and no matter what country you come from or in what language your name for God is spoken, you can go out in the morning and see holy writing in the tracks of little birds in the dust, in the tracks of deer and coyotes in the mud and snow. All that is good is here right now. God is in heaven and so, dear readers, are we.

Will There Be Any Toads in Heaven?

by Keith Helmuth

We have a great fondness for toads on North Hill Farm and they seem to have great fondness for us—or rather for the particular environment we have helped shape. There seems to be a direct, positive correlation between garden development and toad population. Toads, of course, are champion insect eaters and we value them as working members of the farm  crew. I suppose they must value us as champion insect growers since gardening brings on great blooms of insects as well as vegetables and flowers.

I am concerned about toad populations. According to a variety of recent studies, toad and frog populations world-wide are crashing. Whole species have disappeared from what were thought to be relatively pristine environments. Their disappearance indicates that yet another level of environmental deconstruction has been reached. Ecological collapse *is not* a fantasy of doom-minded environmentalists. It is happening! Now! Toads and frogs are among the oldest species in the community of life. Their sensitivity to the generalized toxification of Earth's environment is an omen of Biblical proportions.

What is going on here? More and more I have come to the conclusion that the destruction of Earth's biotic integrity has to do with much more than just the overt necessities of economic behavior. The struggle to center our lives in Creation—in Earth process as we have come to understand it—is also about excavating the deep psychic structures of the Judeo-Christian tradition, structures which have created our worldview and have driven our collective behavior in ways that are often antithetical and sometimes stunningly inappropriate with regard to the biotic integrity of Earth.

It has come to me that we need to conduct a kind of archeological dig into the Christian worldview in order to redeem it from a variety of ecological errors. In my effort to do this "spiritual" archeology I have received particular assistance from the toads with whom we share North Hill Farm. Encountering toads always brightens my mood, and good humor sometimes opens the door on an innovative thought.

One summer day a few years ago, while weeding in the herb garden and having met a toad in the basil, a question popped into my mind: "Will there be any toads in heaven?"

Now the juxtaposition of such a down-to-earth creature with such a lofty theological concept may seem whimsically absurd, and, in fact, it was exactly this dissonance that intrigued me. Why does the thought of toads in heaven seem so incongruous? The answer is not hard to find.

Looking back over the centuries we see how theological interests have risen and fallen in popularity. One of the interests that has enjoyed a consistently high profile until recent times is the nature of heaven. Based on the references in the Bible, an image of heaven has been built up in the Christian tradition that has had profound social, economic and ecological consequences.

Even though, in modern times, it has become increasingly difficult for Christian thinkers to undertake sustained speculation on the nature of heaven, the old image of this promised land has remained a *sub rosa* component of the Western world-view. It seems, in fact, that the eclipse of heaven as a topic of theological inquiry and general public interest has not diminished the tenacity of the cultural orientation that arises from its history. If anything, the promised land orientation in our culture has grown stronger even as its theological prominence has faded. It has simply shifted from the eternal to the temporal and re-emerged in economics, technology, and social planning.

The idea of Heaven derived from the Bible, and developed over many generations by orthodox theologians and preachers, is based entirely on the image of an urban environment—a heavenly city, the city of God. As far as I am aware, there are no rural or wilderness images of heaven in the Bible. The Isaiahian image of the peaceable kingdom on Earth has generally been regarded as a temporary arrangement. The ultimate goal, the environment of heaven, has always been portrayed as a great and good city.

What is this heavenly city, this promised land orientation? As a package of cultural values, it has a variety of notable features: ultimate convenience and total leisure. No work, no struggle required. Total peace, joy, and contentment. No conflict, sadness or suffering. No decline, decay or death. And all this is framed within an entirely urban environment. The concept of the heavenly city is the exact opposite of a rural or wildland life and economy. Nor does it draw on the social and economic arrangements of small town or village life. The concept of heaven like the design of our central urban environments, is based on transcending the fundamental meteorological, biophysical energetic, metabolic, and economic conditions of Earth process.

The hold of this vision on the collective imagination of Christendom as it turned into Western Civilization did not wane. It simply moved from the ethereal to the concrete, from the sky to the earth, from theologians and preachers to the political economists, engineers and entrepreneurs. The whole modern project of economic development—both capitalist and socialist— has been driven by the utopian image of overcoming, through technology, the basic conditions of Earth process, and the establishment of human habitation in an environment which realizes as fully as possible the values and conditions of the heavenly city.

Is this a noble vision worthy of allegiance? Many intelligent persons over the past ten centuries have thought so and worked hard to achieve it. Or is it a recipe for ecological and social disaster'? A dissenting minority has been voicing this warning. It seems to me the issue is now clear. The roots of the economic and technological behaviors which are poisoning and disabling the Earth are lodged in an image of deliverance and salvation; lodged in a wish for privilege and exemption which starts in the Bible, which has been carried and nourished in Western culture, and has now, through the agency of the capital-driven market economy, exploded in ecologically and socially damaging consequences over the whole Earth

An image which started with a theological warrant—the image of the heavenly city—has now been translated into a license for bulldozing the ecosystem, undermining the value and dignity of labor and offering shopping malls and theme parks in their place.

If this seems exaggerated, consider the meaning of the toxic, metallic tasting haze that now routinely overspreads vast regions of our continent and makes public respiratory warnings almost as common as weather forecasts. We are talking about the breath of life. Cancer rates climb. Forest environments collapse. Lakes go dead. Loons diminish. Toads vanish. However we conceive of it—as an urban rest home in the sky or the promised land of total convenience on Earth—the answer to the question in my title is, "No. There will be no toads in heaven."

Obviously, a great confusion has occurred. The attempt to establish the heavenly city of maximum convenience is wrecking the Earth. Somehow we must pull this image—this "ghost in the machine"—out of the driver's seat and put ecological wisdom in its place. I'm not sure what should be done with the idea of the heavenly city. It is a powerful image. Perhaps theologians could issue a recall and try to make appropriate modifications in its character.

Personally, I would not want to inhabit a heaven without toads, and since a heaven of total convenience and ease—wherever it is located—seems to rule them out, I vote for a new image of heaven; an image which includes trees and turtles, birds and insects, labor and rest, and plenty of toads. I want a heaven that jumps around my feet.

In the past, those who understood the ecological dissonance of the Biblical tradition mostly just ignored it and worked to create an ecologically accurate worldview in the hope of altering the environmentally destructive behavior of modern culture. This re-education is not working, or at least not working fast enough. It appears to me we should now raise the ecologically dissonant elements of the Biblical worldview into full consciousness. Perhaps if we can gain a freeing perspective on these elements of our cultural heritage we will awaken the clarity and courage of the changes we need to undertake the changes of adaptation to the way our amazing natural home actually works and the changes that enable human communities to lift their social relations into a better harmony.

Growing Connection:
The Ecovillage Vision and the
Future of Community

by Diana Leafe Christian

I'm laughing so hard I almost fall out of my chair. Six of us are sitting around a dining room table recalling some of our favorite lines from Woody Allen's time-travel movie *Sleeper*. ("It's 2025!? Oh no! I'm 50 years behind in my rent!").

We're having dinner in the White Owl Lodge, a two-story timber framed building we use as our village pub at Earthaven, a 10-year-old aspiring ecovillage in the mountains of North Carolina. The people at my table range from a young mother in her 30s to my own mom, who's 89. Other people of all ages are gathered in small groups at other tables, and some sit at the bar. Two young men are drinking mead as they bend over a chessboard at a small round table. People are laughing and joking, going back to the bar for seconds, or stopping at other tables to schmooze and catch up on the day's news. Others are snuggled in conversation by the fireplace. Children are scrambling around the floor. World music—tonight it's Arabic—plays on the sound system.

Everywhere I look my eye falls on beauty. All the lumber in here, from round-pole timber-frame posts to knee braces, wain-edged ceiling beams, golden hardwood floor, and even the oak bar itself is from lumber logged and milled on our land. The building was built by many of our young loggers and carpenters, including our White Owl host who cooked and served the dinner. The massive Russian masonry fireplace was faced with round river rocks by a community member who's a stonemason. The blue and peach-colored counters and floors in the kitchen were tiled with left-over tiles from construction sites. Water in the kitchen is piped from one of our springs. The lights over the tables, the Arabic music, and all the kitchen appliances are running on power from our microhydro system in a nearby stream. The kitchen's graywater flows to a bark-chip graywater trench, cleaned by microorganisms before it sinks into the soil below.

Outside in soft spring night, children dart through the shadows, as their parents walk back from the composting toilet structure a short distance through the woods. All around us are gravel roads, paths, and footbridges we built ourselves. Beyond are our three closest neighborhoods, where many of us live in small passive solar homes or large multi-household residences we've built ourselves, mostly of natural materials, and always without bank loans. Most have solar panels. Beyond this central part of our village are ten more neighborhoods, several campgrounds, and a small valley that will remain permanent wilderness, nestled in the perpetual forest stands of our 320 acres.

Since Earthaven is an aspiring ecovillage, our off-grid utilities, natural-built dwellings, ecospiritual aspirations, and close-knit social life are both an expression of ecovillage values and the reason we're all here.

"An ecovillage," write Robert and Diane Gilman in their 1991 book, *Ecovillages and Sustainable Communities*, "is a human-scale, full-featured settlement in which human activities are harmlessly integrated into the natural landscape in a way that is supportive of healthy human development, and which can be successfully continued into the indefinite future." This is my favorite definition. The Global Ecovillage Network (GEN), an international organization of ecovillage activists, says an ecovillage can be a traditional third-world village with an ecologically and culturally sustainable lifestyle, a sustainability education center, or an intentional community, and we're the latter. (An intentional community is a group of people who live with, or adjacent to, or near enough to one another to carry out their common purpose together.) GEN estimates more than 15,000 identifiable ecovillage projects exist today. But back to the Gilmans' definition.

'"Human-scale" means the settlement is small enough so that everyone knows everyone else, and everyone has input in the decisions that affect their lives. We're 60 people at Earthaven going on 160. We all know each other at this size, and we'll still know everyone (though not equally well) when we reach our maximum size.

"Full-featured settlement" means ecovillage residents live there, can work there, can buy many goods and services there, their social life is there, their spiritual life is there. While we leave Earthaven's property—some to jobs in town, or to shop, or to see movies or visit friends—we can also choose to do much of that here. Many of us at Earthaven earn a living on the land, either because we're self-employed, telecommute, or work for one of several businesses owned by various other community members, such as Permaculture Activist magazine or Red Moon Herbs. When we need unskilled labor, carpentry, plumbing, electrical services, or computer repair, we hire each other. Some of us sell each other eggs or salad greens; our small general store supplies basic necessities. Our town shopper picks up groceries and building supplies twice a week from Asheville. Some of us manage to not leave the community for weeks at a time if we choose to.

"Human activities harmlessly integrated into the natural landscape" means how the people live, work, grow their food, generate their power, and so on. They don't harm the air, water, soil, or the creatures they share the land with. We're not harmless yet at Earthaven, though we aim to be. We practice sustainable logging so we don't disturb the soil unduly or create runoff in the creeks, and we leave trees by the streams to keep the water shaded and cool for the fish. We build with the least toxic materials we can, given economies of scale and the need to use building materials that are structurally sound and not prohibitively expensive. We recycle our waste and garden organically. But we still drive through two of our creek crossings because we haven't built bridges over them yet. We still use concrete and plywood in some of our buildings. We still drive cars and use gasoline. We're a long way from harmless.

"In a way that's supportive of healthy human development" means the people doing all this are thriving. They're healthy, happy, and not burnt out. We're not there yet either. Many of us work far too hard for too many hours a day. We're building this place from scratch, in the mountains, in a forest, and most of us were city dwellers. We've had to learn permaculture design, site planning, excavation, building construction, plumbing, electrical wiring—trades many of us never had a clue about. And, since an ecovillage is as much human interactions as solar panels, we've also had to learn consensus decision-making, meeting facilitation, agenda planning, honest self-revealing communication, and counseling and mediation skills—which most of us never had a clue about either. We're a long ways from our ideal of "healthy," but we're aiming for it.

"Successfully continued into the indefinite future" means that generations later our descendents will still be able to live like this on Earthaven's property. They'll do it better than we are, God willing.

"Ecovillages are intentional communities dedicated to creating and demonstrating ecological, social, economic, and spiritual sustainability," writes ecovillage activist Manda Gillespie in *Communities* magazine. "They take many forms, from rural to urban, from small experiments to large districts in transition, and exist in many cultures and geopolitical climates. All have made a commitment to model community development while considering how present actions affect future generations."

Consider Dancing Rabbit Ecovillage in rural northeastern Missouri, founded in 1993, where twenty ecovillagers dwell in a gently rolling prairie setting. At Dancing Rabbit you'll also find small, natural-built passive solar buildings or large multi-household residences, many solar panels and a wind generator, and people earning a living whenever possible in small, onsite businesses or telecommuting. Like us, they generate their own social and cultural lives onsite and make decisions by consensus. However, there are striking differences. Earthaven members are clearing trees so we can one day grow our own food; Dancing Rabbit is already bursting with produce from their abundant organic gardens. When they want to go somewhere, they mostly bicycle. No one owns a private car, so when they do drive, they car pool using cars and vans from their community-owned car-coop, powered with biodiesel they make themselves or recycled cooking oil. They use local, natural materials when they can, and any lumber must be recycled or from locally salvaged buildings.

Both Dancing Rabbit and Earthaven are rural, and built from scratch on raw land. But it's more sustainable to retrofit existing buildings, and that's what residents of Los Angeles Eco-Village have done. Most of the 35 "intentional neighbors" of this 11-year-old intentional community live in two adjacent apartment buildings in a two-block inner city neighborhood. They've renovated their buildings with environmentally friendly materials, removed the fences between their yards, established several small organic gardens, set up shared compost and recycling facilities, and planted 100 fruit trees. They make decisions by consensus and gather for Sunday potlucks in the courtyard. About a dozen residents earn a living onsite, through maintenance and repair, remodeling, and housecleaning services. Several residents have started a bike repair co-op. To encourage bicycling and riding the bus, all car-free households get $20 off on their rent. Thirteen LA Eco-Villagers moved to the community without cars; seven more have given up their cars since moving there. They're redesigning their street to slow traffic, and the city of Los Angeles has committed over $250,000 to implement the plan.

Dancing Rabbit, Earthaven, and LA Eco-Village are fairly "alternative," appealing mostly to pioneers, eco-activists, and countercultural folk. But an ecovillage model you could take your grandmother to is EcoVillage at Ithaca (EVI), founded in 1992. There, 120 people live in two adjacent cohousing neighborhoods in a rural area two and a half miles from downtown Ithaca, New York. As in most cohousing communities, their two neighborhoods consist of two facing rows of townhouse-style apartments with common gardens and children's play areas in-between, and a large shared community building where residents dine together three nights a week. Each housing unit has its own kitchen, living room, bathroom, and bedrooms, and uses the shared common facilities in the common house, including community kitchen and dining room, laundry room, children's play room, meeting rooms, and so on.

Unlike Dancing Rabbit and Earthaven, which look fairly

countercultural, and Los Angeles Eco-Village, deep in the inner city, EcoVillage at Ithaca is as attractive and comfortable as any suburban neighborhood—although green. Its residents enjoy their own onsite CSA (community-supported agriculture) farm where they pick up organic produce every week. They dwell in energy-efficient, passive-solar homes, recycle almost everything they use, share ownership of their common facilities, and make community decisions by consensus. Half the adult wage earners work at least part-time on site in home offices or those in the community building. They carpool extensively, share cars, and ride the bus (they successfully lobbied the local bus company to make a stop by their entry road). They've preserved 90 percent of their property as open space for organic agriculture, woods, meadows, and wetlands, and set aside 50 acres as a permanent conservation easement administered by a local land trust.

Ecovillages aren't just a North American phenomenon. Some of the more well-known ecovillage projects include Crystal Waters in Australia (founded in1988), Findhorn in Scotland (1962), and Lebensgarten in Germany (1985). The 100-household Munksoegaard Ecovillage near Copenhagen won first prize in a Danish competition in 2000 for the best sustainable design for the 21st century. And Kobunaki Ecovillage, the first such project in Japan, will soon break ground for a 250-home settlement on 30 acres near Kyoto.

Global Ecovillage Network (GEN) has broadened the definition of ecovillages beyond the ecological aspect of sustainability to include social sustainability (cooperation and democratic decision-making) and spiritual sustainability (supports its members' shared or diverse spiritual beliefs and processes). Many, like Earthaven, offer workshops and internships in permaculture, natural building, and other aspects of ecovillage living.

In 1998, the United Nations named ecovillages in their "Top 100 List of Best Practices." Ecovillage activists are striving to be living models of sustainability—examples of a new/old way of life and actions we can undertake now to counter dangerous trends.

"We stand at the junction between two millennia," observes

GEN activist and Ecovillage Training Center Director Albert Bates in *Communities* magazine. "The past millennium was about building societies that ran on fossil sunlight and militarism. The next one, still a mystery, must be more conscientious and humane or we won't survive. It's on the shoulders of ecovillage pioneers that the dream we all have now rest—for peace, security, prosperity, family, and happiness into the community generations of our children—whether we, or they, recognize it yet."

Yet however lofty our goals and potentially significant our long term impact, ecovillage residents are also just people like you and me trying to learn to live together congenially and do the right thing by the planet on a day-to-day basis. And keep our sense of humor. At tonight's dinner at the White Owl, maybe we'll we get into Monty Python.

Celebration

*We celebrate the human role as a positive, life-enhancing agent in
Earth's unfolding story.*

*In so doing, we live in the wonder and mystery
of the living Universe.*

Do I remember to give thanks for life's gifts, both large and small?
Do I make time for the things that bring joy and enhance life?
Do I keep a child-like openness to nature and new experiences?
Am I willing to share my joy and wonder with others?
Am I willing to laugh, especially at myself?

"I thank you, God, for this most amazing day, for the leaping greenly spirits of trees, and for the blue dream of sky and for everything which is natural, which is infinite, which is yes."
—*e.e. cummings*

"Everybody needs beauty as well as bread, places to play in and pray in, where nature may heal and give strength to body and soul." —*John Muir*

"If a child is to keep alive his inborn sense of wonder...he needs the companionship of at least one adult who can share it, rediscovering with him the joy, excitement and mystery of the world we live in."
—*Rachel Carson*

"Wake at dawn with a winged heart and give thanks for another day of loving."
—*Kahlil Gibran*

"If the only prayer you said in your whole life was, 'thank you,' that would suffice."
—*Meister Eckhart*

Children of the Light

by John Fowler

In the beginning was Power—intelligent, loving, energizing. In the beginning was the Word, supremely capable of mastering and moulding whatever might come into being in the world of matter. In the beginning there were not coldness and darkness. There was Fire. This is the truth."
—*Pierre Teilhard de Chardin*

At the base of the serene tropical rainforest sits this cosmic hurricane. At the base of the seaweed's column of time is the trillion degree blast that begins everything.
—*Brian Swimme and Thomas Berry*

All of the energy that ever will be came forth in primal fire and light. During the last century, a huge amount of attention was focused on the nature and behavior of that light. Einstein held it as a constant; a yardstick for the physical cosmos. Max Planck and Werner Heisenberg began mapping its properties and our relationships to them. These were to become the foundations of quantum mechanics.

While Einstein, Planck, Heisenberg, and others detailed the mysteries of the physical cosmos, Maria Montessori observed and charted the life of the child. By 1948 she was convinced that "Human consciousness comes into the world as a flaming ball of imagination. Everything invented by man, physical or mental, is the result of someone's imagination."

Her nearly fifty years of working with children led her to believe that the story of the universe was equally primary. She claimed that:

> If the idea of the universe be given to the child in the right way, it will do more than just arouse his interest, for it will create in him admiration and feeling loftier and more

satisfying. The child's mind then can become fixed and can work. The knowledge he then acquires is organized and systematic; his intelligence can become whole and complete because of the vision of the whole that has been presented to him, and his interest spreads to all, for all are linked and have their place in the universe on which his mind is centered.

That story must now begin with fire and light. More importantly, light can be understood as the underpinnings of both the physical and the psychic cosmos. In fact, the two aspects can readily be seen as part of one seamless universe. I am a Montessori teacher daily engaged in the lives of nine, ten, and eleven-year-old children. The practical question has been paramount: How can these principles be merged in the ongoing classroom life of children?

It is here that Thomas Berry and Brian Swimme have been so helpful as they remind us that it's all about story. Stories of beginnings and stories of creation have always held the greatest fascination for children and do so for many reasons. Perhaps chief among these is that, as Erich Neumann, the eminent Jungian, has claimed, creation stories are really about the birth of human consciousness (1973, p. 6). They follow the same patterns. They sweep over the same metaphoric and archetypal ground.

With this much as guide, the "Timeline of Light" curriculum was created for the children in my classes in our large public Montessori school in Denver, Colorado. The curriculum received its name from *The Timeline of Light,* a colorful, scientific, archetypal, and mythical portrayal of the first 14 billion years of cosmic emergence. But the curriculum drew its strength from the imagination and insight of the children. In turn, the imagination of the children received its spark from the creative flame of personal experience.

The experiences offered in the curriculum are integral. The original goal was for each child to approach a state where she was at once the subject and the object of personal experience, what my dear late friend and mentor, Sherman Stanage, called the "*coject,*" that place where the individual merges with the universe. The goal was to merge the flaming ball of the imagination with an understanding of light as the primal substance of our universe. Their meeting was arranged through the medium of metaphor, not metaphor in the limited sense of comparing two words to create a third sense of meaning, but metaphor in the grand sense described by Bob Samples [author of *Open Systems, Open Mind*s: *Reflections on Consciousness and Education*]. In this view, the metaphoric mind is the mind that contains "nature's own expression" in the immediate way found in the Taoism of Lao-Tzu, the *satori haiku* of Japanese sages, or the visual vitality that children so often bring to their art.

There is nothing new here. In a very concrete sense, metaphor has always been handmaiden to science. Galileo metaphorically insisted that the book of nature was written in the language of mathematics, and note the lasting impact his metaphor has had! Then turn to the Gaia theory made popular by James Lovelock and Lynn Margulis. In the cases of both Galileo and Gaia, metaphoric roots have shouted their truth. So it is with all science, whether the domain of that science is internal or external.

For children, the foregoing holds little interest. For them, the real import lies in feeling. So that is where we begin. The metaphors always follow, pouring forth naturally from their expanded feeling for the cosmos. The first lesson in the curriculum is a recalling of the primordial flaring forth, the primal fire of creation. In as poetic a way as possible, the children are invited to hear this most important of all stories. The lights are dimmed. Vangelis' *Opera Sauvage* (1979) plays softly in the background. As I recount the emergence of the universe, the children are invited to relax and enjoy the story for some 20 or so minutes. Their feelings and impressions combine with the effect of the environment to invoke a shift of consciousness. At story's end the children are invited to express their feelings, impressions, and thoughts in artistic form using any and all of the materials available in the classroom. We can see that these moments are precious to the children. They have told us so, not only through their art, but in oh so many voices.

A fascinated Natto said that he felt like he was right there every step of the way, from the primordial flaring forth to the very first atoms. Monica found the story amazing but felt cheated that it was still unfinished. Tamara described the impact of the tale as "mind blowing" and drew a picture that could well have been found in a physics text, complete with the bounding, spiraling dance made by subatomic particles, a dance never before seen by her physical eyes. Alondra was so fascinated by what the story evoked that she simply burst out saying that she wanted more. Let me add the inspired and evocative voice of Julio to this list, a voice that clearly and mystically stated:

"I felt like I was there when the universe was being born. And I felt like I was born again at the very same moment. I saw a star about to be blasted into a galaxy."

Julio and the rest of the children have been truly touched by the depth and breadth of the universe story. They are far from alone—and no wonder! The story of creation, properly set and told, is the grandest of all tales, at once the most personal and the most far-reaching that we can offer.

After a few weeks we extend the story into traditional metaphor. The children are asked to compare the creation of the universe to a birthday party, an extremely personal and significant event in the life of any eleven-year-old! Here again the natural and creative mind has leapt forth. As though it were yesterday, I can recall Elizabeth proclaiming that the birth of the universe must have been a lot like a birthday party because at a birthday party you get a lot of gifts and when the universe was created the "endless gifts of sound and color poured into space creating all that there is." Crystal's voice rang just as true. She noted that one of the differences between a birthday party and the birth of the universe is that after a birthday party, even a sleepover, the children go to sleep and rest, "but the universe never sleeps." Several years ago Mo noted that "the universe itself is like a big chocolate cake and when we celebrate its birthday the stars are present like candles, and as one is going out another is coming into existence, kind of an endless celebration of light and color."

Celebration is a constant, a cornerstone, a *sine qua non* of the curriculum. We sing songs, we write collective poetry, we dance, perform experiments, explore geometric constructs and intuitions, and, most frequently, the children draw. One of their favorite themes is the way that we are held by the Sun. After several months of lessons, the children receive the following brief bit of information.

> We are held by the gravity of the Sun. If it were not so, we would be without the pattern of the seasons and the magic of day and night. Were we not held just as we are and just where we are, life as we know it would never have been shaped, the flowers would never bloom, the moon would not cast its mystery and the great flocks of geese would never soar south with the coming of winter. Our Sun holds us in the precious grasp of its gravity, never pulling too much or too little, ever keeping us in balance with its warmth.

The children are then asked to respond in the most glorious and artistic way imaginable. By now their creative readiness has grown considerably. Many show the Sun in feminine form, others in bifurcated dark and light shading as if to indicate the positive and negative aspects of too much and too little heat. One archetypal gem depicted a primordial sun blowing a spirited breath of life into our fair planet. Yet other versions have been in three dimensions, with the Earth extended from the Sun by a piece of black yarn. Without fail, each and every depiction of the miracle of solar fire, heat, gravity, and balance has reached beyond the longest stretch of my imagination, an occurrence for which I am extremely grateful.

Of course the integral perspective of cosmology is ever present in the classroom. It announces itself in literature discussions, class government, poetry, and myriad other ways. The children always ask for more, always want to hear the stories and have the experiences again.

This article has only skimmed the surface of their experience. It falls short of an ideal vision in two distinct ways. The first is that the breadth and depth of any cycle of five months duration cannot be painted in so brief a space. The present vehicle can only suggest and hope that you join in the celebration. The second restriction lies in the very essence of our time on earth. The children are young but their lives will be long. As they live those lives it would be my great joy to glean but a fraction of the ways they can go forth and make the planet a better place. It is my belief that the personal and ecological insight gathered from their work will be significant.

That insight is also, as this article has hinted, beyond quantification. However, we are fortunate that young authors such as Tara, have given us a peek into that qualitative well of feeling and understanding that has quenched the thirst of so many children. Let her words be the last:

Light
Expanding, Radiant
Rushing, Giving, Receiving.
It burns in all of us,
The Giver.

Life as Play: A Simpler Way

by Meg Wheatley and Myron Kellner-Rogers

Life is creative. It plays itself into existence, seeking out new relationships, new capacities, new traits. Life is an experiment to discover what's possible. As it tinkers with discovery, it creates more and more possibilities. With so much freedom for discovery, how can life be anything but playful?

What has kept us from seeing life as creative, even playful? At least since Darwin, Western culture has harbored some great errors. We have believed that the world is hostile, that we are in a constant struggle for survival, that the consequence of error is death, that the environment seeks our destruction. In such a world, there is no safety. Who wouldn't be afraid?

Darwinistic thought solidified the belief that life was not supposed to happen. Life was an accident, just one of many random events. Because the world had never intended for life to appear, the world had no obligation to sustain it. Life had to fight for every breath, tested constantly by an unwelcoming and unforgiving environment. Species appeared by chance. Individuals that stumbled on lucky genetic errors survived. The environment loomed over every living thing, ready to challenge, ready to destroy. It was an awesome responsibility life faced: Get it right, or die.

These errors of thought have guided most of our decisions. They have kept us from seeing a world that is continuously exploring and creating. Life is about invention, not survival. We are here to create, not to defend. Out beyond the shadows of Darwinistic thought, a wholly different world appears. A world that delights in its explorations. A world that makes it up as it goes along. A world that welcomes us into the exploration as good partners.

Images of life as creative and playful have been with us for thousands of years in many spiritual traditions, but modern Western thought makes it difficult to approach life as play.

Life's process of creating is quite different from what we had thought. There are enough underlying principles to this process that we could call it a logic, a logic of play. In fact, we would like to call it the logic of life. The key elements of this logic are evident in recent work by scientists who explore how life comes into being:

• Everything is in a constant process of discovery and creating. Everything is changing all the time: individuals, systems, environments, the rules, the processes of evolution. Even change changes. Every organism reinterprets the rules, creates exceptions for itself, creates new rules.

• Life uses messes to get to well-ordered solutions. Life doesn't seem to share our desires for efficiency or neatness. It uses redundancy, fuzziness, dense webs of relationships, and unending trials and errors to find what works.

• Life is intent on finding what works, not what's "right." It is the ability to keep finding solutions that is important; any one solution is temporary. There are no permanently right answers. The capacity to keep changing, to find what works now, is what keeps any organism alive.

• Life creates more possibilities as it engages with opportunities. There are no "windows of opportunity," narrow openings in the fabric of space-time that soon disappear forever. Possibilities beget more possibilities; they are infinite.

• Life is attracted to order. It experiments until it discovers how to form a system that can support diverse members. Individuals search out a wide range of possible relationships to discover whether they can organize into a life-sustaining system. These explorations continue until a system is discovered. This system then provides stability for its members, so that individuals are less buffeted by change.

• Life organizes around identity. Every living thing acts to develop and preserve itself. Identity is the filter that every organism or system uses to make sense of the world. New information, new relationships, changing environments—all are interpreted through a sense of self. This tendency toward self-creation is so strong that it creates a seeming paradox. An organism will change to maintain its identity.

• Everything participates in the creation and evolution of

its neighbors. There are no unaffected outsiders. No one system dictates conditions to another. All participate together in creating the conditions of their interdependence.

There is no such thing as survival of the fittest, only survival of the fit. This means that there is no one answer that is right, but many answers that might work. The puzzle in biology is not how natural selection forces an organism into one right solution. The puzzle is how so much diversity, such rampant profligacy, can be tamed sufficiently to develop organisms that are similar enough to reproduce. Why are there so many different plants and animals? Perhaps it is because life has only these simple criteria: Whatever you become, make sure you can survive and reproduce. These are very broad constraints, not strict rules. Given so much freedom, organisms take off in all directions, exploring what's possible.

Nature encourages wild self-expression as long as it doesn't threaten the survival of the organism. The world supports incredible levels of diversity, playful additions to one's physical appearance, unique excursions into color and flair. There is no ideal design for anything, just interesting combinations that arise as a living thing explores its space of possibilities. Yet we have terrorized ourselves as a species by the thought of evolution, driving ourselves into positions of paralyzing conformity for fear of getting things wrong.

This world of wild exploration is one which tinkers itself into existence. Tinkerers have skills but no clear plans. They make do with the materials at hand. Does such tinkering make life appear indifferent, relativistic, crassly opportunistic? Or does it reveal life's delight in exploration, in discovering what's possible? Tinkering opens us to what's possible in the moment. Analytic plans drive us only toward what we think we already know.

But life's tinkering has direction. It tinkers toward order—toward systems that are more complex and more effective. The process used is exploratory and messy, but the movement is toward order. In human attempts to construct functioning ecosystems, scientists cannot predict what will work. But they do know that the system will seek stability. Almost always, what begins in randomness ends in stability. Life seeks solutions, tends toward support and stability, generates systems that sustain diverse individuals. Life is attracted to order.

But how it gets there violates all of our rules of good process: Life is not neat, parsimonious, logical, nor elegant. Life seeks order in a disorderly way. Life uses processes we find hard to tolerate and hard to believe in—mess upon mess until something workable emerges.

All this messy playfulness creates relationships that make available more: more expressions, more variety, more stability, more support. In our exploration of what's possible, we are led to search for new and different partners. Who we become together will always be different than who we were alone. Our range of creative expression increases as we join with others. New relationships create new capacities.

This creative world is playful even in its processes. None of us struggles to create ourselves in isolation, fighting to survive in a world of fixed rules and unyielding circumstances. The world is more playful than this, more relational. Life invites us to create not only the forms but even the processes of discovery.

The environment is invented by our presence in it. We do not parachute into a sea of turbulence, to sink or swim. We and our environments become one system, each influencing the other, each co-determining the other. Geneticist R. C. Lewontin explains that environments are best thought of as sets of relationships organized by living beings. "Organisms do not experience environments. They create them."

This co-determination is evident in the evolution of our planet. In its nearly four billion years of experimentation, life has created Earth as a set of relationships that are hospitable to life. It has discovered both new forms and new processes. Science writer Louise B. Young describes this process beautifully:

> Life altered the atmosphere and gentled the sunlight. It turned the naked rocks of the continents into friable soil and clothed them with a richly variegated mantle of green which captured the energy of our own star for the use of living things on earth, and it softened the force of the winds. In the seas life built great reefs that broke the impact of storm-driven waves. It sifted and piled up shining beaches along the shores. Working with amazing strength and

endurance, life transformed an ugly and barren landscape into a benign and beautiful place.

In a universe where the desire to experiment and to create is so inescapable, it seems important to ask why. Why are novelty and experimentation so encouraged? Why does life seek to organize with other life?

When living beings link together, they form systems that create more possibilities, more freedom for individuals. This is why life organizes, why life seeks systems—so that more may flourish.

Evolution as survival of the fittest has inhibited our observation of coevolution. We are not independent agents fighting for ourselves against all others. There is no hostile world out there plotting our demise. There is no "out there" for anyone to occupy. We are utterly intertwined. Always we are working out conditions for life with others. We play an essential role in shaping each other's behavior.

If we see life as a brutal contest among separate entities, we focus on individual contribution, individual change. This worldview not only makes us feel afraid and isolated but it also causes us to hope for heroes. If evolution is the result of changes in individuals, what we need are a few individuals who can outsmart nature and win out over the competition. Yet in a systems-seeking, coevolving world, there is no such thing as a hero. Not even a visionary leader. Everything is a result of interdependencies—systems of organization where we support, challenge, and create new combinations with others. It's hard to think about individuals at all.

We make the world lonelier and less interesting by yearning for heroes. We deny the constant, inclusionary creating that is going on; we deny our own capacity to contribute and expand.

No one forges ahead independently, molding the world to his or her presence while the rest trail admiringly behind. We tinker ourselves into existence by unobserved interactions with the players who present themselves to us. Environment, enemies, allies—all are affected by our efforts as we are by theirs. The systems we create are chosen together. They are the result of dances, not wars.

soulstice

by Drew Dellinger

every ounce of matter is frozen light
roses, clouds, bones, tears
all slowly moving light

everything is shining in glory
everything singing a story

and if love is a language
then I am just learning to spell
while there's a story that the stars have been
burning
to tell

everything is blazing
like a diaphanous theophany

everything is shining
like the radiant mind of a child
like the eyes of a saint
like the dawn on the Nile
where the pyraminds track the arc
of the spinning earth

sometimes I wander the streets and curse the darkness
with a heart that's
frozen as the arctic

and winds are forming
as the planet's turning
and I'm thinking about 500 years of oppression
and I'm thinking about 500 years of resistance
and I'm thinking

what if the trade winds had blown the other way?
would we not have been spared the middle passage?

and I wander the streets and curse the darkness
with a heart that's
frozen as the arctic

because the capital of government has
succumbed to the
government of capital

and I know the longest night gives way to the
strongest light
so I prolong this fight 'til what's wrong is right

every second in the universe a supernova is
exploding
every second a star is shattering

and flames were leaping off the moon last night
flames were leaping off the moon last night

like binary stars we
circle each other

like binary stars we
circle each other

and the more I see of you
the more I love the view

let me be a fierce clear mirror
in a cosmos made of passions

open the window
let me feel the star-filled night

if you can stand before the cosmos

until your form becomes transparent
the stars will pour beams
through your
emancipated borders

open the window
let me feel the star-filled night

and if love is a language
then I am still learning to spell
while there's a story that the stars have been burning
to tell

Play: The Movement of Love

by Gwen Gordon

Not long ago, I lived in an apartment that overlooked a preschool playground. At 8:00 a.m., as I ate my granola every morning, the doors to the school yard burst open and preschoolers spilled onto the yard. I sat staring out the second floor window, happily buffered from the full volume of their blood curdling screeches, and watched, mesmerized. Children hurled themselves into the day, bumping, tripping, bouncing, building things, smashing them down, hitting, kicking, laughing, hugging. Everything was there—trial, disappointment, grief, success, connection, creativity, celebration, belonging, not belonging—all in one little playground. I had the distinct feeling I was watching the raw business of the universe, the workings of evolution itself.

An angel hovering above the world must feel the same way, gazing down at this one big rumpus with all its scraped knees and first kisses. Myriad life forms emerging out of the primordial seas, gathering together, creating more life forms, making cities, cities falling apart, people fighting, others writing poems, the aurora borealis, jellyfish, fleas that jump into the nostrils of hummingbirds, two-thousand-year-old Sequoias. The qualities that are so exuberantly displayed in childhood play are writ large in the evolutionary process on a cosmological scale. The whole Universe is one big playground, and evolution one great big, gorgeous rumpus.

Watching the play every morning my heart would burst with delight because the cosmos is delightful. Then it occurred to me—I was feeling waves of love watching the children play, not because they are so adorable and I have a biological clock, but because play itself is the movement of love.

Most of us were taught that the Universe is a deadly serious place, run by fixed laws, chance and necessity—like a machine: Our human world a small island of meaning and civility in a vast sea of violence and indifference. The image has no romance, no delight. Is it any wonder that we now live in deadly serious times, full of terror and madness? We have created the world that fits our worldview.

But the view of the Universe as a collection of fixed objects is not fixed. It is shifting to a view of the Universe as, what Thomas Berry calls, a "communion of subjects." Everything in the Universe is intimately relating to everything else. Eros is running the whole show with attractions of every kind pulling for communion, physically, emotionally, and spiritually in every curve of the cosmos. There's no such thing as empty space anymore. Space is as empty as the space between lovers' eyes. It's teeming with desire, electrical charges, and sexy curves in the Universe's wild embrace.

It might seem as if we've come a long way from child's play. What I saw on the playground, though, was immensely erotic and intimate. It was pure, raw, and lusty life force impelling those children to grapple with gravity and their own coordination to discover what a human can do and make. By far the most common use of words for play in most languages is in an erotic context. Diane Ackerman tells us that: "the Sanskrit word for copulation is kridaratnam, which translates as 'the jewel of games.' In German, a *spielkind* (literally a "play child") is a baby born out of wedlock. In English we make a play for, play up to, indulge in love play." We also have foreplay and *Playboy* magazine with playmates-of-the-month. If the evolving Universe is a communion of subjects then evolution is love play, the intimately creative adventure of Eros.

Until recently, evolutionary theory was a grim picture— "nature, red in tooth and claw" where only the fittest survived, new species emerging only through chance and necessity. Now we have a slightly kinder, juicier, and more mischievous picture. Stephen Jay Gould gave us the term "exaptation" to describe how nature improvises by co-opting previously evolved functions to do new things. This helps explain flight. Imagine a bug in the tropics. It can't regulate its own body temperature so it has to grow elaborate fans on its back to stay cool. One particularly hot summer afternoon, a bug with a pair of fans the size of which no other bug had ever seen before sits fanning itself dreamily. Suddenly—Whooooooooaaaaa—a flying bug. Improvisation lifts us up and out of our daily habits to see things from a new perspective. Now that's a playful Universe!

Exaptation is pure improvisation. It's like the character in the movie *Airplane* who, when given a document and asked what he makes of it, answers, "Well, I could make a hat, or a broach, or maybe a little paper airplane." Nature takes what's there and makes stuff up. Before I got a Master's degree I used to put the initials M.S.U. after my name. They stood for "Make Stuff Up." I had no idea that making stuff up was wired right into the human brain. Gould says that the human brain is par excellence the chief exemplar of exaptation. This is because, about 150,000 years ago the hominid brain expanded massively. When it did, it acquired neural circuits that are not closely tied to any specific function but can be used in a variety of ways. It is this neural plasticity that enables the blind person to develop acute hearing and sensitive fingers for reading Braille, and the right-handed pianist to have as much coordination in the left hand. Neural plasticity has enabled a frontal lobe designed for hunting and gathering to be repurposed into Beethoven's *Sonata Pathetique,* Shakespeare's sonnets, and the Beatles' *Abbey Road.* The human is the only species that specializes in being unspecialized.

If the Universe were a collection of fixed objects governed by fixed laws, then it would be wise to stay rigid. But the Universe is a fluid current of living play, so our own improvisational play and flexibility is essential for going with the flow of the cosmos, responding creatively moment to moment to the changing needs, demands, and opportunities we meet. When we play, we enter the creative current of possibilities, the self-organizing force of the whole cosmos, as active participants. Before the human, all animals were specialized for particular niches. We have the flexibility of the cosmos dancing right in our neurons, enabling us to move into any niche and explore the whole world as a playground.

While play is built right into the cosmos, it's generally agreed that playfulness didn't come on the animal scene until about 150-200 million years ago, with mammals and birds in the Jurassic period. As I write this, my dog Luna is shaking her rope toy, insisting I stop what I'm doing this instant and play tug-of-war. Meanwhile, my neighbor has a diabolic African Gray Parrot who repeatedly calls the dog, Patrick, over to her cage yelling, "Patrick!!" then spills the water dish over his head and laughs out loud, "Ar ar ar."

Most animals outgrow the playfulness of their youth, but humans are curious and playful, exploring the world, learning, playing practical jokes, and inventing things throughout our whole lifetimes. That's because in some sense we never really grow up. Compared to other animals, the human rate of development is extremely slow. As a result, childhood qualities extend all the way into old age. This phenomenon is called *neoteny*. Neoteny causes us to retain qualities like curiosity, sensitivity, imagination, wonder, flexibility, humor, optimism, honesty, and spontaneous expression and remain in an unending state of development potentially through our whole lives. Humans are developmentally adolescent chimps that have become sexually mature.

Remaining childlike enhances our capacity for communion. Like Cupid, a Greek image for Eros, neoteny is the romantically savvy child who, with an impish, knowing wink, shoots Eros onto the scene. Because of neoteny the human pelvis doesn't rotate like it does with most large primates, enabling humans to make love face to face. Our extended childhood makes us softer, rounder, smoother, and more sensitive. Compared to our primate ancestors, we are much less aggressive, far more cooperative, and capable of depths of emotion and care that are the basis of art and culture.

While we can thank neoteny in general for the finest aspects of civilization, it is the resulting intensity of the mother/child bond that deserves most of the credit. The mother/child bond has to be extraordinarily intense because humans are born extremely premature. As newborns, we are utterly helpless little fetuses. In contrast, picture the newborn colt standing and walking within the first day of being born. We, on the other hand, leave the physical womb before we have even finished gestating. We can't crawl for three to six months and require eight years of protective care to finish our development. We are utterly and completely dependent on our caregiver's constant, nurturing care. Our bond with her is our second womb.

This means that an amazing and mysterious thing has to happen if the baby is to survive. The caretaker has to embody the profoundly nurturing qualities of the mother's womb, the compassion of the womb of the whole Universe, or the baby will die. And this is exactly what happens. Many new mothers never imagined they were capable of so much love, they're drunk with it. This is the compassion of the Universe awakening in the human to serve its ongoing play. The child's adventurous play and the mother's loving care emerge together through the dance of the baby's exquisite intimate dependence.

The Indo-European word *plegan*, the root for play, means to risk, chance, expose oneself to hazard. Adventurous play is risk. We can risk to the extent that we feel safe and held in love. In turn, what we hold in love can open to the world and play. The cosmos wouldn't be in a dance of evolving play if it weren't held by the caring curvature of spacetime in a tender gravitational embrace. This curve, the mother's embrace, enables the whole play of evolution. Play and care are the order and chaos of a creative cosmos, but through the human the cosmos can play with and care for itself like never before.

So why, if care and play are so essential to our nature, are we violently destroying ourselves and the planet? What went wrong? We have not grown into our destiny as cosmic playmates because we do not feel ourselves held in a loving cosmos. Care and play in balance generate ingenious inventions that add to the life and beauty of the world. Out of balance, they wreak havoc. Care with a lack of play is static, while play with a lack of care is disconnected and cruel. Milan Kundera writes about the laughter of devils and the laughter of angels in *The Book of Laughter and Forgetting*. He describes the laughter of devils as laughter at the meaninglessness of things, and the laughter of angels as laughter with the meaning of things. The laughter of devils is play without care.

On the playground, I watched the occasional outburst of tears when someone got too rough, bossy, mean, or exclusive. There were others who stayed on the edge of the playground cut off from the play. Play is a sign of health. When a child is overly aggressive or withdrawn from play, something is wrong. In the '60s, psychiatrist Stuart Brown did extensive research on the personal histories of horribly violent mass murderers and others "on the fringe," and found that all of them had lacked natural, spontaneous, free-spirited play during their childhood. A lack of nurturing care combined with a lack of play is deadly because it goes against the grain of the whole Universe.

As a culture we are like the child sitting on the edge of the playground, unaware of the playmates all around us. Thinking that we're separate from the world, we are cut off from the sense of being held that makes play possible. Our play impulses are lacking the tempering influence of care. The disproportionate amount of money spent on the military and prisons instead of education and social programs is a portrait of a homicidal, play-deprived culture sitting on the edge of the playground. We have yet to come into our true nature and powers as cosmic playmates.

The Buddha described how the noblest qualities have "near enemies," qualities that are often mistaken for the noble ones, but which lack deep care and connection. In the Buddha's teachings, the near enemy of equanimity is disinterest. I propose that the near enemy of play is entertainment and recreation. Competitive sports, video games, luxury cruises, and high stakes gambling on the stock market are not play. Neither is drug use, or shopping sprees. They are attempts to get relief from the gray backdrop of our play-deprived lives through forms of near-play that lack intimacy with the world. That is why near-play quickly becomes compulsive. It can never satisfy our deepest urges for true play as intimate participation in the cosmos. The free-spirited true play that is our birthright has become so dangerously distorted by a play-deprived culture that we confuse it for war.

The philosopher James Carse, in a brilliant little book called *Finite and Infinite Games*, describes the difference between finite and infinite play. Finite play has rigid limits, rules, winners and losers, and does not include everybody in the game. Infinite play, on the other hand, changes the rules as needed and includes everyone. The whole purpose of infinite play is to keep the play going. Now we can see a little more clearly what has gone awry in our world. Without caring connection, infinite play becomes finite. With high stakes, winners and losers, it takes itself very seriously; and when you take things too seriously you end up dropping bombs. The ultimate expression of finite play is war.

But in infinite play, everything—war, death, deadlines, annoying bosses, barbed wire fences, fear and terrorism—can all be brought into the play. This implies that it's possible to get to the source of being that lets you sing and dance no matter what else is going on. When our sense of well-being comes from a deep enough intimacy with the Universe, there's nothing to win or lose. We can risk anything. We can trust that no matter how foolish, confused, or inept we might be, we will not fall out of the web of life. Being held keeps us from holding back from the world and lets us participate playfully.

Spiritually realized people tend to be the most mischievous, childlike, and playful of all. Infinite play is the natural expression of a liberated consciousness that recognizes itself as the ground of being. This is our own true, infinite, unbounded nature that we share with the whole cosmos. We meditate for hours, do prostrations, chant and tie ourselves in pretzels, in order to touch the Absolute, to feel held in the wild embrace of the Divine. We touch the Absolute in order to play in the relative. With the divine mother's spiritual maturity and the divine child's flexibility and enthusiasm, our perceptions of the world are as fluid as the world itself. We can sense reality as the intimate movement of the Divine, the *[Hindu concept] Lilla, [which means]* "illusion or Divine play." The word for illusion literally means "in play." The ultimate goal of spiritual practice is enlightenment, the lightness of being that comes from recognizing the world as play. It is the liberation from a finite identity in a finite game to the infinite.

So how do you stay light in heavy times? In the Diné Navajo culture, a person with imbalances is given a special blessing ritual to heal them. This involves the whole tribe coming together to hold them in beauty and tell the cosmic creation story for many nights on end. Beauty and the story of the Universe remind us that we are held in the compassionate embrace of the cosmic mother. Our greatest challenge and opportunity in this time is to find our way to feeling profoundly held. Our hearts are aching for it. When we have this, we can include everything we experience into the play. As Rainer Maria Rilke wrote, "Let everything happen to you, beauty and terror, no feeling is final." Whatever you're feeling, if you greet it as a playmate, it will begin to move.

Play is movement. When something has play, it has wiggle room. It isn't rigid or fixed. With play a regular stiff stick becomes a joy stick. There is inherent joy and ecstacy in the movement of play. Ecstasy or *ex-stasis*, literally means, standing aside, or getting off our spots. You can't play unless you can move, whether physically, emotionally, or spiritually. If you're stuck, then play will help. Wiggle your grief, your pain, your depression. Give it breath, find its edges, exaggerate it, paint it, sing it, put a clown nose on it. Play gets us off of our spots, our tragic stories, our habitual ways of thinking and being, and brings us present with the constant movement of love that is the Universe. There can be pain in the present moment, but in the infinite play, pain is felt fully and then moves into something else, and something else after that.

If we forget to play, we lose our love for life, and loving life is what will save our world, not fearing destruction. We're desperate to be invited into our joy, into our energy source, the belly laugh, the burst of giggles, wild abundance, bright color and zest for life of play. The laughing Buddha is fat to show that even the most massive bulk can lift off the ground—with a big enough laugh. Laughter is the sound of play and a doorway into play. Right now, wherever you are, put this article down and laugh. Not because there's anything funny going on, but because you're free to laugh. It may seem awkward at first, but stretch into it. Get off your spot. You will discover that you can find ecstasy just by moving toward it. Play is the movement of love, and love is what moves the Universe. Never underestimate, especially during a time of crisis, the power of play to move the world. Indeed it's the only thing that ever did.

"And we should consider every day lost on which we have not danced at least once. And we should call every truth false which was not accompanied by at least one laugh."
—Nietzche, *Thus Spoke Zarathustra*

Discovering the Divine Within the Universe

by Gail Worcelo, CP

The bell rings at 5 a.m., an early morning call to prayer. It is the beginning of our monastic day here in Vermont. It is time for Morning Vigil. At this hour, all is in darkness except for the one candle lighting our prayer space. I take my place on the cushion and join the others gathered for our hour of contemplative prayer.

This time of Vigils is the night watch hour, a time to touch the mysterious presence of God at the heart of the Universe. We discover, as the Gospel of John tells us that "the Light shines in the darkness."

This morning I experience this literally. There is a large skylight above my head and in this predawn darkness I can see the shining stars of the Milky Way galaxy. The words of the Psalmist come to mind, "Praise God, sun and moon; praise God, shining stars!"

I reflect on the fact that I am made of that same star stuff. The luminous fire that burns in those stars has burned through 15 billion years of Universe unfolding and burns in me this morning. It burns in my hunger for the Holy. It burns in every leaf, animal, stone and bird. It is the Fire within the fire of all things.

This is the same fire that ignited the burning bush that jolted Moses and made him take off his shoes and exclaim, "This place is Holy Ground." I try to absorb these words from the Old Testament: "This place is Holy Ground."

I want to situate myself within the fullness of this understanding and push my contemplation beyond old limiting notions which subscribe God to some abstract heaven. The book of Wisdom declares: "The Spirit of God fills the whole world!" I want to know this world filled with the Spirit of God and situate myself in its larger context.

Towards the end of his life Teilhard de Chardin wrote: "Less and less do I see any difference between research and adoration." For Teilhard as for other poets and mystics, prayer was a meditation on the Universe, informed by knowledge open to Mystery.

I reflect upon how technology has given us the capacity to extend our senses, to be able to see and hear what has always been there but what we were unable to know with unaided senses. We have suddenly been given a glimpse of the footprints of God embedded in the cosmos as we come to understand how the Universe works.

We come out of 15 billion years of unfolding, we are vital dust, a further development of the original fireball. In this morning prayer I try to locate myself in our galactic neighborhood. The galaxy in which I pray is 100,000 light years wide. A single light year is equal to six trillion miles. Our nearest neighbor, the Andromeda galaxy, is 2.3 million light years away.

This takes some time to absorb. We are located in vastness, in the vast heart of God. Although I sit still and firm during this time of meditation, I reflect upon the fact that the Earth is revolving at 900 miles an hour. It is orbiting the sun at 19 miles per second. We are moving as a solar system at 40,000 miles per hour around the center of our galaxy, and our galaxy is expanding at 12 million miles per minute.

This is the context in which I find myself as I sit down to pray. Things are anything but still. I imagine God dancing with wild abandon through the farthest reaches of the cosmos. In today's Gospel of John, the words "Abide in me as I abide in you" take on new meaning. The place where the Divine abides is much vaster than we can imagine. "Abide in me" means "abide in my vastness, abide in my Universe."

There is a realization taking place within me, as my eyes reach out through the skylight, that the deeper I go in prayer the farther out I go in the cosmos. Inner and outer are one. This is what the mystics of our Christian tradition understood as they went deeper into the inner experience of God. They experienced a harmonization of their lives with the greater rhythms of existence. They knew by faith what science knows empirically, that the Universe is charged with the presence and reality of the Divine.

These mystics allowed the fire of contemplation to transform them into a union of love with all of creation. They understood that Divine Radiance floods the Universe making all things holy.

I know this, too, in a deep, intuitive way. I think we all do. The night sky begins to give way to the dawn as the Milky Way becomes a faint memory this morning. Before the bell rings to call this hour of prayer to a close I remember the words of Annie Dillard, "The world has two kinds of nuns, there are those inside and those outside of convents. Whichever kind she is, the nun's vocation is contemplation of the real."

The bell rings as the first glimmer of dawn appears in the morning sky. The hour of prayer is over. I blow out the prayer candle, extinguishing the flame. Yet I know full well that the Fire within the fire of all things still burns in every creature, galaxy, and star, and in every person who hungers for the Holy.

Evening Thoughts

by Thomas Berry

Thomas Berry Award and Lecture
August 30, 2000

Sponsored by the Center for Respect of Life and Environment and the Forum on Religion and Ecology at the UN Millennium World Peace Summit for Religious and Spiritual Leaders, Waldorf Astoria Hotel, New York City.

During these past two days much has been accomplished to advance the cause of peace by our discussions and simply by our being with each other. We learned to trust and admire each other and to share with each other the traditions we represent.

This evening I suggest that we continue this presence to each other by looking beyond ourselves to the larger universe we live in. If it were convenient I would suggest that we go outside this building, that we go beyond all the light and noise of the city and look up at the sky overarching the Earth. At this time in the evening we would see the stars begin to appear as the sun disappears over the horizon. The light of day gives way to the darkness of night. A stillness, a healing quiet, comes over the landscape. It's a moment when some other world makes itself known, some numinous presence beyond human understanding. We experience the wonder of things as the vast realms of space overwhelm the limitations of our human minds.

This moment, as the sky turns golden and the clouds reflect the blazing colors of evening, we participate for a moment in the forgiveness, the peace, the intimacy of all things with each other.

Parents hold their children more closely and tell stories to the children as they go off into dreamland, wonderful stories of times gone by, stories of the animals, of the good fairies, adventure stories of heroic wanderings through the wilderness, stories of dragons threatening to devour the people and of courageous persons who saved our world in perilous times.

These final thoughts of the day are continued in the minds of children as even in their sleep they begin to dream of their own future, dreams of the noble deeds that would give meaning to their lives. Whether awake or asleep, the world of wonder fills their minds, the world of beauty fills their imagination, the world of intimacy fills their emotions.

When we look back over our own lives we realize that whatever of significance we have achieved in our own personal lives and in the larger domain of the cultural context of our lives has been the fulfillment of thoughts and dreams that we had early in our lives, dreams that sustained us when we encountered difficulties through the years.

Beyond the dreams of our personal future, there are the shared dreams that give shape and form to each of our cultural traditions. Because this other world cannot be explained by any technical or scientific language, we present this other world by analogy and myth and story. Even beyond childhood this is the world of the human mind.

So tonight as we look up at the evening sky with the stars emerging faintly against the fading background of the sunset, we think of the mythic foundations of our future. We need to engage in a shared dream experience. The experiences that we have spoken of as we look up at the starry sky at night and in the morning and see the landscape revealed as the sun dawns over the earth, these reveal a physical world, but also a more profound world that cannot be bought with money, cannot be manufactured with technology, cannot be listed on the stock market, cannot be made in the chemical laboratory, cannot be reproduced with all our genetic engineering, cannot be sent by email. These experiences require only that we follow the deepest feelings of the human soul.

What we look for is no longer the *Pax Romana,* the peace of imperial Rome, nor is it simply the *Pax Humana,* the peace among humans, but the *Pax Gaia,* the peace of Earth and every being on the Earth. This is the original and the final peace, the peace granted by whatever power it is that brings our world into being. Within the universe the planet Earth, with all its wonder, is the place for the meeting of the divine and the human.

As humans we are born of the Earth, nourished by the Earth, healed by the Earth. The natural world tells us:

> I will feed you, I will clothe you, I will shelter you, I will heal you. Only do not so devour me or use me that you destroy my capacity to mediate the divine and the human. For I offer you a communion with the divine. I offer you gifts that you can exchange with each other. I offer you flowers whereby you may express your reverence for the divine and your love for each other.

> In the vastness of the sea, in the snow-covered mountains, in the rivers flowing through the valleys, in the serenity of the landscape and in the foreboding of the great storms that sweep over the land, in all these experiences I offer you inspiration for your music, for your art, for your dance.

All these benefits the Earth gives to us individually, in our communities and throughout the entire Earth. Yet we cannot be fully nourished in the depths of our being if we try to isolate ourselves individually, or if we seek to deprive others of their share by increasing our own; for the food that we eat nourishes us in both our souls and our bodies. To eat alone is to be starved in some part of our being.

We need to reflect that our individual delight in the song of the birds or the sound of the crickets and cicadas in the evening is enhanced not diminished when we listen together in the evening with our families and our friends. We experience an easing of the tensions that develop between us, for the songs that we hear draw us into the intimacy of the same psychic space. So with music, our folk music as well as the symphonies of Mozart or Beethoven, draw an unlimited number of persons into the same soul space.

Perhaps our greatest resource for peace is in an awareness that we enrich ourselves when we share our possessions with others. We discover peace when we learn to esteem those goods whereby we benefit ourselves in proportion as we give them to others. The very structure and functioning of the universe and of the planet Earth reveal an indescribable diversity bound in an all-embracing unity. The heavens themselves are curved over the earth in an encompassing embrace.

Here I would recall the experience of Henry Thoreau, an American naturalist of the mid-19th century who lived a very simple life with few personal possessions. At one time he was attracted to purchase an especially beautiful bit of land with a pasture and a wooded area. He even made a deposit. But then he realized that it was not necessary to purchase the land because, he reasoned, he already possessed the land in its wonder and its beauty as he passed by each day. This intimacy with the land could not be taken away from him no matter who owned the land in its physical reality.

So, indeed, that same bit of land could be owned in its wonder and beauty by an unlimited number of persons, even though in its physical reality it might be owned by a single person.

Such was the argument of Mencius, the Chinese writer who taught the emperor that he should open up the royal park for others, since it would be an even greater joy to have others present with him; as at a musical concert each person enjoys the music without diminishing but increasing our own joy as we share it with others. So, too, for those in the Boddhisattva tradition of

India. There were those such as Shanti Deva, in the fifth century of our era, who took a vow to refuse beatitude itself until all living creatures were saved. For only when they participated in his joy could he be fully caught up in the delight of paradise.

It has taken these many centuries for us to meet with each other in the comprehensive manner that is now possible. While for the many long centuries we had fragments of information concerning each other, we can now come together, speak with each other, dine with each other. Above all we can tell our stories to each other.

Tonight we might recall the ancient law of hospitality, whereby the wanderer was welcomed. So it was with Ulysses in his long voyage home after the Trojan war. When exhausted and driven ashore on occasion and surrounded by a people that he had never met before, he was consistently rested, invited to dine with the people of the place, and then in the quiet moment afterward, was invited to tell his story. So it has been, I trust, with each of us in these past few days. To some extent we have been able to tell our stories to each other. Now a new phase in all our stories has begun as we begin to shape the Great Story of all peoples as we move into the future.

As a final reflection, I would suggest that we see these early years of the 21st century as the period when we discover the great community of the earth, a comprehensive community of all the living and non-living components of the planet. We are just discovering that the human project is itself a component of the Earth project, that our intimacy with the Earth is our way to intimacy with each other. Such are the foundations of our journey into the future.

Now night has advanced. The stars are more brilliant than ever. Yet the time has come for us to return to the dining room of the Waldorf to enjoy our final moments with each other as we continue our journey on into the 21st century.

A Suspended Blue Ocean

by Hafiz

as translated by Daniel Ladinsky

The sky
is a suspended blue ocean.
The stars are the fish
That swim.

The planets are the white whales
I sometimes hitch a ride on,

And the sun and all light
have forever fused themselves

Into my heart and upon
my skin.

There is only one rule
on this Wild Playground,

For every sign Hafiz has ever seen
reads the same.

They all say,

"Have fun, my dear; my dear, have fun,
in the Beloved's Divine
Game,

O, in the Beloved's
Wonderful
Game."

Appendix

Friends and the Earth Charter

by Ruah Swennerfelt

For me, September 9, 2001, was a day filled with hope and joy, in contrast to the tragic events that took place two days later. I had the privilege of joining more than 500 people who came together at Shelburne Farms in Shelburne, Vermont, to celebrate and honor the Earth Charter, a worldwide movement to replace war and injustice with peace and justice for the life community. Paul Winter offered sensuous music that evoked the sounds and rhythms of nature as well as the human longing for beauty and connection. Steven Rockefeller (one of the co-creators of the Earth Charter) shared the history of the Earth Charter and the unique democratic process that created it. Jane Goodall explained how the Earth Charter gives her another reason for hope for a peaceful, just, and sustainable planet. And all the participants celebrated through music, ritual, and art.

Quakers have a long and rich history of working for peace and justice, not just from their own perspective, but side-by-side with other faith groups and organizations. But we're often seen as a fringe group by the dominant culture. What better way to convince that culture to join our work for peace and justice than to develop a common language, a common vision, and a common set of principles by which to live? I believe that is what the Earth Charter offers.

The Earth Charter is the product of a decade-long, worldwide, cross-cultural conversation about humanity's common goals and shared values. Although it was inspired in part by the 1992 UN Conference on Environment and Development in Rio de Janeiro, its persuasive power is due largely to the fact that it has evolved independently of conventional governmental and corporate processes, fashioned not by heads of state, but by a variety of citizens of many classes, of many countries. John Scull of Canadian Yearly Meeting reminded Canadian Friends that it is important to understand that the Earth Charter is not just about ecological integrity, but includes social and economic justice, democracy, peace, and respect for diversity. The great power of the Earth Charter comes from its emphasis on the interconnectedness of all these concerns, as the following text makes clear.

Earth Charter

Preamble to Earth Charter

We stand at a critical moment in Earth's history, a time when humanity must choose its future. As the world becomes increasingly interdependent and fragile, the future at once holds great peril and great promise. To move forward we must recognize that in the midst of a magnificent diversity of cultures and life forms we are one human family and one Earth community with a common destiny. We must join together to bring forth a sustainable global society founded on respect for nature, universal human rights, economic justice, and a culture of peace. Towards this end, it is imperative that we, the peoples of Earth, declare our responsibility to one another, to the greater community of life, and to future generations.

Earth, Our Home

Humanity is part of a vast evolving universe. Earth, our home, is alive with a unique community of life. The forces of nature make existence a demanding and uncertain adventure, but Earth has provided the conditions essential to life's evolution. The resilience of the community of life and the well-being of humanity depend upon preserving a healthy biosphere with all its ecological systems, a rich variety of plants and animals, fertile soils, pure waters, and clean air. The global environment with its finite resources is a common concern of all peoples. The protection of Earth's vitality, diversity, and beauty is a sacred trust.

The Global Situation

The dominant patterns of production and consumption are causing environmental devastation, the depletion of resources, and a massive extinction of species. Communities are being undermined. The benefits of development are not shared equitably and the gap between rich and poor is widening. Injustice, poverty, ignorance, and violent conflict are widespread and the cause of great suffering. An unprecedented rise in human population has overburdened ecological and social systems. The foundations of global security are threatened. These trends are perilous—but not inevitable.

The Challenges Ahead

The choice is ours: form a global partnership to care for Earth and one another, or risk the destruction of ourselves and the diversity of life. Fundamental changes are needed in our values, institutions, and ways of living. We must realize that when basic needs have been met, human development is primarily about being more, not having more. We have the knowledge and technology to provide for all and to reduce our impact on the environment. The emergence of a global civil society is creating new opportunities to build a democratic and humane world. Our environmental, economic, political, social, and spiritual challenges are interconnected, and together we can forge inclusive solutions.

Universal Responsibility

To realize these aspirations, we must decide to live with a sense of universal responsibility, identifying ourselves with the whole Earth community as well as our local communities. We are at once citizens of different nations and of one world in which the local and global are linked. Everyone shares responsibility for the present and future well-being of the human family and the larger living world. The spirit of human solidarity and kinship with all life is strengthened when we live with reverence for the mystery of being, gratitude for the gift of life, and humility regarding the human place in nature.

We urgently need a shared vision of basic values to provide

an ethical foundation for the emerging world community. Therefore, together in hope we affirm the following interdependent principles for a sustainable way of life as a common standard by which the conduct of all individuals, organizations, businesses, governments, and transnational institutions is to be guided and assessed.

PRINCIPLES

I. RESPECT AND CARE FOR THE COMMUNITY OF LIFE

1. **Respect Earth and life in all its diversity.**
   a. Recognize that all beings are interdependent and every form of life has value regardless of its worth to human beings.
   b. Affirm faith in the inherent dignity of all human beings and in the intellectual, artistic, ethical, and spiritual potential of humanity.

2. **Care for the community of life with understanding, compassion, and love.**
   a. Accept that with the right to own, manage, and use natural resources comes the duty to prevent environmental harm and to protect the rights of people.
   b. Affirm that with increased freedom, knowledge, and power comes increased responsibility to promote the common good.

3. **Build democratic societies that are just, participatory, sustainable, and peaceful.**
   a. Ensure that communities at all levels guarantee human rights and fundamental freedoms and provide everyone an opportunity to realize his or her full potential.
   b. Promote social and economic justice, enabling all to achieve a secure and meaningful livelihood that is ecologically responsible.

4. **Secure Earth's bounty and beauty for present and future generations.**
   a. Recognize that the freedom of action of each

generation is qualified by the needs of future generations.

b. Transmit to future generations values, traditions, and institutions that support the long-term flourishing of Earth's human and ecological communities.

In order to fulfill these four broad commitments, it is necessary to:

II. ECOLOGICAL INTEGRITY

5. Protect and restore the integrity of Earth's ecological systems, with special concern for biological diversity and the natural processes that sustain life.

a. Adopt at all levels sustainable development plans and regulations that make environmental conservation and rehabilitation integral to all development initiatives.

b. Establish and safeguard viable nature and biosphere reserves, including wild lands and marine areas, to protect Earth's life support systems, maintain biodiversity, and preserve our natural heritage.

c. Promote the recovery of endangered species and ecosystems.

d. Control and eradicate non-native or genetically modified organisms harmful to native species and the environment, and prevent introduction of such harmful organisms.

e. Manage the use of renewable resources such as water, soil, forest products, and marine life in ways that do not exceed rates of regeneration and that protect the health of ecosystems.

f. Manage the extraction and use of non-renewable resources such as minerals and fossil fuels in ways that minimize depletion and cause no serious environmental damage.

6. Prevent harm as the best method of environmental protection and, when knowledge is limited, apply a precautionary approach.

a. Take action to avoid the possibility of serious or irreversible environmental harm even when scientific knowledge is incomplete or inconclusive.

b. Place the burden of proof on those who argue that a proposed activity will not cause significant harm, and make the responsible parties liable for environmental harm.

c. Ensure that decision making addresses the cumulative, long-term, indirect, long distance, and global consequences of human activities.

d. Prevent pollution of any part of the environment and allow no build-up of radioactive, toxic, or other hazardous substances.

e. Avoid military activities damaging to the environment.

7. Adopt patterns of production, consumption, and reproduction that safeguard Earth's regenerative capacities, human rights, and community well-being.

a. Reduce, reuse, and recycle the materials used in production and consumption systems, and ensure that residual waste can be assimilated by ecological systems.

b. Act with restraint and efficiency when using energy, and rely increasingly on renewable energy sources such as solar and wind.

c. Promote the development, adoption, and equitable transfer of environmentally sound technologies.

d. Internalize the full environmental and social costs of goods and services in the selling price, and enable consumers to identify products that meet the highest social and environmental standards.

e. Ensure universal access to health care that fosters reproductive health and responsible reproduction.

f. Adopt lifestyles that emphasize the quality of life and material sufficiency in a finite world.

8. Advance the study of ecological sustainability and promote the open exchange and wide application of the knowledge acquired.

a. Support international scientific and technical cooperation on sustainability, with special attention to the needs of developing nations.

b. Recognize and preserve the traditional knowledge and spiritual wisdom in all cultures that contribute to environmental protection and human well-being.

c. Ensure that information of vital importance to human health and environmental protection, including genetic information, remains available in the public domain.

III. SOCIAL AND ECONOMIC JUSTICE

9. Eradicate poverty as an ethical, social, and environmental imperative.

a. Guarantee the right to potable water, clean air, food security, uncontaminated soil, shelter, and safe sanitation, allocating the national and international resources required.

b. Empower every human being with the education and resources to secure a sustainable livelihood, and provide social security and safety nets for those who are unable to support themselves.

c. Recognize the ignored, protect the vulnerable, serve those who suffer, and enable them to develop their capacities and to pursue their aspirations.

10. Ensure that economic activities and institutions at all levels promote human development in an equitable and sustainable manner.

a. Promote the equitable distribution of wealth within nations and among nations.

b. Enhance the intellectual, financial, technical, and social resources of developing nations, and relieve them of onerous international debt.

c. Ensure that all trade supports sustainable resource use, environmental protection, and progressive labor standards.

d. Require multinational corporations and international financial organizations to act transparently in the public good, and hold them accountable for the consequences of their activities.

11. Affirm gender equality and equity as prerequisites to sustainable development and ensure universal access to education, health care, and economic opportunity.

a. Secure the human rights of women and girls and end all violence against them.

b. Promote the active participation of women in all aspects of economic, political, civil, social, and cultural life as full and equal partners, decision makers, leaders, and beneficiaries.

c. Strengthen families and ensure the safety and loving nurture of all family members.

12. Uphold the right of all, without discrimination, to a natural and social environment supportive of human dignity, bodily health, and spiritual well-being, with special attention to the rights of indigenous peoples and minorities.

a. Eliminate discrimination in all its forms, such as that based on race, color, sex, sexual orientation, religion, language, and national, ethnic or social origin.

b. Affirm the right of indigenous peoples to their spirituality, knowledge, lands and resources and to their related practice of sustainable livelihoods.

c. Honor and support the young people of our communities, enabling them to fulfill their essential role in creating sustainable societies.

d. Protect and restore outstanding places of cultural and spiritual significance.

IV. DEMOCRACY, NONVIOLENCE, AND PEACE

13. Strengthen democratic institutions at all levels, and provide transparency and accountability in governance, inclusive participation in decision making, and access to justice.

a. Uphold the right of everyone to receive clear and timely information on environmental matters and all development plans and activities which are likely to affect them or in which they have an interest.

b. Support local, regional and global civil society, and promote the meaningful participation of all interested individuals and organizations in decision making.

c. Protect the rights to freedom of opinion, expression, peaceful assembly, association, and dissent.

d. Institute effective and efficient access to administrative and independent judicial procedures, including remedies and redress for environmental harm and the threat of such harm.

e. Eliminate corruption in all public and private institutions.

f. Strengthen local communities, enabling them to care for their environments, and assign environmental responsibilities to the levels of government where they can be carried out most effectively.

14. Integrate into formal education and life-long learning the knowledge, values, and skills needed for a sustainable way of life.

a. Provide all, especially children and youth, with educational opportunities that empower them to contribute actively to sustainable development.

b. Promote the contribution of the arts and humanities as well as the sciences in sustainability education.

c. Enhance the role of the mass media in raising awareness of ecological and social challenges.

d. Recognize the importance of moral and spiritual education for sustainable living.

15. Treat all living beings with respect and consideration.

a. Prevent cruelty to animals kept in human societies and protect them from suffering.

b. Protect wild animals from methods of hunting, trapping, and fishing that cause extreme, prolonged, or avoidable suffering.

c. Avoid or eliminate to the full extent possible the taking or destruction of non-targeted species.

16. Promote a culture of tolerance, nonviolence, and peace.

a. Encourage and support mutual understanding,

solidarity, and cooperation among all peoples and within and among nations.

b. Implement comprehensive strategies to prevent violent conflict and use collaborative problem solving to manage and resolve environmental conflicts and other disputes.

c. Demilitarize national security systems to the level of a non-provocative defense posture, and convert military resources to peaceful purposes, including ecological restoration.

d. Eliminate nuclear, biological, and toxic weapons and other weapons of mass destruction.

e. Ensure that the use of orbital and outer space supports environmental protection and peace.

f. Recognize that peace is the wholeness created by right relationships with oneself, other persons, other cultures, other life, Earth, and the larger whole of which all are a part.

THE WAY FORWARD

As never before in history, common destiny beckons us to seek a new beginning. Such renewal is the promise of these Earth Charter principles. To fulfill this promise, we must commit ourselves to adopt and promote the values and objectives of the Charter.

This requires a change of mind and heart. It requires a new sense of global interdependence and universal responsibility. We must imaginatively develop and apply the vision of a sustainable way of life locally, nationally, regionally, and globally. Our cultural diversity is a precious heritage and different cultures will find their own distinctive ways to realize the vision. We must deepen and expand the global dialogue that generated the Earth Charter, for we have much to learn from the ongoing collaborative search for truth and wisdom.

Life often involves tensions between important values. This can mean difficult choices. However, we must find ways to harmonize diversity with unity, the exercise of freedom with the common good, short-term objectives with long-term goals. Every individual, family, organization, and community has a vital role to play. The arts, sciences, religions, educational institutions, media, businesses, nongovernmental organizations, and governments are all called to offer creative leadership. The partnership of government, civil society, and business is essential for effective governance.

In order to build a sustainable global community, the nations of the world must renew their commitment to the United Nations, fulfill their obligations under existing international agreements, and support the implementation of Earth Charter principles with an international legally binding instrument on environment and development.

Let ours be a time remembered for the awakening of a new reverence for life, the firm resolve to achieve sustainability, the quickening of the struggle for justice and peace, and the joyful celebration of life.

Contributors

EarthLight wishes to acknowledge and express deep appreciation to all of the contributors who generously gave permission to reprint their materials for this anthology:

INTRODUCTORY MATERIAL, pp 9-29

Cindy Spring is an environmental activist and a writer. She co-leads a bioregional awareness program called Close to Home: Living with Wildlife in the East Bay. She was the coordinator of Earth Day 2000 for the Bay Area. Cindy also participates in several Bay Area environmental organizations and writes a column for *Bay Nature* magazine. She has co-authored two books with her husband, Charles Garfield, including *Wisdom Circles: A Guide to Self-Discovery and Community Building in Small Groups*.

Anthony Manousos joined the Religious Society of Friends (Quakers) in 1985 and is currently editor of *Friends Bulletin*, the official publication of independent Western Quakers. He has edited two Quaker books, *A Western Quaker Reader* (2000) and *Compassionate Listening and Other Writings* by Gene Knudsen Hoffman (2003). He is married to a United Methodist minister whom he met at Pendle Hill, a Quaker study center near Philadelphia. They currently live in Torrance, California, where they tend their garden together.

Eric Sabelman, PhD, is a biomedical engineer on the neurosurgery staff of Kaiser Hospital in Redwood City, CA. He began attending Quaker meeting in Pasadena, CA, in 1969, and became a member of Palo Alto (CA) Friends Meeting about 20 years later. He has been clerk of Pacific Yearly Meeting Unity with Nature Committee and Quaker representative to Stanford Associated Ministries. He is currently clerk of College Park Quarterly Meeting Ministry and Oversight Committee and secretary of the *EarthLight* Board of Directors. Stories that he writes from inspiration during Quaker worship have been recorded on CD by Tom and Sandy Farley (www.spont.com).

K. Lauren de Boer was editor and executive director of *EarthLight* magazine from 1996 through 2005, a publication that explored the intersection of ecology, cosmology, consciousness, and spirituality. His essays, articles, and interviews have appeared in a number of anthologies and publications, including *Parabola, Yes!,* and *Connotations.* Lauren is a founding board member—with Brian Swimme, John Seed, Connie Barlow, and others—of the Epic of Evolution Society, a group of scientists, theologians, and artists whose purpose is to explore the meaning and implication of the sacred Universe Story for our time. He currently serves on the editorial advisory board for the Center for Ecozoic Studies in North Carolina, is a board member for the Institute for Sacred Cinema, and for the OCTAVE Alliance, a non-profit that brings together musicians and sustainability groups. He currently offers a graduate program in ecology, cosmology, and sustainability through the Institute for Educational Studies. In addition to his interests in cosmology, Lauren is a poet, essayist, pianist, and amateur naturalist and birder of 25 years. He is at work on a book, *Imagining Earth: the Practice of Spiritual Ecology in Everyday Life.*

Marshall Massey has been involved with the Religious Society of Friends (Quakers) since 1970 and is presently a member of Omaha Friends Meeting, Iowa Yearly Meeting (Conservative). He was co-founder of Quaker Earthcare Witness, the North American Quaker environmental organization. He was also former treasurer, in the 1980s, of the Colorado Environmental Coalition, which was at that time an umbrella coalition of many of the big environmental organizations in the state. He is the author of numerous articles and pamphlets and has led numerous workshops and given talks about the environment. Reprinted with permission of author.

Sandy Moon Farley created the queries, or self-examination questions, that appear at the beginning of each chapter. She is a teacher of English as a Second Language, storyteller, and writer, also co-author and illustrator of *Earthcare for Children* and co-editor of *Earthcare for Friends*. She has served on the board of Quaker Earthcare Witness, *EarthLight* Magazine, and the *Friends Bulletin.*

Conscious Evolution, pp 30-118.

The Great Turning by Joanna Macy (*EarthLight* Issue 29 Spring 1998) Joanna Macy, PhD, is a scholar of Buddhism, Systems Theory, and Deep Ecology, known widely for her workshops and trainings for activists. Her many books include *Coming Back to Life* and *Widening Circles.* www.joannamacy.net. Reprinted with permission of author

Odyssey of a Quaker Earthcare Activist by Louis Cox, writer and Publications Coordinator for Quaker Earthcare Witness, member of Burlington Friends Meeting, New England Yearly Meeting. Louis has been working in the environmental movement for the last 35 years and has developed back-to-the-land and alternative-energy skills while living in southern Missouri and northern Vermont. Printed with permission of author.

The Great Work —Thomas Berry in His Own Words (*EarthLight* Issue 34 Summer 1999). Berry is a leading cultural historian and environmental thinker. For more than 40 years he has been developing a comprehensive vision of a viable future for the Earth community. In emphasizing the magnitude of our current global ecological crisis he observes that we are ending the Cenozoic era and entering into an Ecozoic period. Reprinted with permission of author.

Our Children: Their Future by Thomas Berry (*EarthLight* Issue 22 Summer 1996). See above.

Science as Wisdom: The New Story as a Way Forward, an interview with Brian Swimme by K. Lauren de Boer (See bio above) (*EarthLight* Issue 26 Summer 1997) Reprinted with permission of author. Swimme is a mathematical cosmologist and author of *The Universe is a Green Dragon* and *The Universe Story*, a collaboration with Thomas Berry. Swimme's media work includes the video series, *Canticle to the Cosmos* and *The Hidden Heart of the Cosmos*.

Scientists find universe awash in tiny diamonds by Pat Mayne Ellis (*EarthLight* Issue 39 Fall 2000). Ellis is a semi-nomadic West Coast Canadian writer who is awed and rejoices that her poem continues to speak to readers and listeners. Reprinted with permission of author.

Declaring the Holy: interview with Pattiann Rogers by Maryanne Hannon(*EarthLight* Issue 51 Fall 2004). Hannan has published poems and essays in numerous publications. She lives in upstate New York with her husband. They have two married daughters and one grandson. Reprinted with permission of author.

The Possible Suffering of a God During Creation poem by Pattiann Rogers. (*EarthLight* Issue 51 Fall 2004). Rogers has published numerous books of poetry, including *Generations, Song of the World Becoming: New and Collected Poems*, 1981-2001; *Firekeeper: New and Selected Poems* (1994), and *Eating Bread and Honey* (1997). The mother of two sons and two grandsons, Rogers lives with her husband, a retired geophysicist, in Colorado. Reprinted with permission of author.

The Motherhouse of Reinvention, by Sharon Abercrombie (*EarthLight* Issue 43 Fall 2001). Abercrombie served as EarthLight's assistant editor for seven years. A staff writer for the *Oakland Catholic Voice*, she is a frequent contributor on eco-spiritual topics for *National Catholic Reporter*. Reprinted with permission of author.

The Practice of the Presence of the Wild by David Oates *(EarthLight* Issue 1 Spring 1990). Oates currently teaches at Clark College, a community college in Vancouver, Washington. A former attender of Santa Monica (CA) Friends Meeting, Oates is the author of numerous articles as well as books of poetry and prose dealing with environment, nature, etc: *City Limits: Walking Portland's Boundary; Channeling Walt in Time of War; Peace in Exile; Earth Rising: Ecological Belief in an Age of Science*. Reprinted with permission of author.

Camas Lillies poem by Lynn Ungar (*EarthLight* Issue 41 Spring 2001) Ungar lives in California with her partner, their daughter, three dogs and a cat. She is a Unitarian Universalist minister by ordination and a dog trainer by avocation. Reprinted with permission of author.

SACRED RELATIONSHIP, pp 78-118

Invocation, Prayer for the Earth by John Seed (*EarthLight* Issue 3, Spring 1991). **Rainforest and Psyche** by John Seed (*EarthLight* #3 Spring 1991). Seed is director of the Rainforest Information Centre, PO Box 368, Lismore, New South Wales, 2480 Australia. With Joanna Macy, Arne Naess and others he co-authored the book *Thinking Like a Mountain*. He travels extensively around the world lecturing on the plight of the rainforests and conducting Councils of All Beings and other "re-Earthing" workshops. A major portion of this article is taken from his paper presented to the Ecopolitics Conference, University of Hobart, May 1987. Reprinted with permission of author.

Animal Allies by Brenda Peterson (*EarthLight* Issue 20 Winter 1995-96). Peterson is the author of three novels, the collection of essays *Nature and Other Mothers* (in which "Animal Allies" appeared), and *Living by Water*, another collection of essays chosen as one of the best books of the year by the American Library Association. She lives in Seattle, WA. Reprinted with permission of author.

Picking Up Roadkill by Susan Tweit (*EarthLight* Issue 38 Summer 2000). Tweit is a field ecologist-turned-writer-and-radio-commentator. She is the author of ten books on humans and the rest of nature, including several that have won national awards. Her latest book is *The San Luis Valley: Sand Dunes and Sandhill Cranes*. She lives in rural Colorado with her husband and dog. Reprinted with permission from author.

Turning the Compost by Barbara Meyn (*EarthLight* Issue 23 Fall 1996). Meyn has been a newspaperwoman, teacher, writer and poet. She lives in Sonoma County, CA.

The Voice of the Turtle by Linda Souma Seebeth (*EarthLight* Issue 30 Summer 1998). Seebeth is an author and educator, having taught elementary school through college, specializing in working with so-called learning disabled (learn differently). She lives in the woods with her husband, John Seebeth, two dogs and various wildlife critters. Reprinted with permission of author.

Garden of Eden on your Dinner Plate? by Connie Barlow (*EarthLight* Issue 50 Summer 2004). Barlow is author of *Green Space, Green Time* and *Evolution Extended.* She travels with her husband, Rev. Michael Dowd, speaking on cosmology, ecology, and the Great Story of evolution. Connie is an *EarthLight* editorial advisor. This article draws insights from her 2001 book, *The Ghosts of Evolution.* Reprinted with permission of author.

Grace at the Table by Molly Anderson (*EarthLight* Issue 50 Summer 2004). Anderson is focused on how science can better inform public policy for ecological integrity, social justice and sustainable food systems. She clerks the Earthcare Ministry Committee of New England Yearly Meeting, and is a member of Friends Meeting at Cambridge, Massachusetts. She serves on the North American Steering Committee of the Agribusiness Accountability Initiative. Reprinted with permission of author.

My Religion Is Rain by Cindy Spring, editor.

COLLECTIVE WISDOM, pp 119-171.

Confessions from the Buddhist Frontier by Kurt Hoelting (*EarthLight* Issue 25 Spring 1997). Hoelting is Director of the Inside Passages Project, based on Whidbey Island in Puget Sound. Drawing on Buddhist and Judeo-Christian contemplative practice, Inside Passages combines kayak wilderness trips with meditation practice, forging a closer link between inner and outer wilderness exploration. Reprinted with permission of author.

How to Regain Your Soul by William Stafford (*EarthLight* Issue 49 Summer 2003). Stafford authored more than 65 volumes of poetry and prose. Among his many honors and awards were a Shelley Memorial Award, a Guggenheim Fellowship, and a Western States Lifetime Achievement Award in Poetry. In 1970, he was the Consultant in Poetry to the Library of Congress (a position currently known as the Poet Laureate). He died in 1993. Reprinted with permission of his family.

Thomas Berry's Intellectual Journey by Mary Evelyn Tucker (*EarthLight* Issue 34 Summer 1999). Mary Evelyn Tucker is a visiting professor at Yale and Research Associate at the Harvard-Yenching Institute. She is the author of *Worldly Wonder: Religions Enter Their Ecological Phase* (Open Court, 2003). She also edited the ten volume series on *World Religions of the World and Ecology* (Harvard University Press 1997-2004) with John Grim. Reprinted with permission of author.

The Meadow Across the Creek by Thomas Berry (*EarthLight* Issue 34 Summer 1999). See bio above. Reprinted with permission of author

First Nations and the Future of the Earth by Rebecca Adamson. (*EarthLight* Issue 40, Winter 2000-01). Adamson, Cherokee, is Founder and President of First Nations Development Institute. She has worked directly with grassroots tribal communities, and nationally as an advocate of local tribal issues for 25 years. Reprinted with permission of author.

Wlomsen Mgaeso by Joseph Bruchac (*EarthLight* Issue 43 Fall 2001). Bruchac is a poet, storyteller and writer whose work often reflects his Abenaki Indian heritage and his commitments to peace and respect for the natural world. Reprinted with permission of author.

The Spirituality of Native African Culture by Malidoma Some (*EarthLight* Issue 10 Spring 1993). Some, PhD, from Burkina Faso, West Africa, sent by his elders to the West, shares indigenous wisdom that has allowed his people to live in balance on the planet for thousands of years. Reprinted with permission of author.

The Goddess and the Garden, interview with Starhawk by Ruah Swennerfelt (*EarthLight* Issue 30 Summer 1998). Swennerfelt serves as General Secretary of Quaker Earthcare Witness. She lives in rural Vermont with her husband, Louis Cox. The offices are in their solar-electric, hand-built home where they grow most of the vegetables they eat and try to live in harmony with the land. She is a member of the Burlington Monthly Meeting and New England Yearly Meeting. Reprinted with permission of author. Starhawk is author of many works celebrating the Goddess movement and Earth-based, feminist spirituality. She is a peace, environmental, and global justice activist and trainer, a permaculture designer and teacher, a Pagan and Witch.

Our Sacred Relationship to Animals: an Islamic Perspective by Iftekhar A. Hai, (*EarthLight* Issue 38 Summer 2000). Hai is Director of Interfaith Relations of United Muslims of America, a San Francisco Bay Area organization. He represents American Muslims on ten interfaith organizations, regionally, nationally and internationally. He teaches ecumenical and universal aspects of Islam destroying stereotyping and building bridges of understanding. Reprinted with permission of author.

Befriending the Earth by Rex Ambler (*EarthLight* Issue 2, Fall 1990). Ambler, a British Friend, is author of many books on Quaker theology and spirituality, including *Experiments with Light, Light to Live by, The End of Words*, and *Truth of the Heart, an Anthology of George Fox*. Reprinted with permisssion of author.

The Spark by Chris Hoffman (*EarthLight* Issue 48 Spring 2003). Hoffman's publications include *Cairns* (a collection of poetry) and *The Hoop and the Tree: A Compass for Finding Deeper Relationship With All Life*. Reprinted with permission of author.

MUTUAL LEARNING, pp 172-218.

The Lucky Little Seaweed: A Great Story Parable by Mark McMenamin (*EarthLight* Issue 50 Summer 2004). McMenamin is Professor of Geology at Mount Holyoke College. A paleontologist, he is the author of *The Garden of Ediacara* and *Hypersea: Life on Land.* Reprinted with permission of author.

What We Bless, Blesses Us by J. Ruth Gendler (EarthLight Issue 51 Fall 2004). Gendler is an exhibiting artist, author of *The Book of Qualities* (on the personification of human emotion), and editor of *Changing Light.* Reprinted with permission of author

Cultivating Relational Intelligence by Nina Simons (*EarthLight* Issue 53 Spring 2005). Simons is co-executive director, with her husband Kenny Ausubel, of Bioneers/Collective Heritage Institute. Bioneers promotes practical environmental solutions and innovative social strategies to restore the Earth and our communities. Permission from author © Nina Simons/Bioneers Conference.

Watering the Seeds of the Future, interview with Michael Meade, by K. Lauren de Boer (*EarthLight* Issue 44 Winter 2001-02). See bio above. Michael Meade is an author, master storyteller and scholar of mythology. He is founder of Mosaic: Multicultural Foundation, which focuses on youth at risk.

Beyond a Culture of Fear by K. Lauren de Boer, see bio above (*EarthLight* Issue 47 Winter 2002-03). Reprinted with permission of author.

The Clan of One-Breasted Women by Terry Tempest Williams (*EarthLight* Issue 37 Spring 2000). Williams is an author, speaker and environment activist. She says her ideas are shaped by the Great Basin, the Colorado Plateau and her Mormon culture. Adapted from *Refuge: An Unnatural History of Family and Place* by Terry Tempest Williams. Excerpted with permission by Vintage Books, a division of Random House, Inc.

Native Ways, Our Ways: A Personal Journey by Alan Strain (*EarthLight* Issue 11 Summer 1993). Strain was a Quaker educator with a deep concern for Native Americans. He served as Western field secretary for Central Committee for Conscientious Objectors. He was associate Dean of Student Affairs and interim Dean of Native American Affairs at Stanford University during the 1970s, where he helped organize the first annual spring Inter-Tribal Pow Wow. He also was active in Palo Alto and Santa Cruz Friends Meetings. He died in 2003. Reprinted with permission of his family.

Ten Caterpillars Yawning by Cindy Spring, editor (*EarthLight* Issue 54 Fall, 2005).

All the Time in the World by Anthony Manousos, co-editor.

CONSCIOUS CHOICE., pp 219-253.

Conscious Living by Cindy Spring, editor (*EarthLight* Issue 42 Summer 2001).

Ecozoic Activism by Michael Dowd and Connie Barlow (*EarthLight* Issue 42 Summer 2001). Dowd, MDiv, DMN, is a community organizer, evolutionary evangelist, and well-known popularizer of the Great Story. A former United Church of Christ minister and author of *EarthSpirit: A Handbook for Nurturing an Ecological Christianity*, he now manages Global Action Plan's Sustainable Lifestyle Campaign in Rockland County, NY. Connie Barlow (see bio above) Reprinted with permission of authors.

Redwood Seder: interview with Rabbi Arthur Wascow by Richard Sheinin (*EarthLight* Issue 25 Spring 1997). Scheinin is the classical music and jazz writer at the *San Jose Mercury News*, where he previously spent eleven years (1992-2003) covering the religion and ethics beat. He lives in Santa Cruz, CA, with his family. Reprinted with permission of the author. Rabbi Arthur Waskow is director of the Philadelphia-based Shalom Center, an international network that brings Jewish thought and action to bear on protecting the Earth and celebrating community.

The Entire Universe in a Piece of Bread by Thich Naht Hanh (*EarthLight* Issue 50 Summer 2004). Hanh is a Vietnamese Zen Buddhist master, poet, and peace and human rights activist. He founded Plum Village in France to alleviate the suffering of refugees and political prisoners in the Third World. Permission to reprint given by Parallax Press.

Eating for Peace by Thich Nhat Hanh (*EarthLight* Issue 39 Fall 2000). See above. Thich Nhat Hanh also has over 85 published titles of wisdom and poetry. Permission given by Parallax Press.

Wonders of the Watershed by Gary Synder (*EarthLight* Issue 15 Fall 1994). Snyder is a widely published Pulitzer Prize-winning poet (*Turtle Island*) and author. He writes on the relationship of humans and nature, and now teaches literature and 'wilderness thought' at the University of California at Davis. This essay was later published in an expanded version in *A Place in Space* (Counterpoint Press, 1996). © Gary Snyder, 1994 and 1996. Reprinted with permission of author.

Animal Grace by Mary Lou Randour (*EarthLight* Issue 38 Summer 2000). Randour is a professional psychologist and director of programs for Psychologists for the Ethical Treatment of Animals. Her latest book is *Animal Grace: Entering a Spiritual Relationship with our Fellow Creatures*. She lives with her husband and two dogs, Toshi and Sophie, in Chevy Chase, Maryland. Reprinted with permission of author.

Jim Corbett, Goatwalker, Cowbalist by David Ray, author of many volumes of poetry, including most recently *Music of Time: Selected & New Poems* and *The Death of Sardanapalus and Other Poems of the Iraq Wars*. David lives in Tucson, Arizona, and is a member of Pima Monthly Meeting.

Jim Corbett was born in Wyoming in 1933, and ranched in Arizona during much of his adult life. He has also been a sheep and goat herder, librarian, range analyst, and teacher of wildland symbiotics. He became active with Quakers in 1962. He was the author of numerous books and pamphlets, the most noted being *Goatwalking/a Guide to Wildlife Living, a Quest for the Peaceable Kingdom* (1992) and *Sanctuary of All Life* (published posthumously in 2005). Reprinted from *Friends Bulletin* with permission of author.

INCLUSIVITY, pp 254-281.

On the Pulse of the Morning by Maya Angelou (*EarthLIght*, Issue 10, Spring 1993). Angelou is a poet, best-selling author, civil rights activist and playwright. She travels the world spreading her legendary wisdom. (Public domain.)

Spirituality in Place-based Community by Freeman House (*EarthLight* Issue 45 Spring 2002). House is a co-founder of the Mattole Restoration Council in Northern California and became its executive director. His book, *Totem Salmon: Life Lessons from Another Species*, was awarded the American Academy of Arts and Letters' Harold Vursell Award for quality of prose. Reprinted with permission of author.

Free Range Salmon by Cindy Spring (*EarthLight* Issue 45 Spring 2002), editor.

Our Father Which Art in Birds and Fish by Jordan Fisher-Smith (*EarthLight* Issue 17 Spring 1996). Smith lives in the northern Sierra Nevada. He is the author of *Nature Noir: a Park Ranger's Patrol in the Sierra* (Mariner, 2006). Reprinted with permission of author.

Will there be any toads in Heaven? by Keith Helmuth. (*EarthLight* Issue 26 Summer 1997). Helmuth is a writer, market farmer, community development activist, and Quaker living near Woodstock, New Brunswick. Along with his wife, Ellen, and sons Eric and Brendan, he established North Hill Farm in 1972 in the Saint John River watershed of New Brunswick, Canada. Since retiring from farming, they have been sojourning residents of Philadelphia, PA. Keith is a founding Board member and Secretary of Quaker Institute for the Future. Reprinted with permission of author.

Growing Connection: The Ecovillage Vision and the Future of Community, by Diana Leafe Christian (*EarthLight* Issue 53 Spring 2005). Christian is editor of *Communities* magazine, and author of *Creating a Life Together: Practical Tools to Grow Ecovillages and Intentional Communities* (2003). She lives at Earthaven Ecovillage in North Carolina. Reprinted with permission of author

CELEBRATION, pp 282-315.

Children of the Light by John Fowler (*EarthLight* Issue 39 Fall 2000). Fowler, has been teaching in a public Montessori school in Denver for the past fifteen years. He has also taught classes at Naropa University, the Endicott/TIES MEd program, and given numerous workshops on his Timeline of Light. Reprinted with permission of author.

Life as Play: A Simpler Way, by Meg Wheatley and Myron Kellner-Rogers (*EarthLight* Issue 26 Summer 1997). Wheatley and Rogers lead the Berkana Institute, a non-profit educational and research foundation seeking to discover new organizational forms. Reprinted with permission of authors.

Play: the Movement of Love, by Gwen Gordon, (*EarthLight* Issue 48 Spring 2003). Gordon received her Master's degree in Philosophy, Cosmology, and Consciousness from the California Institute of Integral Studies. She started a life of play building Muppets for Sesame Street, has been an artist-in-resident in prisons, corporations, and think tanks, and is currently offering playshops as a transformative path. Reprinted with permission of author.

soulstice by Drew Dellinger (*EarthLight* Issue 42 Summer 2001). Dellinger is a spoken word poet, teacher, and activist. He is founder of Poets for Global Justice, and author of the collection of poems, *love letter to the milky way.* He is associate professor at John F. Kennedy University. Reprinted with permission of author.

Discovering the Divine within the Universe by Gail Worcelo, CP (*EarthLight* Issue 39 Fall 2000). Worcelo is a Catholic nun, formerly from the Passionist Order, and co-founder, of Green Mountain Monastery, dedicated to the healing and protection of Earth and its life systems. She has been a student for the past 20 years of Thomas Berry. Reprinted with permission of author.

Evening Thoughts by Thomas Berry (*EarthLight* Issue 39 Fall 2000). See bio above. Reprinted with permission of author.

A Suspended Blue Ocean Hafiz poem translated by Daniel Ladinsky. (*Earthlight* Issue 48 Spring 2003). Ladinsky, born in the Midwest, made his home for six years in a spiritual community in western India. He has published three volumes of translations of the great Persian poet Hafiz: *The Gift, The Subject Tonight Is Love,* and *I Heard God Laughing.* His latest book is an anthology titled *Love Poems from God* (2002). Reprinted with permission of author.

Contributors of Artwork

Kathleen Edwards is an award winning illustrator, painter and sculptor whose work has been exhibited nationally. She lives in Northern California. Drawing on p. 111.

Meganne Forbes is a watercolor artist who draws her inspiration from nature. Dolphins, whales and sea turtles are especially dear to her. She lives in Carpinteria, CA. www.meganneforbes.com Artwork on p. 9.

Jesse Wolf Hardin is the founder of Anima earth-informed practice and author of *Gaia Eros.* He co-hosts retreats, vision quests and events at the riverside sanctuary, Anima Wilderness Center. Drawings on pp. 78, 147, 254, 274.

Karen Hess and Scott Hess co-create *Dragonfly Graphics,* a freelance creative arts design studio in Sonoma County, CA., providing web design, print design and copywriting. www.dragonflygraphicarts.com Photograph on p. 3.

Marion C. Honors, CSJ, says her art is rooted in the New Story of Creation. Her current work is primarily monotype printmaking with water-based media. Her award-winning art has been exhibited nationally and internationally. Drawing on p. 30.

Dawn Raymond is a Midwest girl by upbringing, a West Coast woman in spirit, who does most of her artwork using a variety of media in a community context. She is a core member of the *EarthLight* community. www.sharemorehavemore.net Drawing on p. 229.

Mary Southard, CSJ, is a life adventurer whose fascination is the Divine, the ever-present Source, beauty, wonder and on-going creativity of the Cosmos, most especially our Earth. Besides being a painter and sculptor, she is also an experienced educator, retreat director and spiritual companion. She lives and has her studio in La Grange, IL. Drawing on p. 41.

Gary Tonhouse is dedicated to creating an appreciation, awareness and concern for our environment through the power of photography and education. His workshop is in Ankeny, Iowa. www.reflectiveimages.com Photograph on p. 29.

Jean Triol taught clinical laboratory science with a specialty in cytology for 35 years. She is now exercising her talents as an original watercolorist. During the past decade her award winning paintings have been exhibited in juried art shows around the United States. She holds signature membership in the Montana Watercolor Society. She is a member of the board of *Friends Bulletin*. Watercolor on cover and back.

Cathy Weber grew up in midwestern USA, studied at the Herron School of Art and Indiana University, and later completed a formal painting apprenticeship in Mexico City. In 1981 she moved to Dillon, Montana. Though Weber executes the bulk of her work in watercolor, she is skilled at working in a variety of media. Her artwork is on p. 183.

Students of John Fowler created the children's drawings while they were in his Montessori classroom. Their artwork appears on pp. 142, 146, 281, and 289.

ACKNOWLEDGEMENTS

This anthology was guided by a core committee of Cindy Spring and Eric Sabelman from *EarthLight*, and Anthony Manousos and Sandra Farley from the Religious Society of Friends (Quakers),

ACKNOWLEDGEMENTS FROM CINDY SPRING: My deep appreciation first and foremost goes to Anthony Manousos, the co-editor, whose vision and persistence made this book possible. He has been a joy to collaborate with in this project. We received bountiful support from the Religious Society of Friends (Quakers) and especially from the Pacific Yearly Meeting of Friends. Eric Sabelman and K. Lauren de Boer were generous with their assistance in selections and permissions. Many thanks to the people on the Selection, Art, and Poetry Committees (see below) who took seriously their job of making thoughtful comments and careful choices. From the end of the publication of *EarthLight* magazine in 2005 to the debut of this anthology, the EarthLight Community was held together primarily by five other people besides myself: Dawn Raymond, Loren Haralson, Joyce Rybandt, Bill Collins and Deb Collins. Without their holding the vision of *EarthLight* and their commitment to "keeping the lights on" in the dark days of early 2006, this book would have never been completed. We are indebted to Dawn, in particular, for her selfless dedication to maintaining the office and, more importantly, for her unflagging faith in living the principles of *EarthLight*. I also want to acknowledge my friend and hiking partner, Sandra Lewis, whose wise counsel helped shaped this book. Finally, I am so grateful to have a life partner, Charlie Garfield, who inspires and supports all my endeavors. He continuously teaches me what engaged spirituality is all about.

ACKNOWLEDGEMENTS FROM ANTHONY MANOUSOS: First, I want to express appreciation for the generous support of the Elizabeth M. Chace Fund, Helen Bross, and the many other generous donors who made this project possible. Working with Cindy Spring has been a joy as well as a privilege, for which I am very grateful: Cindy is a radiant earth spirit as well as a tireless worker. I have also enjoyed collaborating with my co-editors Eric Sabelman and Sandy Farley, as well as with Lauren de Boer, whose work as an editor and environmental advocate I have always deeply admired. Louis Cox and Ruah Swennerfelt provided both practical help and spiritual inspiration as I endeavored to deepen my understanding of spiritual ecology and figure out how to put this book together. This project could not have moved forward without the thoughtful discernment and caring support of the Board of *Friends Bulletin*: Norm Pasche, Polly Kmetz, Jean Triol, Rob Roy Woodman, Sandy Farley, Tom Vaughan and Stephen Matchett. Finally, I would like to thank my wife Kathleen Ross, without whose love, good sense, and proofreading skills I could not accomplish what I do.

ACKNOWLEDGEMENTS FROM K. LAUREN DE BOER: Acknowledgements from K. Lauren de Boer: While I guided the EarthLight process, it was always carried out through extensive collaboration with dozens of people. There were so many people, too many to list, who gave their time, money, and life wisdom in support of my ministry at *EarthLight*. I am deeply grateful. It was truly the work of a community dedicated to Earth and the future. The following people were especially supportive and involved: Jo Hanson, Joanne Lauck, Larry Edwards, Tandra McLaughlin, Karen Hess, Sharon Abercrombie, Meheret Fikre-Sellassie, Dennis Rivers, Mary Evelyn Tucker, Brian Swimme, Joanna Macy, Thomas Berry, Miriam MacGillis, Paul Burks, Bob Schutz, Diana Brooks, Miriam Hurley, Loretta Peters, Cindy Spring, Jean Barker, John and Pat Sullivan, Kevin Peer, Susan Kleihauer, Cathy Holt, Sharon Abercrombie, Dan Turner, Scott Sousa, Jim Duffy, Tom Whiteman, Sandra Lewis, Shelley Tanenbaum, Cheryl Lander, Bill Collins, and Dawn Raymond. I also want to extend gratitude to Paul Hoffman, Billy Holliday, Marion Weber, Frederika and Norman Brooks, Jane Spear, and my parents, Thomas and Beatrice Smith.

ANTHOLOGY SELECTION COMMITTEE: Cindy Spring, Anthony Manousos, K. Lauren de Boer, Loren Haralson, Sandra Lewis and Joyce Rybandt.

ART SELECTION COMMITTEE: Dawn Raymond, Joyce Rybandt, Debra Collins.

POETRY SELECTION COMMITTEE: Eric Sabelman, Nancy Brink.

CONTRIBUTORS TO BOOK PRINTING FUND

The following people generously donated $100 or more toward the printing costs of this book:

Jean Barker * Sarah L. Barnett * Rev Stephen Baxter * Melinda Briscoe * Frederika & Norman Brooks * Helen Bross * Kate Buckner * Mardy Burgess * Paul Burks * David & Virginia Burnight * Ellen Bush * Dr. Dave & Anna Cochran * Congregation of Divine Providence of Texas * David Cooper * Colette & Stan Corwin * Ruth Carey & Jim Crowfoot * Community Connexion * Cultivating Connections * Francesca D'Anneo * Betty Daugherty, FSPA * Ecumenical Institute: Boston Inc. * Claudia Enos * Adelaide & Frederick Finseth * Lis Fleming * Helena Foster * Foundation for Global Community * Charles Garfield * Herman F. Greene * John V. Haralson * Gerald Haynes * Joanne Hawke * Tom Head * Lynn Carol Henderson * Phyllis Hetrick-Bennett * Frank Hill * Doug & Shirley Hitt * Laura Huxley * David Irvine * Marisa S. James * Melissa Lovett-Adair * Vida Kenk & William Minkel * John W. Lau * Frances Lightson * Beal Lowe * Juanita Madison * Kenneth & Freya Mahaffey * Duane R. Manning * Pamela Mayer * Stanley McCracken * Jane & Wayne McKeel * Frances Melvold * Leigh Merinoff * Eleanore & Sebastian Milardo * Gene Mitchell * Monastery of St. Gertrude * Lansing S. Moran * Mary & Ted Mueller * TJ Mullin * Kit Newman * The New Orleans Female Dominican Academy * Astrid Nordness * Roena Osting * Palo Alto Friends Meeting * Shirley & Ray Patterson * Leonard Pavelka * Amy Prater * Robert & Janeene Raymond * Joan and Tom Rawles-Davis * Gertrude Reagan * Laura Reske * Lois Richter * Karla Ristad * The Riverwind Foundation * MaryAnn & Eric Sabelman * Kathy & Harold Saunders * Esther & Herbert Seaman * Neva Schuelke * Marie Schutz * Roberta Schutz * Karla Schutz Herndon * Shimon Schwarzschild * William Scott * Marie L Seckar, OP * Sisters of the Presentation-New York * Sisters of St Joseph of Carondolet of St Louis * Sisters of St Joseph of Chambery –West Hartford, CT * Stanley and Marjorie Smigel * Michael Sohigian * School Sisters of Notre Dame * Miriam Stampfer * Jane & Ron Stavoe * Brian & Denise Swimme * Michael Tompkins & Richard Westberg * Albert Trull * Tom & Cheryl Fields Tyler * Barbara Vaile * Barbara Valocore * Polly Victor * Elizabeth A. Volpe * Barbara & Roland Wentzel * Jane Marvin Whitner * The Woodbury Family * Dr. Judith Wright * Mary Yeakel / Virginia Metcalf * Mary T. Yelenick * Leah & Alex Zaffaroni * Jessica Zeller

EarthLight Publishing History

We want to take this opportunity to acknowledge the many people who provided the vision, and the hard work, that made 54 issues of EarthLight possible:

EDITOR/ASSOCIATE EDITOR, MANAGING EDITOR, POETRY EDITOR: Sharon Abercrombie, Paul Burks, K. Lauren de Boer, Susan Kleihauer, Chris Laning, Sandra Lewis, Jeanne Lohman, David Oates, Robert Schutz.

EDITORIAL ADVISORY BOARD/COMMITTEE, SCIENCE/ART ADVISORS, GUEST EDITORS: Dana Abell, Sharon Abercrombie, Al Baez, Connie Barlow, Gerald Barney, Thomas Berry, Paul Burks, Carl Casebolt, John B. Cobb, Jr., James Conlon, K. Lauren de Boer, Mark Dowie, Michael Dunn, Larry Edwards, Fannie Fonseca-Becker, Micki Graham-Newlin, John Grim, Jo Hanson, Keith Helmuth, Cathy Holt, Bill Howenstine, Julie Knowles, Joanne Lauck, Lew Levenson, Miriam Macgillis, Joanna Macy, Marshall Massey, Patricia Nagle, Paul Niebanck, Chuck Orr, Kevin Peer, Jack Phillips, Gretchen Rudnick, Robert Schutz, B. Shiman Schwartzchild, Charlene Spretnak, Alan Strain, Sparlha Swaby, Brian Swimme, Diana Trimble, Mary Evelyn Tucker, Dan Turner, Vic Yellowhawk White, David Wilson, Susan Kleihauer, Cheryl Lander, John Sullivan, Pat Sullivan.

STAFF: CIRCULATION/SUBSCRIPTIONS, PRODUCTION/LAYOUT/PROOF, FUNDRAISING/DEVELOPMENT, TREASURER, WEBSITE MANAGER. Jean Barker, K. Lauren de Boer, Tom Farley, Meheret Fikre-Sellassie, Jescie France, Susan Kleihauer, Chris Laning, Joanne Lauck, Sandra Lewis, Greg Marshall-Clark, Tandra McLaughlin, Stephen McNeil, Loretta Peters, Lois Richter, Dennis Rivers, Dee Rossman, Joyce Rybandt, Shelley Tannenbaum, Jack Valenta, Doug Van Houten.

PYM CUN EARTHLIGHT COMMITTEE, *EARTHLIGHT* BOARD OF DIRECTORS: Dana Abell, Sharon Abercrombie, Barbara Allen, Jean Barker, Joanna Bramble, William Collins, Louis Cox, K. Lauren de Boer, Jim Doherty, Michael Dunn, Andrea English, Tom Farley, Sandra M. Farley, Jescie France, Rusi Gustafson, Elizabeth I. Jones, Steve Jones, Susan Kleihauer, Mark Koenig, Cheryl Lander, Chris Laning, Sandra Lewis, Bill Miller, Patricia Nagle, Paul Niebanck, Chuck Orr, Dawn Raymond, Eric Sabelman, Robert Schutz, Shelley Tannenbaum, Tom Whiteman.

EARTH LITERACY WEB: William Collins, K. Lauren de Boer, Betty Kissilove, Darlene Pagano, Thomas Zeller.

EARTHLIGHT WEBMASTER: A special note of gratitude to Dennis Rivers who continues to update and enhance the *EarthLight* website www.earthlight.org as his contribution to the community.

ONLINE RESOURCES FOR AN ECOLOGICAL AGE

EARTHLIGHT COMMUNITY: WWW.EARTHLIGHT.ORG

THE EARTHLIGHT COMMUNITY is a local group based in Oakland, CA, engaged in supporting a perspective that is broadly spiritual in its approach to ecological and social issues. Through its networks, it is also a collaboration of individuals and organizations across the US, Canada, and overseas, that is invested in creating a web of support for a deeper relationship to the Earth Community.

QUAKER EARTHCARE WITNESS: http://fcun.quakerearthcare.org. Quaker Earthcare Witness is a spiritually-centered movement of Quakers and like-minded people seeking ways to integrate concern for the environment with Friends' long-standing testimonies for simplicity, integrity, peace, and equality.

OTHER SELECTED LINKS

ORGANIZATIONS

• Anima Wilderness Center: www.animacenter.org (Jesse Wolf Hardin)

• Bioneers: www.bioneers.org (Nina Simons)

• Center for Ecozoic Studies: www.ecozoicstudies.org (Thomas Berry)

• Center for Education, Imagination and the Natural World: www.beholdnature.org (Carolyn Tobin)

• Center for the Study of the Universe: www.brianswimme.org (Brian Swimme)

• Communities Magazine: www.ic.org (Diana Leafe Christian)

• Earth Charter: www.earthcharterusa.org

• First Peoples Worldwide: www.firstpeoples.org (Rebecca Adamson)

• Forum on Religion and Ecology: http://environment.harvard.edu/religion/main.html (Mary Evelyn Tucker)

• Inside Passages: www.insidepassages.com (Kurt Hoelting)

• Parallax Press: www.parallax.org (works of Thich Nhat Hanh)

INDIVIDUALS

- Connie Barlow and Michael Dowd: www.thegreatstory.org
- Joseph Bruchac: www.josephbruchac.com
- Drew Dellinger: www.drewdellinger.org
- Chris Hoffman: www.hoopandtree.org
- J. Ruth Gendler: www.ruthgendler.com
- Joanna Macy: www.joannamacy.net
- Michael Meade: www.mosaicvoices.org
- Brenda Peterson: http://literati.net/Peterson/
- Pattiann Rogers: http://home.comcast.net/~pattiann_rogers
- John Seed: www.rainforestinfo.org
- Malidoma Some: www.malidoma.com
- Starhawk: www.starhawk.org
- Susan J. Tweit: www.susanjtweit.com
- Terry Tempest Williams www.coyoteclan.com

For information on ordering more copies of
EarthLight: Spiritual Wisdom for an Ecological Age,
please contact either:

EarthLight Community
111 Fairmount Ave.
Oakland, CA 94611
(510) 451-4926
email: admin@earthlight.org
www.earthlight.org

Friends Bulletin
c/o Anthony Manousos
(310) 325-3581
email: friendsbulletin@aol.com
www.westernquaker.net

Other books available through *Friends Bulletin* publications:

Compassionate Listening and other writings by Gene Hoffman, Quaker Peacemaker and Mystic. "For more than half a century, Gene Hoffman—through her essays and poetry, her workshops and speeches, her travels and her witness—has been a fountainhead of creative spirituality and courageous peacemaking. This book will be a rich resource for those who come after her." —Richard Deats, Editor of *Fellowship Magazine.* Paperbound, 350 pp. with photos and index. $16.00 (plus $4.50 postage & handling).

Quaker Peace Testimony in Times of Terrorism by Robert Griswold. Reflections upon the spiritual basis for Friends' peacemaking efforts during this time of "perpetual war for perpetual peace." Single copy: $3.95.

Islam from a Quaker Perspective by Anthony Manousos. This pamphlet explores the spirituality of fasting, examines the Islamic faith in relation to Friends' testimonies and provides a brief overview of Quaker involvement in the Middle East. Single copy: $3.95. Two or more: $3 each (incl. postage & handling).

A Western Quaker Reader, Writings by and about Independent Quakers in the Western United States. First historical work about Western Quakerism written from the viewpoint of Independent Friends, provides vivid, first-person testimonies by Friends involved in the "reinvention" of Quakerism in the Western USA from the 1930s to the present. 354 pp. paper. $16.00 (plus $4.50 postage & handling).